THE DICKENS AESTHETIC

AMS Studies in the Nineteenth Century, No. 6
ISSN   0196–657X

Other titles in this series:

1. Anne Aresty Naman, *The Jew in the Victorian Novel: Some Relationships between Prejudice and Art.* 1980.

2. Sue Lonoff. *Wilkie Collins and His Victorian Readers: A Study in the Rhetoric of Authorship.* 1982.

3. William E. Buckler. *Matthew Arnold's Prose: Three Essays in Literary Enlargement.* 1983.

4. Ann H. Jones. *Ideas and Innovations: Best Sellers of Jane Austen's Age.* 1987.

5. *The Two Thackerays: Anne Thackeray Ritchie's Centenary Biographical Introductions to the Works of William Makepeace Thackerary.* Critical Introduction by Carol Hanbery MacKay. 2 vols. 1988.

THE DICKENS AESTHETIC

RICHARD LETTIS

AMS PRESS
NEW YORK

Library of Congress Cataloging-in-Publication Data

Lettis, Richard.
  The Dickens aesthetic.

  (AMS studies in the nineteenth century,
ISSN 0196-657X ; no. 6)
  Bibliography: p.
  Includes index.
  1. Dickens, Charles, 1812–1870—Aesthetics.
I. Title.   II. Series.
PR4592.A34L4   1989   823'.8   87-45808
ISBN 0-404-61486-8

AMS PRESS, INC.
56 East 13th Street
New York, N.Y. 10003

Manufactured in the United States of America

Table of Contents

To Lucy, my own Inimitable, who didn't believe the book would ever be finished, but always believed in the book.

Acknowledgments

I wish to thank the Faculty Research Committee, C. W. Post College, for several grants of released time so that I might work on The Dickens Aesthetic. I am grateful to Professor Fred Kaplan of the editorial board of *Dickens Studies Annual* for his assistance in tightening and ordering of versions of Chapters 1 and 4. And I give heartfelt thanks to Mrs. Ruth Sullivan of the Computer Center of Long Island University, without whom the book would never have been seen in print, and to Professor Edmund Miller, who also helped generously in making letters stay together, and accents come right.

Introduction

"The twentieth century will understand Dickens better than the nineteenth century has understood him." James L. Hughes, *Dickens as Educator.*

Dickensian criticism in the twentieth century has been obliged to rescue Dickens from that series of misunderstandings to which all but a few of his contemporaries—and more than a few of their successors—subjected him. Our age first found it necessary to save him from those who, like Lewes in his own time and Leslie Stephen shortly after and F. R. Leavis alarmingly close to ours, would make of him a great entertainer, but hardly a serious artist (Leavis, without *mea culpa*, subsequently participated in the saving process): Earle Davis said of the Dickens centennial that ". . . The most important result of all the attention paid to Dickens in the year 1970 has been to document the thesis that Dickens was more than a 'natural' novelist."[1]

Close upon the heels of this redemption of Dickens' art were attempts to retrieve from legend the man himself. First, it was necessary to answer or better still remove from importance the assertion that he was not a gentleman. Still more recently, scholars have saved him from sainthood. But while some valuable spadework had already been done as early as his own lifetime, only in the last few decades has anything like a widespread effort been made to demonstrate that Dickens had a brain—to elevate him above the level of, as Chesterton called him, "inspired Cockney"—a man without education or indeed much taste or intelligence, who somehow managed to write great novels.

Dickens was certainly not a well-educated man for his time, but this truth, like many truths about him, has been expanded to an untruth—in this case, that he had virtually no intellectual life beyond the writing of his novels, and that any study of such things as his opinions about the fine arts and literature would simply be effort wasted. Probably this assumption owes much to the fact that Dickens was an autodidact: when someone, assuming Dickens had enjoyed the conventional upbringing of a gentleman, asked his father where he had been educated, the embarrassed parent choked out, "Why, indeed, Sir—ha! ha!—he may be said to have educated himself." Despite evidence to the contrary, it has long been decided that he did not do a very good job; some of his friends—and many scholars—seem to have been unable to forgive him for failing to be his own Oxbridge. When G. H. Lewes visited the Dickens residence at Doughty Street, he was shocked to find that the library consisted of "nothing but three-volume novels and books of travel, all obviously the presentation copies from authors and publishers. . . ." Other friends expressed (with a rather surprising frankness) the opinion that his mind was little suited to scholarly study. The actor Macready said that he "would not care to linger for contemplation," and Humphrey House tells us that "Carlyle used to call him 'little Dickens', as if the adjective applied to more than his body." George Augustus Sala said that he knew nothing of French literature, except perhaps Hugo and Alexandre Dumas. John Forster wrote that "apart from that wonderful world of his books, the range of his thoughts was not always proportioned to the width and largeness of his nature," and said that he was "never bookish in the smallest degree" (meant as a compliment, but contributing to the legend that Dickens did not read), though he added that "He was quite up to the average of well-read men. . . ." Several of Dickens' contemporaries agreed that Dickens did not like to

talk about ideas. Richard Hengist Horne, though he said of Dickens
that "In private, the general impression of him is that of a first-rate
intellect," also made his intelligence seem Houyhnhnm-like: "He hates
argument; in fact, he is unable to argue—a common case with impul-
sive characters who see the whole truth, and feel it crowding and
struggling at once for immediate utterance."   Robert Shelton
Mackensie concurred:

> He hated argument,—indeed, he would not, and could not, go
> into it. He used to observe, "no man but a fool was ever
> talked *out* of his own opinion and *into* your state of mind.
> Arguments are only cannon-balls, fired at a sandbank, or
> water poured into a sieve,—a sheer waste of time and
> trouble. I won't argue with a man: it is going down, on all
> fours, to an obstinate dog. In emphatic cases the only ar-
> gument is a punch on the head."

Others were openly disparaging. "Compared with that of Fielding or
Thackeray," said Lewes, "his was merely an animal intelligence, i.e.
restricted to perceptions."[2]

The opinion of Dickens' friends has been accepted by later
writers: among the best and most enthusiastic Dickensian scholars of
the past one finds, either by clear assertion or damning faint praise or
embarrassed silence, the opinion that whatever he might be as
novelist, gentleman, or human being, Dickens was not a man of intellect or culture—or at the very best, that he was not a man to trouble
himself about such abstractions as aesthetic theory. House speaks of
"the slight history of Dickens's opinions," Monroe Engel says that he
was "not a great reader," and Edgar Johnson agrees that he was not
a learned reader all his life. The best biographies either imply by
silence or openly state that he had little or nothing to say about art,
music, literature, sculpture, poetry, or much of anything else—except
drama, where most have allowed him to excel. Neither in his defini-
tive biography nor in the Introduction to his collection of some of

Dickens' letters, does Edgar Johnson give much attention to anything his great subject had to say about such matters. The Introduction summarizes what the letters have to offer; there is no mention of Dickens' critical judgment, nor anything else pertaining to the world of culture except "his editing, his play-acting and directing. . . ." Yet Johnson concludes with the statement that "The whole man is here in these letters." Similar ignoring or deprecation of Dickens' ideas about the arts occurs in Dobree and Batho, Santayana, Inge, Engel, R. C. Churchill, Harry Stone, K. J. Fielding, and Walter Phillips, among many others.[3]

Faced with so much smoke, it would be foolhardly to argue that there is no fire. But it may be worthwhile to peer through the obliterating screen of adverse judgment to determine whether the Dickensian intellect must be left in ashes, or whether something may be rescued, like Dickens' novels and social status and human nature, from the flames. Certainly it is worthwhile to find out what he had to say about aesthetics, to see if he was capable of intelligent and coherent pronouncement, or if he had no aesthetic theory worth considering. Before we begin, however, it may be useful to review the little that is known about Dickens' education, both formal and self-acquired.

Since, as Edgar Johnson says, "The full range of any writer's knowledge is seldom mirrored in his books," we may best begin to trace Dickens' learning not in the books he wrote but in those he read. With virtually no real schooling, Dickens was never guided (or bullied) into the liberally educated ideal of his time: he felt no obligation to read in areas in which he had no interest. Small as was the pick-up library Lewes was surprised to find in the home of a supposed gentleman, Dickens freely confessed that he had not read everything in it: "I don't pretend that I read all the books that are sent me. . . ." He would seem never to have become acquainted with more than the rudiments of philosophy or theology; John Towne Danson said that "of political Economy, or of political finance, he knew nothing." Lewes claimed that he also knew nothing about science or "the higher literature." Among the major novelists he perhaps did not read Austen (he does not mention her, and Forster indicates that at least to 1838 he had not read her). It was said that he had not read the Brontës, though books by all three Brontës were in his library at his death. Greek and Latin literature were almost certainly beyond him: though occasional Latin phrases and allusions to classical literature can be found in his works, his exposure to Latin was, if anything, rudimentary, and his contact with the classics slight— most of it probably second-hand. He did read some things in translation: Homer was in the library at Gad's Hill, and John R. Warner has suggested that Pip in *Great Expectations* is loosely based on Telemachus.[4]

Despite such reservations, it can be argued that Dickens was better than "average well-read" (even while admitting the vagueness of the term), and that reservations concerning his erudition are owing at least in part to the insistence that to be well read, one must have read like a nineteenth-century gentleman. It was foolish of Lewes to be shocked by the young Dickens' small library and limited reading. His mistake was founded on an assumption of class, and he was too intelligent to have made it, if he knew anything about Dickens' life up to that time. When Dickens lived at Doughty Street, he was still in his early twenties, an age at which young gentleman were well advanced in education, but at which the intelligent young Englishman without the gentleman's advantages not infrequently had just begun his. There had been no time or opportunity in Dickens' life for a leisurely progress through the educational system, picking up along the way a broadening interest in many fields of learning as well as the foundations of a liberal library. From the time he was pulled out of school to work in that terrible blacking warehouse, his formal education—apparently not of the best, to begin with—had (despite the three years he was later to spend at the Wellington Academy) virtually ended, and his time was devoted first to an abortive study of law, then to mastering shorthand (as no other man ever seems to have mastered it) for his work as a parliamentary reporter, and at last to the writing of the millions of words that poured out of him to the end of his life, not only in his fifteen novels but in short fiction, reviews, essays, speeches, letters, plays, and other writing; before long, too, there was the added huge task of editing journals and occasional books. No one who knew of these things should have expected to find in the young Dickens any more than they did find: Lewes' shock was a form of class snobbery. But what was worse was the prejudice apparently thus begun: the older Dickens was forever to be judged by the handicap suffered by the younger.

Moreover, Lewes erred in judging Dickens' erudition by his library: all things considered, Dickens had done pretty well as a reader, even by his early twenties. According to Gladys Storey, he could be found as early as the age of five, "his custom being to sit holding a book in his left hand, the wrist of which he clasped with the other, swaying his body to and fro, while his eyes eagerly scanned the pages." By the age of ten Dickens had read Smollett, Fielding, Goldsmith, Cervantes, Le Sage, Defoe, *The Arabian Nights*, Sterne, Irving, Addison, Steele, Johnson, and many others including Mrs. Inchbald, *The Scottish Chiefs* by Jane Porter, *The Life of Baron Frederic Trenck*, and *The Adventures of Philip Quarll*—most of them not once, but "over and over again." This is no bad beginning for one who was to be characterized as "average well-read"; possibly some graduates of Eton had not read a great deal more (at least not "over and over again"). In his youth, the reading became wider. While learning shorthand to become a newspaper parliamentary reporter, Forster tells us, Dickens,

> became an assiduous attendant in the British Museum reading-room. . . . No man who knew him in later years, and talked to him familiarly of books and things, would have suspected his education in boyhood, almost entirely self-acquired as it was, to have been . . . rambling or haphazard. . . .

Beyond what has already been quoted, the only opinion to the contrary
is that of John Black, editor of the *Morning Chronicle*, who said of
Dickens at age twenty-two or-three that "he has never been a great
reader of books or plays, and knows but little of them. . . ."[5]
Perhaps Black was deceived by Dickens' oft-recognized reluctance to
parade his knowledge: certainly no one else who knew Dickens ever
accused him of lack of familiarity with drama.

Despite his mountainous work schedule, Dickens continued to
read steadily if not widely throughout his life. By the time of his
residence at Devonshire Terrace, his library, described by Mrs.
Gaskell as a place of "books all round, up to the ceiling, and down
to the ground," had grown to "a goodly array of standard works,"
and Lewes found him capable of conversation on "graver subjects"
than theater and London life, though he remained "completely outside
philosophy, science, and the higher literature. . . ." Thomas Hill
undertook to trace the allusions to literature in Dickens' "major
works," and reported, "I have been amazed at the number of books
with which Dickens must have been acquainted and with the scope of
his reading, considering all we know of his early education."[6] Blank
spots notwithstanding, his reading appears to have become increasingly
eclectic: Forster says that on just one of Dickens' vacations he read
"all the minor tales as well as the plays of Voltaire, several of the
novels (old favourites with him) of Paul de Kock, Ruskin's *Lamp of
Architecture*, and a surprising number of books of Africa and other
travel for which he had an insatiable relish: but there was never
much notice of his reading in his letters." Out of those books on
Africa, it should be mentioned, the "little Dickens" got enough to
catch the great Carlyle in an error about that continent in his *French
Revolution*, which Dickens said he had been reading "again for the
500th time. . . ."[7] If Dickens read but half as much during other
vacations, it is difficult to understand why Forster called him merely
averagely well-read; Forster often seems curiously ambivalent about his
friend, complimenting with one hand while qualifying with the other,
or offering a negative assessment only to supplement it with redemptive

information. It must have been difficult for a man with a good
formal education to praise an autodidact too highly, perhaps even as
highly as he deserved. In any case, even Forster's limited evaluation
of Dickens as reader places him well above the half-educated cockney
others have made him out to be.

Books cited by Dickens not only in his works but in his letters
amply bear out Edgar Johnson's assertion that his reading in later life
was "more numerous and more varied than he is ordinarily given
credit for . . ."; Johnson adds that his comments on these books are
"always vividly alive, and often sharply penetrating." He mentions
Richardson, Cooper, Scott, several Elizabethan dramatists including
Shakespeare and Jonson, as well as Congreve, Sheridan, "and all the
comic playwrights, down to an almost endless number of nineteenth-
century comedies and farces." The list continues with Aubrey's *Brief
Lives*, Pepys, Boswell, Gibbon, Macauley, Carlyle, Buckle, Cobbett,
De Quincy, and Landor; Johnson says that Sydney Smith's *Lectures on
Moral Philosophy* "was one of his favorite books. He was among the
earliest to realize the genius of Browning and Tennyson; he published
some of the poems of the young Meredith and praised his *Shaving of
Shagpat.* . . ." Finally, Johnson mentions Gaskell and Eliot, and
says that Dickens knew and admired Chateaubriand, Lamartine,
Dumas, and Hugo, was on terms with the leading Parisian dramatists,
and was among the first Englishmen to praise Turgenev.[8]

Many more names must be added, with no thought of including
everything Dickens read. He enjoyed biography, though he had
serious reservations about exposing the private life of writers; he
burned all letters received by him to discourage such activity in connection with his own life, and thought it a good thing that little was
known about the life of Shakespeare. As for fiction, he not only
knew Godwin's *Caleb Williams* but wrote to Poe (whose work he also
read) about the way it was written. Sala's assertion that Dickens
knew only Hugo and Dumas among French writers is simply wrong:
Paul Feval said that "He knew us all," and while Philip Collins suggests that Feval may have been thinking more of the writers than their

works, he accepts the assertion that, in addition to French writers already named, Dickens knew Balzac, Sand, Leon Gozlan, Joseph, Mery, and Alphonse Daudet. Dickens read nearly all the poets of his century. Forster adds that he had read *Tales of the Genii* and George Colman's *Broad Grins.*[9]

In his letters Dickens claimed to be "rather strong on Voyages and Cannibalism . . ." and mentioned that he had read Dallas's *The Gay Science of Art and Criticism.* In history, Dickens had read and admired the works of J. A. Froude, and recommended to Constance Cross works by him, Buckle, and Macaulay. He also talked to Miss Cross about "Schiller and Goethe and Lessing," and, negatively, Heine.[10] He read widely in geography and travel, and knew a number of books of a more or less scientific nature; Hill concluded that he "really studied" medicine. In 1854 he wrote to Mrs. Watson to recommend two new books on astronomy: Whewell's *On the Plurality of Worlds* and Brewster's *More Worlds Than One.* He was familiar with the work of Baroness von Bulow, who introduced the kindergarten system to England, and with the philosophy of the educator Froebel. (As educational reformer, Dickens has been called "the greatest that England has produced," and "one of the first great advocators of a national system of schools. . . .")[11]

If he lived among us today, Dickens surely would be viewed as a man who, like many autodidacts, had holes in his cultural credentials, but was nevertheless a very well-read man. Though as Forster says, Dickens did not refer frequently in his letters to his reading, enough mention of books is made to demonstrate clearly that "average well-read" is the very least that can be said of him.

To list the books and writers Dickens read is a simple matter; to decide just what he got out of them is more difficult, especially since Dickens was not given to parading his knowledge. But some of his contemporaries attested to his ability to speak intelligently and informatively. The Reverend Whitwell Elwin found him "full of knowledge," and said that "his reading was beyond what could have

been anticipated from his brief and broken studies." Not a few critics
have found something like intellect—abstract, as well as concrete—in
Dickens' writing; indeed, many of those who speak of his limitations
also mention his strength. Walter Phillips follows his remark about
Dickens as non-thinker with this:

> Yet instinctive and unbookish as Dickens' art was, it would
> be the gravest mistake to assume uncertainty in his narrative
> creed or practise. How he wanted a story told he knew
> quite as well as the most philosophical of novelists; amd in
> his capacity as editor of a periodical and mentor extraor-
> dinary to Wilkie Collins, he had recorded a suffcent number
> of impressions and preferences to enable some understanding
> of the dramatic method.[12]

Harry Stone says that he collected the unpublished pieces Dickens
wrote for his journals partly because they "make it possible to study
. . . [Dickens'] theory of art. . . ." Despite his reluctance to
descend to the technical, Stone says, "Dickens was willing to speculate
and theorize." Edgar Johnson qualifies his own negative judgment:
"Not primarily a systematic thinker, but a man of feeling, intuitive
and emotional, Dickens had nevertheless a sharp intelligence. . . ."
After noting that "commentators as varied as Dean Inge and Bernard
Shaw have claimed he was unaware of the cultural upheavals of the
nineteenth century and indifferent to all its fierce revivals and revolu-
tionary movements in art, in philosophy, in science, in social theory,
and in religion," and quoting Inge—"the number of great subjects in
which Dickens took no interest whatever is amazing"—Johnson adds
that

> The generalization is far too sweeping. Dickens was himself
> a revolutionary movement in the art of literature, and had
> strong and considered judgments on its practise. . . . He
> was fully alert to the developments of the age, and was at
> least as well informed as most educated men, not excluding

men of letters.

Angus Wilson said that if Dickens "did not always see very clearly, he saw very deeply into the world he lived in; perhaps indeed not clearly because so deeply." If, as Wilson continues, his seeing was impaired by his limited formal education, his disagreements with more learned men were not always owing to his defects, but sometimes to theirs:

> . . . He thought many answers of intellectuals and experts on matters which concerned human beings to be too clear, too simple; that they left out feelings. . . .
>
> He was not dismissive of intellect or reasons, but only of what he thought monstrous or absurd perversions of it. . . . He refuses . . . to join "with the unreasonable disciples of a reasonable school. . . ."[13]

One must understand and forgive the friends who belittled Dickens' intelligence and learning; it is difficult for the well-rounded product of formal education (especially in the nineteenth century, when there was far more rounding) to penetrate the uneven and spotty surface of the self-taught man to his essential qualities. Certainly Dickens got very little from the small amount of formal education tossed his way. In Chatham he attended the school of the Reverend William Giles, an Oxford-educated scholar who was impressed with and gave much help to his young pupil, and said he "made rapid progress." But then came the move to London and, during hard times there, no school at all. When Dickens returned to classes at the Wellington Academy House, from 1824 to 1827, he did not impress his schoolmates; years later Dr. Henry Dawson said he did not distinguish himself, and another former chum reported that "He was not particularly studious. . . . As for education, he really received hardly any."[14]

Therefore Dickens lacked some of the earmarks of the educated man. But if, for example, he never learned to read Greek or Latin, he did acquire some knowledge of continental languages, which would identify him as an educated man today. While he knew nothing of German, comically protesting when his son Charley sent home compositions from school in that country that "I can't read a word!," he read, wrote, and apparently spoke French quite fluently; it was the only foreign language in his library. Though erratic in his use of accent marks in French—and though Forster in his usual way compliments his writing in French but says that he "Never spoke the language very well, his accent being somewhat defective . . . ,"—Dickens not only wrote well enough so that by 1848 his letters to his French friends were all in their language, but he was able to report that at least one Frenchman, M. Pichot, said that "he had rarely met a foreigner who spoke French so easily as your inimitable correspondent. . . .[15] By 1844 Dickens had "long been accustomed to read French almost as easily as English," and the following year he dropped the "almost." But his first attempt to speak French was, Forster tells us, amusing. On a trip to Marseilles (on his way to Italy),

> His first experience in a foreign tongue he had immediately on landing, when he had gone to the bank for money, and after delivering with most labourious distinctness a rather long address in French to the clerk behind the counter, was disconcerted by that functionary's cool inquiry in the native-born Lombard Street manner, "How would you like to take it, sir?"[16]

A similar anecdote told by Dickens about Forster may explain why the biographer was reluctant to compliment his friend's French too highly. Coming to Boulogne to visit Dickens, he had, in response to customs officals who had asked in French if he had anything to declare, "not at all understanding the enquiry, said after a moment's reflection with the sweetness of some choice wind instrument

'Bon jour!' and was immediately seized. . . ." But even if Forster was right in asserting Dickens' limited ability to speak French, there is no doubt that Dickens could understand the spoken word well. He always attended the theater while in Paris, and by 1855 was able to say that "My ear has gradually become so accustomed to French, that I understand the people at the theatres (for the first time) with perfect ease and satisfaction." In the same letter, almost as if anticipating his friend's qualification of his ability, he added, "I walked about with Regnier for an hour and a half yesterday, and received many compliments on my angelic manner of speaking the celestial language." Dickens insisted that both speaking and hearing a language are essential: in "Somebody's Luggage" he argued that "It is with language as with people,—when you only know them by sight, you are apt to mistake them; you must be on speaking terms before you can be said to have established an acquaintance."[17]

Italian was another matter: the best Dickens claimed was that he could "understand, and be understood, without difficulty." As early as 1843, he studied Italian in preparation for his first trip to Italy; he applied himself again in 1844, and acquired enough not only to get by in his vacations in that country but to read the language fairly well. He wrote a paragraph of Italian in a letter to Lewes that the editors of Pilgrim Edition *Letters* call "very good" but for one unusual spelling and one incorrect one. Forster tells us that during his vacation in Albaro in 1844 he again took lessons; in 1853 he wrote from Boulogne, whence he planned a short trip to Italy, that he had "recovered my Italian, which I had all but forgotten. . . ."[18] He relearned enough to laugh at the error of a friend, Emerson Tennent, when the latter in ascending Mount Vesuvius with his family demanded "una chiesa"—a church, not a chair—for his daughter. He liked the sound of Italian; as spoken in and around Milan, he said, "The language has a pleasant sound in my ears, . . . which no other has except my own." Some years later, he remembered enough of the language to correct words in *All the Year Round*.[19]

One can only speculate on how much his familiarity with

foreign languages helped Dickens' education, but surely there must have been at least as much contribution as we would expect in any intelligent man.   Edmund Wilson believed that Dickens "had partly made up for the education he had missed by travelling and living on the Continent and by learning to speak Italian and French."[20] No books in Italian were found in Dickens' library at his death, but the books in French bear marks of careful reading.

It is to the library that we must turn at last for our final sense of Dickens as educated man.   Dickens' collection of books was far from achieving the excellence of the collection of such a well-read novelist as, say, his predecessor Henry Fielding.   Still, the library at Gad's Hill was not only better than the pick-up collection Lewes found years earlier, but superior to the Tavistock library concerning which friends found good (though qualified) things to say.   It was described by a visitor thus: "The bookshelves were full of novels, poetry, history, not suggesting a library but simply individual taste."[21] Perhaps.   But at his death the library contained some three thousand books—as Hill says, not "a bad general library as private collections go."   It contained twelve books on philosophy, one hundred and eighty-two on travel, one hundred and thirty-three on history, biography, and autobiography, thirty-eight on art, three on language, one hundred and seven of or on poetry, twenty-one on religion, twenty-five on literature—and seventy-eight works of literature plus seventy-five novels—, forty-nine related to drama, forty-four on science, nine on politics, three on names, twenty reference works, nine books on music, seven anthologies, one on architecture, and sixteen miscellaneous works.   To this must be added a catalog of "Pictures and Objects of Art" which totalled one hundred and nineteen.   True, there are few classical authors, which marked Dickens in his own time as not formally educated, but in our modern usage of the word there are "classics" galore: Addison, Bacon, Balzac, Beaumont and Fletcher, Boccaccio (in translation), Boswell, the three Brontës, Thomas Browne, the Brownings, Bunyan, Burns, Burton, Samuel Butler, Byron, Carlyle, Cervantes, Chatterton, Chaucer (original and modern),

Coleridge (prose and poetry), Collins, Congreve, Cooper, Cowper, Crabbe, Darwin, Defoe, Thomas Dekker, De Quincy, Mme. de Stael, Lope de Vega, Disraeli, Dryden, Alexandre Dumas, Maria Edgeworth, George Eliot, Emerson, J. Evelyn, Farquhar, Fielding and his sister, Samuel Foote, C. Fournier, Benjamin Franklin, Mrs. Gascoyne, Elizabeth Gaskell, Gibbon, Goethe, Gogol, Goldsmith, Hawthorne, Hazlitt, Homer (translation), Horace (translation), David Hume, Washington Irving, Samuel Johnson, Keats, Kingsley, Lamartine, Lamb, Landor, Le France, Le Sage, Longfellow, Lowell, Lytton, Macaulay, Henry Mackenzie, Marvell, Massinger, Melville, Milton, Montaigne, More, Otway, Pepys, Plautus, Plutarch, Poe, Pope, Rabelais (translation), Reade, Richardson, Schiller, Scott, Shelley, Smollett, Southey, Spenser, Sterne, Swedenborg, Swift, Talfourd, Jeremy Taylor, Tennyson, Thackeray, Thoreau, Trollope, Turgenev, Vanbrugh, Waller, Walpole, Daniel Webster, John Webster, Whitman, Wordsworth, and Wycherley. Many a man in our time, if not in Dickens', who had read no more than these authors would be thought to have a solid foundation in the humanities.

As the world knows, though many an earlier voice was raised in Dickens' defense, it was Edmund Wilson who launched the first concerted counterattack of the twentieth century against the Dickensian deprecators.

> . . . Of all the great English writers, Charles Dickens has received in his own country the scantiest serious attention from either biographers, scholars, or critics. He has become for the English middle class so much one of the articles of their creed—a familiar joke, a favourite dish, a Christmas ritual—that it is difficult for British pundits to see in him the great artist and social critic that he was. Dickens had no university education, and the literary men from Oxford and Cambridge, who have lately been sifting fastidiously so much of the English heritage, have rather snubbingly let him alone. The Bloomsbury that talked about Dostoevsky ignored

Dostoevesky's master, Dickens.[22]

So began the crusade, one anticipated by such writers as Forster and
Chesterton and Gissing and Shaw, though each of these writers, while
elevating Dickens as novelist, contributed a few phrases to the ever-
more-certain lilliputization of him as thinker, critic, dealer in such an
abstract thing as aesthetics. Even Wilson, we may note in the above
declaration of war, limits (at least by implication) Dickens to artist and
social critic, leaving one free to conclude that little aesthetic activity is
to be found in the man.

But in the wave of critical activity that followed Edmund
Wilson's clarion call, a few scholars have begun to consider the
Dickens aesthetic worthy of study. His interest in drama has always
received attention, including compliments which are, if anything, overstated. Every biography notes his activities in the theater—though none
attempts a full examination of his aesthetic principles, or studies such
activity as a whole—and two books offer representations from his
novels, and a fair sampling from his letters, of what he had to say
about the theater. But recent writers have also directed our attention
to Dickens' aesthetic comments in other areas, and to argue against
the notion that he had nothing useful to say. By 1976 Harvey
Sucksmith could protest against Dickens' being "so often thought of as
an uneducated upstart isolated from the intellectual and cultural life of
his time. . . ."[23]

Dickens' interest in art has been examined, most notably in Jane
R. Cohen's *Dickens and His Original Illustrators* and Leonee Ormond's
valuable essays, "Dickens and Painting: the Old Masters," and
"Dickens and Painting: Contemporary Art." In an earlier period
James Lightwood glanced at his experience with music and more
recently Arthur Adrian examined his knowledge of poetry. Monroe
Engel offered the first serious scholarly examination of Dickens among
the arts. In his *The Theory of the Novel in England, 1850-1870*,
Richard Stang gave careful attention to Dickens' ideas about prose
fiction. But it was not until 1970 that Harry Stone called attention to

the importance of the early reviews written by Dickens, especially in the *Examiner*, which "provide us with early examples of Dickens' critical values and judgments."[24]

To date, the only full-length study of the Dickens aesthetic is an unpublished doctoral dissertation by Dolores Lehr, entitled *Charles Dickens and the Arts*. It is a good seminal examination of Dickens' activities in music, drama, poetry, sculpture, and other areas, to which I am in part indebted, but it also continues the negative chorus: Dickens was "a novelist rather than a theoretician or a reviewer," whose critical comments "never really deal with intricate technical details. . . . His response often reveals a lack of sophistication and, at times, almost a Philistine outlook."[25]

The time has come (and more than come) for a thorough examination of all those places in which Dickens expressed ideas about aesthetics—his letters, speeches, reviews, articles, incidental writing, and recorded conversation—so that we may decide much more clearly than anyone has done before exactly to what extent—to the extent that one can ever know—Boz did deal with theory, did involve himself in technical detail, did, no doubt to the amazement of some readers even in our time, think. Our aims, then, are two: to follow him into the world of drama, art, music, poetry, even as we may into sculpture and architecture, and see how active and how effective he was there, and to begin what must become an important part of Dickensian criticism in the last years of the twentieth century: a definition of his own aesthetic judgment. It is not our purpose to assess Dickens the active novelist—though at times our study may be assisted by allusion to his fiction—but to observe Dickens the resident in and observer of and commenter upon the world of the arts. It is important to remember as we do so that we have before us not always the deliberate and carefully reasoned statements of a man who has presented his thought in finished form, but rather a most diverse body of writing. Working with bits and pieces presents obvious difficulties: words themselves become confusing, especially in an age which had not developed a critical vocabulary. What, for example, did Dickens mean by *true?*

Did he mean faithful to fact? Verifiable by reference to the real world? Consistent with feeling? The truth of God? Had Dickens written a book on literary theory, he would have defined his terms, but in his letters, speeches, and magazine pieces he used *truth* to mean different things, and one must try to decide which (and sometimes how many) of several meanings is applied in each case. The point is not that Dickens wrote carelessly: whatever he did for the public was painstakingly done, and even in his private letters he took the time to write well; but much of what we will examine is written offhand, hastily, on the spur of the moment; it is not the product of calm consideration but rather the expression of a momentary state of mind, to meet the exigency of the situation.

Comments are made under quite different conditions, some of them published reviews, some compliments directed to an author, some careful criticism for an aspiring writer, some confidential asides to a friend. Each condition, obviously, must color our response to the thought presented. Dickens' letters are a mine of information, as Ada Nisbett said, "a much more reliable key to an understanding of the man who wrote them than are his works. . . ." But as we read them we must take Dickens' own advice: "We should always remember . . . that letters are but ephemeral. . . ."[26] Perhaps, because Dickens never wrote at length about his art or the art of others, we may never understand his aesthetic as well as we do that of those who offered treatises. But we must begin to try.

1

Art: For the Sake of the Story

My Constant Fortune

Studies of Dickens' experience with painting and related art have been limited to cursory summaries of his activities and to still shorter comments by his biographers on the quality of his critical pronouncements. Most of the latter have been disparaging, though a few in recent years have expressed limited, at times almost grudging, approval.[1] But attackers and defenders of Dickens' opinions on art are not as sharply divided as they at first appear to be: the difference between them is rather of degree than of kind. And those who minimize his critical ability err not so much in the specific points they make, which are often correct, as in the impression they leave with the reader that Dickens' understanding of art is negligible. Despite the defects, it is not; a reading of his comments on painting, illustration, and related arts reveals an intelligent, thoughtful, and consistent pattern of aesthetic judgment, based on principles he applied to all the other arts as well, including that in which he himself excelled. It also shows a considerable development from a fairly narrow and insular idea of what art could be to a much fuller ability to enjoy art

in a broad, if never quite the broadest, range. We need neither
Dickens' daughter nor his biographer to tell us, as they have,[2] that he
had no training in art: he tells us so himself. "I am not mechanically acquainted with the art of painting," he says quite simply in
Pictures from Italy.[3] But then, he had little if any formal training in
anything else, yet managed to write great novels, to read widely in the
areas of his interest, to become the foremost parliamentary reporter of
his time and one of the best editors, and to establish a reputation for
greater knowledge of the theater than any other man of his age.
Certainly his immersion in the world of art—through friendships, attendance of art exhibitions, acquiring of paintings by gift and by purchase, writing on art for his journals and editing of such writing by
others, and most of all through his intense involvement with the artists
who illustrated his novels—must have been very nearly the equivalent
of a formal education. If he lived as intimately as he seems to have
done among the artists of his time and still could manage nothing
more than the commonplace opinions which some critics find in him,
Dickens must stand convicted of limited aesthetic ability indeed.

Dickens knew most of the artists of any repute in his time—
knew them as men, whatever limitations may have existed in his
knowledge of their work. "Since I first entered the public lists," he
said in a speech at the Royal Academy Banquet, "a very young man
indeed, it has been my constant fortune to number amongst my
nearest and dearest friends members of the Royal Academy who have
been its grace and pride."[4] Dickens, indeed, had more artists than
writers as friends. The first, his daughter tells us, was David Wilkie,
whose influence on Dickens is described in some detail by Leonee
Ormond, especially in regard to truth in painting, a preoccupation
with the hearth and the poor, and a break with eighteenth-century
classicism in favor of art to which all could respond.[5] Another early
acquaintance was George Cruikshank.[6] One of his lifelong friends was
the Irish painter Daniel Maclise; others more or less within the
Dickens circle were Ary Scheffer, George Cattermole, W. P. Frith,
Clarkson Stanfield, John Leech, Hablôt Knight Browne, Frank Stone

(and his son, Marcus), Augustus Egg, and Charles Collins (who became the first husband of Dickens' daughter, Kate, herself an accomplished amateur painter). The names of dozens of other artists are to be found in his letters and minor writings: Turner, Richard Doyle, William Oliver, Samuel Palmer, William Mulready, Benjamin Robert Haydon, Charles Robert Leslie, Thomas Webster, Canaletto, Samuel Tovey, John Tenniel, Francis Topham, Robert Scanlon, John Branvard, Edward Ward, Benjamin West, Thomas Sully, David Roberts, William Boxall, Hogarth, Godfrey Kneller, Reynolds, Gainsborough, Watteau, Washington Alston, Francis Alexander, Robert and Fanny M'Ian, and Bamfylde Moore Carew, not to mention such amateur artists as Mrs. Shipton, Count D'Orsay, George Putnam, and Mrs. Richard Watson;[7] a number of these were also acquaintances of Dickens. Wherever he went, he seems to have sought out artists; Forster says that during his stay in Paris in 1855, "Dickens's life was passed among artists. . . . His associations were with writers, painters, actors, or musicians. . . ." And several of his other friends, like Wilkie Collins and John Forster, were known for their knowledge and appreciation of art. Only a few of these friends disparaged Dickens' knowledge of art. George Sala said, "He rarely said anything about art; and for what is usually termed 'high art', I think that he had that profound contempt which is generally the outcome of lack of learning." Dickens did say that "All this high art is out of my reach,"[8] but if contempt is to be read in the statement, it is hardly profound; Dickens' reluctance to make pronouncements, coupled with a fierce desire to avoid platitude and jargon when he did speak, is probably at least as responsible for the statement as is the untutored man's dislike of that with which he is not familiar.

Curiously, Dickens' constant contact with artists never led to an inclusion of them in his novels; as Kate Perugini said, "in the numerous volumes which contain my father's writings . . . never once has he introduced an artist as one of his important leading characters." But if Dickens did not allow artists into his world, he very actively entered into theirs. We can trace Dickens' interest in art back as early as his childhood. In an 1859 piece for *Household Words* he says that among his first possessions were "some coloured engravings of Bamfylde Moore Carew, Mrs. Shipton, and others, in a florid state of art. . . ." It has been argued from a reading of *Sketches by Boz* that Dickens remembered the plates in many of his childhood books more vividly than the texts. This continuing interest, many believe, exerted an important influence upon his fiction. The strongest evidence of such continuing interest is obviously his close work with the illustrators of his novels, but there is ample evidence too in the many illustrated books found in his library at his death, and in numberous gifts of such books, as well as paintings, which he received throughout his life.[9]

As an adult, Dickens made art an important part of his life. Kate spoke of "the hours he passed in [the] studios" of artists.[10] His letters show him to have attended exhibitions fairly frequently, as when he thanked a friend, Angela Burdett Coutts, for tickets to an exhibition of "Old Masters and English School paintings" at the British Institution,[11] wrote to the American painter John Branvard to express his pleasure at the latter's three-mile-long painting of the Mississippi valley which he had seen in an exhibition at the Egyptian Hall in Picadilly,[12] or, from Paris, informed his friend John Forster that he had been an interested observer of the international exhibition of paintings there in 1855. *Pictures from Italy*, of course, gives ample evidence of his careful attention to the art of Italy, but even in *American Notes*, which makes no pretense of treating the culture of the United States, references to painting are not infrequently made. Art is occasionally the subject of articles by Dickens and others in *Household Words* and *All the Year Round*; in one of these, "The Shop Side of Art," he exposed dealers who victimized the nouveau-riche middle-class buyers of art with forgeries (Meagles is so deceived in *Little Dorrit*).[13]

Evidence of Dickens' constant exposure to art can also be found outside of his own writing. For example, his actor-friend William Charles Macready records in his diary that he and Dickens went to the Royal Academy Exhibit on May 2, 1846.[14] And Dickens not only observed but actively supported the world of art. Twice he chaired Artist Benevolent Fund anniversary festivals, once in 1858 and again in 1862. He attended several of the Royal Academy Banquets, the last on April 4, 1870, just two months before his death, and was a successful speaker at such functions. He seems also to have provided financial assistance to painters: his daughter Kate says that "his earnest desire to help the younger and poorer [artist] is well known. . . ."[15] But in art as in his own discipline, Dickens' assistance stopped short of pushing the product: his one refusal to help an artist came in response to a painter who sought to enlist his influence in getting work: Dickens could not, he said, gain access to employment where the artist's talent had not. Even here Dickens was kind; he complimented the unknown artist's "studies from nature" as "excellent observations of nature, in a loving and healthy spirit."[16] But that opinion, he added, would not influence experts on art.

Dickens was also a purchaser of art, though he was by no means a collector. He perpetrated a "pious fraud" upon his friend Maclise in order to buy a picture the artist would otherwise have given him, and there is record of his acquiring several other works— e.g., from Francis Topham and Samuel Tovey. As the catalog of his library shows, many paintings and drawings were in his possession at the time of his death. It is hardly the gallery of a connoisseur: as with his library, one gets the impression of a casually acquired rather than carefully selected gallery. Nevertheless, it was respectable enough for the artist Marcus Stone to admire it in the Tavistock House, saying that the paintings "were arranged on the wall with great discrimination, [*sic*] the owner showed himself to be an excellent 'hanger'." Leonee Ormond says that the paintings hung at Gad's Hill were arranged to produce "a symmetrical and architecturally satisfying effect."[17]

There is even evidence of some interest by Dickens in the developing art of photography during his later years, though hardly any of his comments on it add to our understanding of his aesthetic. Perhaps he was attracted to the new art form because he found in it that exact likeness which Johnson says he made a principal tenet of his criteria for portraiture. In June of 1859 he wrote to his daughter Mamie, of a photo of her and Kate, "it is not a very pleasant or cheerful presentation of my daughters, but it is wonderfully like for all that, and in some details remarkably good."[18] He could even forgive the photo for being ugly, as long as it was true. But the new art form seems never to have been of more than passing interest to Dickens. There is no mention of it in his novels, and his comments, with the single exception of his preference for "likeness," add nothing to our understanding of his aesthetic, though they do help to demonstrate his range of interest.

Frequent contact with art is no proof of ability to understand it, but it seems clear that Dickens, whatever his limitations in technical training, did learn from his constant association with artists and their work. He was *au courant* with at least some of the artistic movements of his time, as his strong opposition to the Pre-Raphaelite School shows. And he was familiar with the styles of several artists, as is demonstrated by his allusions to them in his letters. He knew and detested the style of Alfred and John Chalon, and told Forster he was glad their friend Maclise had escaped "the maudlin taint of the sweet Chalon school of silk and ermine. . . . "[19] When another friend, Mrs. Gore, wrote a satire on a series of engravings by Chalon and others entitled *Portraits of the Nobility*, he wrote to congratulate her. "Those books," he said of the collected engravings, "are the gall and bitterness of my life. I vow to God they make me wretched, and taint the freshness of every new year. Your satire is most admirable, and to pluck the peacock's feathers from such daws is worthy of you."[20]

Occasionally Dickens uses an allusion to an artist as a part of his description of a person or scene, thereby demonstrating his familiarity with the style, quality, or characteristic subject matter of the painter. In a piece in *Household Words* he mentions a police sergeant who "might have sat to Wilkie for the Soldier in the Reading of the Will."[21] A room in Avignon looks to his eye "exactly like a picture

by Ostade".[22] In writing about Branvard's Mississippi painting he says
that "it is not [comparable to] those delicate and beautiful pictures by
Mr. Stanfield. . . ."[23] A letter to Maclise from Italy comments upon
the artist's use of color:

> Apropos of blue.   In a certain picture, called "The
> Serenade," you painted a sky.   If you ever have occasion to
> paint the Mediterranean, let it be exactly of that colour. . . .
>
> I hardly think you allow for the great brightness and
> brilliancy of colour which is commonly achieved on the
> Continent, in that same fresco painting.   I saw some—by a
> French artist and his pupil— in progress at the cathedral at
> Avignon, which was as bright and airy as anything can be,—
> nothing dull or dead about it; and I have observed quite
> fierce and glaring colours elsewhere.[24]

Writing to Macready from a site two miles above Niagara, Dickens
said that "Turner's most imaginative drawing in his finest day has
nothing in it so ethereal, so gorgeous in fancy, so celestial."[25] (It is
one of the few instances in which Dickens preferred actuality to the
imagination.)   In a letter written in 1841 to Washington Irving, a
friend of Leslie's, Dickens remarked on that painter's "great abilities
and uncommon gift of humour, with his pencil. . . ."[26] And in a
published piece in which he discussed a scene acted by Macready, he
observed that "we seemed to be looking on a picture by Leslie.   It
was just such a figure as that excellent artist, in his fine appreciation
of the finest humour, might have delighted to produce."[27]

Gladys Storey tells of an incident related to her by the artist
Fred Roe that dramatically conveys Dickens' ability to recognize the
style of a painter.

> One morning this gentleman happened to be in the
> vicinity of Seven Dials.   Looking into the window of an old
> junk-shop, which displayed a miscellaneous collection of odds

and ends, he noticed among them a water-colour drawing which, even through the grime of the window-glass, appeared to be very good. He entered the shop. Over the counter lolled a stout female who, upon request, unconcernedly extracted the work of art from amongst old lamps, walking-sticks, fire-irons and the rest, with the tips of her none-too-clean fingers.

"How much do you want for it?" inquired the prospective purchaser.

"Oh—five shillin's" she ventured.

Inspecting the water-colour closely, then holding it at arm's-length, he said he would take it.

"May I look at the drawing?" said a voice.

"Certainly," returned the purchaser: when to his surprise he discovered that the request had come from none other than Charles Dickens, who was sitting unobtrusively, notebook in hand, in the corner of the shop. After scanning the water-colour for some moments, he handed it back to the owner, observing: "T" (meaning Turner).

"Yes," replied Roe.

"I congratulate you," said Dickens..[28]

If it requires no great talent to recognize Turner, it suggests rather more ability than Dickens has been given credit for. And there is much more. Despite his modesty, his reluctance to "talk shop," his concern that aesthetic discussion too often fell into pretense and cant, his belief that all art should speak for itself, and a strong dislike of saying anything that might offend an artist, Dickens spoke and wrote enough about the art he saw to demonstrate a set of firmly-held and, at the least, respectable aesthetic convictions. Victorian that he was, he believed that art should improve the viewer, but he held to no narrow moralistic aim—indeed, he abominated such stuff, for the improvement he sought was through the enrichment of reality by the imagination, bringing beauty where there was little, touching the viewer to generosity of spirit by dramatic representation that should be powerful in its fresh and emotional appeal, and revealing to him a truth that—when Dickens was at his best—took him far beyond mere physical verisimilitude to a deepened comprehension of his world and of himself. If we begin with an examination of this, much of the rest of Dickens' aesthetic will fall into place.

Dickens has often been disparaged because, it is said, he looked in painting for little more than accuracy, as though the artist must limit himself to the reproduction of nature. Without a doubt, Dickens did believe this. Part of his negative response to Italian art was owing to his conviction that it violated nature; in a letter from Italy he said that he refused to "leave my natural perception of what is natural and true, at a Palace door, as I should leave my shoes if I were travelling in the East." He held to this view, in his less felicitous moments, all his life: years later, writing of his wandering through the rooms of Hampton Palace in England, he substitutes for the shoes an umbrella which he had been asked to leave at the door, and speculates upon what else the art would require him to abandon:

> Form, colour, size, proportion, distance, individuality, the true perception of every object on the face of the earth or the face of the Heavens, . . . And now I find the moon to be really made of green cheese; the sun to be a yellow wafer or a little round blister; the deep wild sea to be a shallow series of slate-coloured festoons turned upside down; the human face Divine to be a smear; the whole material and immaterial universe to be sticky with treacle and polished up with blacking. Conceive what I must be, through all the rest of my life, if the policeman should make off with my umbrella and never restore it!

> Of all the Powers that get your umbrella from you, Taste is the most encroaching and insatiate. Please to put into your umbrella, to be deposited in the hall until you come out

again, all your powers of comparison, all your experience,
all your individual opinions. Please to accept with this ticket
for your umbrella the individual opinions of some other personage whose name is Somebody, or Nobody, or Anybody,
and to swallow the same without a word of demur. Be so
good as to leave your eyes with your umbrellas, gentlemen,
and to deliver up your private judgment with your walking-
sticks. Apply this ointment, compounded by the learned
dervish, and you shall see no end of camels going with the
greatest ease through needles' eyes. Leave your umbrella-
full of property which is not by any means to be poked at
this collection, with the police, and you shall acknowledge,
whether you will or no, this hideous porcelain-ware to be
beautiful, these wearisomely stiff and unimaginative forms to
be graceful, these coarse daubs to be masterpieces. Leave
your umbrella and take up your gentility. Taste proclaims to
you what is the genteel thing; receive it and be genteel![29]

That a painter might deviate from reality for some good
purpose—to shock, to force a new way of seeing, to make clear how
the artist saw—does not seem to have occurred to this Dickens. But
an earlier paragraph in the article sounds quite a different note. After
looking at the paintings, he wanders outside to the gardens, only to
see them "with court-suits on." Adopting the style of *A Sentimental
Journey*, he says,

I wonder, Yorick, whether, with this little reason in my
bosom, I should ever want to get out of these same inter-
minable suites of rooms, and return to noise and bustle! It
seems to me that I could stay here very well until the grisly
phantom on the pale horse came at a gallop up the staircase,
seeking me. My little reason should make of these queer
dingy closet-rooms, these little corner chimney-pieces tier
above tier, this old blue china of squat shapes, these dreary

old state bedsteads with attenuated posts, nay dear
Yorick, . . . should make, even of these very works of art,
an encompassing universe of beauty and happiness. The
fountain in the staid red and white courtyard without . . .
would never fall too monotonously on my ear, the four
chilled sparrows now fluttering on the brink of its basin
would never chirp a wish for change of weather; no bar-
geman on the rain-speckled river, no wayfarer rain-belated
under the leafless trees in the park would ever come into my
fancy as examining in despair those swollen clouds, and
vainly peering for a ray of sunshine. I and my little reason,
Yorick, would keep house here, all our lives, in perfect con-
tentment; and when we died, our ghosts should make of this
dull Palace the first building ever haunted happily![30]

Though Dickens probably expects his reader to deprecate to some
extent the happiness he and Yorick would experience were they confined forever within Hampton Palace, there is also a distinct sense of
the genuine pleasure such imprisonment would give. There is a
definite impression of the lure of the unreal—even the unnatural—art-
world, of the attractions that make it in some ways superior to those
of nature which the later paragraphs insist it should copy. For a
moment, at least, he seems to have left behind his insistence upon the
superiority of the natural world.

Not long before, Dickens had written another piece for
Household Words in which he also expressed his sense of the contrast
between art and life. Coming out of an exhibition of paintings, he
said, "I was much impressed by the contrast between the polite
bearing of the Fine Arts, and the rudeness of real life." Inside he
was an important person, recognized, deferred to, assisted; outside he
was a matter of complete indifference to those around him. The
outside had a

barbarous tendency to reality, to change and movement, and

to the knowledge of the Present as a something of interest
sprung out of the Past and melting into the Future . . . insomuch that the passing from the inside of the gallery to the
outside was like the transition from Madame Tussaud's
waxwork, or a tawdry fancy ball in the Sleeping Beauty's
palace during the hundred years of enchantment, to a windy
mountain or the rolling sea. I understand now, what I had
never understood before, why there were two sentries at the
exhibition door. These are . . . allegorical personages,
stationed there . . . to keep out Purpose, and to mount
guard over the lassitude of the Fine Arts, laid up in the
lavender of other ages.[31]

Again the weight of the passage is on the side of reality over art, yet
there is something of fascination, of attraction, in the gallery. Overtly
the comparisons all reflect the writer's preference for the outside,
however barbarous; still, the inside has its "enchantment"—no doubt
with its original meaning of being entrapped, but also carrying something of the modern meaning of delight—and the "lassitude" and
"lavender" are not entirely objectionable. Dickens loved the fairy tale;
his reference here to the palace of the Sleeping Beauty cannot be perfectly pejorative. And though the passage clearly prefers nature to
Madame Tussaud's waxwork, we cannot forget that in his own life
Dickens was far more attracted to a good show of any kind than he
was to the greatest beauties a country setting had to offer. In these
two passages art is neither tied to nature nor required to transcend it;
its value rests entirely within itself. Much that Dickens wrote and
said shows him working toward a concept of truth that was not confined to fidelity to nature, however often he retreated to that simple
standard in some situations.

Many other criticisms of Dickens' comments on art require
similar modification. Even in the small sampling of commentary we
have observed, for example, we have encountered references to color,
light, and shade—aspects of painting which critics have said Dickens

refers to infrequently, if at all.   If references are few, it was not
because Dickens ignored color: James T. Fields said that "bright
colors were a constant delight to him," and Locker-Lampson reported
him as saying that "he had the primeval savage's love for bright positive colours."   It is true that there are not many references to color
throughout Dickens' writing, but there are enough to indicate that he
was aware of its importance.   His confession that he was "not
mechanically acquainted" with art is followed by a description of his
"means of judging a picture" which includes the appreciation of
"graceful combinations of form and colors."   Color is commented
upon occasionally: Dickens objected to "the colour of [the] water" in
the Branvard painting of the Mississippi, deplored the "horrible combinations of color"[32] in the Duke of Wellington's funeral car, noted
that the artist who painted the "votive offerings" on the walls of an
Italian church "had not been sparing of his colors,"[33] and found that
in paintings by Giulio Romano in the Palazzo Te in Mantua "the
coloring is harsh and disagreeable. . . ."[34] He lamented that *The Last
Supper* had lost "its original coloring, . . . because of damp, decay,
and neglect, & because inferior painters have disastrously retouched
it."[35] Writing a review of Maclise's *The Spirit of Chivalry*, he spoke
of "the prodigious force and colour which so separate this work from
all the rest exhibited. . . ."[36] In one instance, Dickens even described
color for an illustration for *Martin Chuzzlewit*, though the picture could
only appear in black and white.[37]

It is hardly possible to decide from such statements whether
Dickens' judgment of color was good or bad, but an incident with the
painter John Leech suggests that in at least one instance it was better
than the artist's.   When Leech was upset by the quality of the printed
colors in the four plates he did for *A Christmas Carol*, Dickens reas-
sured him: "You can't think how much better they will look in a
neat book, than you suppose."[38] Jane R. Cohen says that the critics
sided with Dickens: the *Illustrated London News* found the pictures
"tastefully coloured. . . ."[39] In fairness to Leech, it was probably
Dickens' experience with plates for books that enabled him to make

his better judgment.

Dickens also commented upon details of organization to some extent. He spoke of the "beautiful composition and arrangement"[40] of *The Last Supper*; he complained of a painting in which "a little figure on a mountain has a head-dress bigger than the temple in the foreground, or adjacent miles of landscape."[41] He praised the composition of Tintoretto's *Assembly of the Blest*, "with all the lines in it tending majestically and dutifully to Almighty God in the Centre,"[42] though it is disappointing that he had nothing to say about the vivid contrasts of color which are characteristic of that artist. In the same letter, Dickens commented upon another painting, "in which the surprising art that presents the generals to your eye, so that it is almost impossible you can miss them in a crowd though they are in the thick of it, is very pleasant to dwell upon."[43]

Other comments show that Dickens was aware of how conditions of publication or location can affect the reception of a work of art. A series of drawings by John Leech, originally published in *Punch* and reproduced as *The Rising Generation*, Dickens described as showing "to infinitely greater advantage in the present enlarged and separate form of publication."[44] Examining Italian art, he thought that "in the private palaces, pictures are seen to the best advantage."[45] And of the Egyptian Room in the Vatican he wrote:

> There is a fine collection of Egyptian antiquities, in the Vatican; and the ceilings of the rooms in which they are arranged, are painted to represent a starlight sky in the Desert. It may seem an odd idea, but it is very effective. The grim, half-human monsters from the temples, look more grim and monstrous underneath the deep dark blue; it sheds a strange uncertain gloomy air on everything—a mystery adapted to the objects; and you leave them, as you find them, shrouded in a solemn night.[46]

There are also a few indications that, despite his disclaimer,

Dickens understood at least some technical aspects of painting and the care of paintings.   In October of 1852 he went to Fulham to get a "copy" by an "ancient artist" named Mrs. Brayne for Miss Burdett Coutts.   Dickens decided that it would be injured by light, and so would need a case; he also advised his friend on the size of a frame and on "another slight alteration"[47] which has not been identified.   At another time we find him writing to Mrs. Richard Watson that his "baby collection" of pictures looks better at Gad's Hill—"in country light and air"[48] than in London.

In a comment upon Maclise's painting, *Hamlet*, which he thought "a tremendous production," Dickens noted the artist's use of light and shade; the artist, he said, "so manages the lights in this picture, that on the scene behind, is an enormous shadow of this groupe—as if the real murder were being done again by phantoms! And what a carrying-out of the prevailing idea, it is, to paint the very proscenium of the little stage with stories of Sin and Blood. . . ."[49] Dickens may not have noticed this on his own: Thackeray, who was, among other things, a professional art critic, had made much the same comment in an article in *Ainsworth's Magazine* the preceding month. But Dickens' equally perceptive comments on Maclise's *The Spirit of Chivalry*, in his own article published in Douglas Jerrold's *Shilling Magazine* in 1845, are probably his own.

The Idea In My Mind

That art form with which Dickens was most familiar, and from which he learned much about art, is the illustration of books.   His participation in the task of putting pictures into his novels brought him into close working relationship with many of the major English artists of his day, and developed to a high level his ability to select subjects, decide upon the kind of face and figure characters should have, choose the props and scenery most appropriate for a picture, offer directions upon composition and spatial arrangement, understand methods of printing pictures, and make decisions about locating them in the text.   If, as several scholars have remarked, Dickens' fiction was significantly influenced by this experience, it is also true that his understanding of art was improved.

Much of the work Dickens did with his illustrators gives evidence of his mastery of technical aspects of art.   He was familiar with the several methods of reproducing pictures, and was particularly knowledgeable about engraving.   We find him at the age of twenty-five passing judgment upon an engraver, W. C. Walker, who engraved the frontispiece to W. L. Rede's *The Peregrinations of Pickwick*: Walker was ". . . a line engraver of great promise,"[50] the young author confided in a letter to his much older publisher, Bentley.   In another judgment, rendered to Leopold C. Martin, the engraver (along with one Corbould) of seven of the sixteen illustrations of *The Haunted Man*, Dickens showed himself aware of the different quality of proof and final print in a book: "I am much obliged to you for the proofs you had the kindness to send me, yesterday.   The drawings of course appear to greater advantage in such a form, but I think—all things considered—that they have been *very well* rendered in the book, and especially in the frontispiece."[51] Another comment upon an engraving shows Dickens with a sharp eye for what can be lost when something is omitted from the original picture.   In the second volume of Forster's biography of Landor, he wrote,

> is an engraving from a portrait of the remarkable man when seventy-seven years of age, by Boxall. . . .   The original picture is a singularly good likeness, the result of close and subtle observation on the part of the painter; but, for this very reason, the engraving gives a most inadequate idea of the merit of the picture and the character of the man.
>
> From the engraving, the arms and hands are omitted. In the picture, they are, as they were in nature, indispensable to a correct reading of the vigorous face.   The arms

were very peculiar. They were rather short, and were curiously restrained and checked in their action at the elbows; in the action of the hands, even when separately clenched, there was the same kind of pause, and a noticeable tendency to relaxation on the part of the thumb. Let the face be never so intense or fierce, there was a commentary of gentleness in the hands, essential to be taken along with it.[52]

It has been alleged that Dickens did not see with the eye of an artist. Sometimes he did not: he was too busy seeing paintings with the eye of a novelist. But the two kinds of seeing are not mutually exclusive; Dickens could see some art as well as any painter.

But Dickens' work with his illustrators also reveals limitations in his understanding of art. Although Jane R. Cohen highly values his overall contribution to the quality of the pictures which appear in his works, she also notes instances in which his interference hurt. On several of these occasions Dickens pressured his artist to do more than was possible. Professor Cohen points out that in the "Paul and Mrs. Pipchin" picture for Chapter 8 of *Dombey and Son*, for example, had Browne taken his instructions about placing Paul "in the fireplace corner, with his gaze shadowed by the black drapery as the text specified, the problems of composition and light would have been almost insuperable."[53] Occasionally Dickens seemed unaware of how much an illustration could contain, and would give an artist much more than he could put into his drawing (Dickens almost always chose subjects for his illustrators, and usually described what he wanted in considerable detail). On Dickens' letter to Browne concerning the "second subject" for *Martin Chuzzlewit*, Browne wrote "I can't get all this perspective in—unless you will allow of a long subject—something less than a mile."[54] There is much more than perspective in Dickens' instructions that the most conscientious artist could never get in. There is movement: for a scene in *Martin Chuzzlewit* Dickens advised his artist to draw a picture in which "Mr. Pecksniff hastens in. . . .

The old man in a transport of burning indignation, rises from his chair, and uplifting his stick, knocks the good Pecksniff down. . . ."[55] Dickens' instructions even include the cessation or absence of activity: "Kit . . . stops for a moment . . .";[56] or "a subject representing Master Humphrey's clock as stopped. . . ." (How in the world does a picture show a clock as having stopped?) It is clear that Dickens wants cinema, not stills—or that he would, if he could, endow his pictures with all the powers of his narrative. Yet not even his narrative could accomplish some things his instructions detail: in a carriage scene in *Barnaby Rudge* a character is required to turn on the driver's seat and look into the carriage while menacing with his cudgel someone running beside the carriage.[57]

Obviously Dickens did not intend his artists to get all that he mentioned in his instructions into their pictures. Much of the information is supplied to assist their imagination, to prepare them for the still life they are to draw, to help them acquire a sense of mood, of feeling. But if this much is clear, it is equally clear that he wished they could "get it all in." Could they have done so, could Dickens have had motion pictures, each illustration would have invested his story with more life than even his gifted pen could bring to it; the characters would have lived more completely than even his prose could make them live.

It is this, one suspects, that attracted Dickens so strongly to art: he felt in it the potential to create life beyond the limits of (at least, in a different way from) his own genre. His fascination with drama is surely of a similar nature; his perceptive comments on the dramatic in painting show how close he thought the two arts to be. In one such comment he drew a distinction between dramatic and theatrical: "in the former case a story is strikingly told, without apparent consciousness of a spectator, and . . . in the latter case the groups are obtrusively dressed up, and doing (or not doing) certain things with an eye to the spectator, and not for the sake of the story. . . ."[58] "For the sake of the story"; certainly everywhere in his work with his illustrators, Dickens' first concern is that. The fault in an illustration which provoked his strongest reaction was the artist's failure to follow the narrative. The worst such instance occurred when John Leech put the wrong character in a scene near the end of Part II of *The Battle of Life.* Dickens wrote Forster:

> When I first saw it, it was with a horror and agony not to be expressed. Of course I need not tell *you*, my dear fellow, Warden had no business in the elopement scene. He was never there! In the first hot sweat of this surprise and novelty, I was going to implore the printing of that sheet to be stopped, and the figure taken out of the block. But when I thought of the pain this might give to our kind-hearted Leech; and that what is such a monstrous enormity to me, as having never entered my brain, may not so present itself to others, I became more composed; though the fact is wonderful to me.[59]

Important facets of the critical Dickens are to be found here, perhaps the most important being that no criticism, not even of the most devastating flaw of which Dickens can conceive, is worth giving offense to a friend; in the above letter, he recovered from his anguish enough to go on to praise the work Leech had done for *The Battle of Life.* But almost equally important is the fact that a picture drawn contrary to his story is a "monstrous enormity," almost a kind of threat to the imagined reality that the story is as it existed within his brain. It is "wonderful" to Dickens that anything contrary to that imagined reality could exist; he has to convince himself that others will not find it monstrous too. It is almost like science fiction, in which some departure from cosmic law may threaten existence itself.

There is no doubt that Dickens felt a powerful connection between his illustrations and his stories. He did not spend time on them simply because he wanted the finished book to be as good as it could be, though that was no doubt an important consideration. He labored over them as exhaustingly as he did because they lived for him exactly as his fiction did, and he felt the integrity of the second threatened by any lapses in the first.   Seeing so much, one understands far more clearly than before such a statement as Dickens wrote into a speech for Frank Stone, to be delivered at the Manchester Athenaeum on October, 1845, in which he said that painting was "an art which had ever been allowed to possess a kindred, nay, sisterly relation, to the spirit of literature. . . ."[60] Siamese sisters, one might add.

I think no one[61] has quite understood the mortal intensity of this linkage before, though several have noticed the influence of drawing upon Dickens' writing.   Jane R. Cohen suggests that working with artists both helped to form Dickens' vision of his world and taught him ways of conveying it to his readers through details of character and setting.[62]   Others have commented upon the similarity between Dickens' prose and the technique of painting.   Van Gogh, whose letters give evidence of the closest reading of Dickens, said that "there is no writer, in my opinion, who is so much a painter and black-and-white artist as Dickens.   His figures are resurrection."[63]   Dickens himself said, "I don't invent it—really do not—but *see* it, and write it down."[64]   In a sense this is as much as to say that, as a novelist, Dickens worked from a picture.

But if drawing influenced Dickens' writing, it was all too often simply in terms of his writing that he viewed the drawings of his illustrators: they were to be judged not so much as art on their own terms as merely another kind of writing.   Though they turned out to be among the best of their kind, it was not their excellence as art that he concentrated on, but their fidelity to his story and their support of his characters.   He never doubted, from the moment when his first novel began with his changing his publishers' plan to have him write a story for Robert Seymour's illustrations (saying, as he put it in his Preface to *Pickwick Papers*, that "it would be infinitely better for the plates to arise naturally out of the text"), the primacy of story over picture.   His letters sometimes show a nervous fear, not that an illustrator may draw an artistically poor figure, but that he may not catch the idea of the character which Dickens felt the need to present. (Certainly quality and accuracy often overlapped: a drawing that captured Dickens' conception was for that reason a good piece of art.)

> The points for illustration, [he wrote to Forster, who often helped him with all aspects of his novels] and the enormous care required, make me anxious. The man for Dombey, if Browne could see him, the class man to a T, is Sir A___ E___ of D___'s. Great pains will be necessary with Miss Tox. The Toodle family should not be too much caricatured, because of Polly.[65]

Forster says that Dickens "expressed his anxiety about Browne's illustrations for Dombey, with a nervous dread of caricature in the face of Mr. Dombey. 'I do wish he could get a glimpse of A, for he is the very Dombey.'"[66] But Browne could not get his glimpse, and so Dickens required him to supply a "sheetful" of "actual heads as well as fancied ones,"[67] so that he might select the face most like that of his imagined reality.

Just a few months later, Dickens was upset by Browne's handling of other characters in *Dombey & Son*; he wrote Forster that the illustration of Paul and Mrs. Pipchin was "frightfully and wildly wide of the mark. Good Heaven: in the commonest and most literal construction of the text, it is all wrong. . . . I can't say what pain and vexation it is to be so utterly misrepresented."[68] Again, one has the sense that Dickens' imagined characters are as real to him as any actual being: to be "utterly mispresented" is damaging not only to them, as a poor photograph in a magazine might be to a public person, but to their creator, as though some of nature's journeymen had made a man and not made him well, and thereby had offended the image in the creator's mind. If his most severe criticism is leveled against those who got the story wrong, his highest praise is given not to those who drew the finest pictures but to those who managed what Dickens told John Leech he had done in his drawings for *Master Humphrey's Clock*: "this is the very first time any designs for what I have written have touched and moved me, and caused me to feel that they expressed the idea I had in my mind."[69] When Cattermole sent him watercolors of two of his illustrations for *The Old Curiosity Shop*—one of Little Nell's grave, and one of the interior of the shop—Dickens expressed similar satisfaction:

> It is impossible for me to tell you how greatly I am charmed with those beautiful pictures, in which the whole feeling and thought and expression of the little story is rendered to the gratification of my inmost heart; . . . [70]

And when W. P. Frith, after doing a picture of Dolly Varden for *Barnaby Rudge*, later painted Dolly again, and also Kate Nickleby, Dickens is reported to have said, "All I can say is, they are exactly what I meant."[71] "The idea I had in my mind"; "the whole feeling and thought and expression of the little story"; "exactly what I meant"; it is this, more than artistic excellence, that Dickens looked for in the illustrations of his novels.

Some of his critical commentary, however, was directed to the improvement of a picture as picture, not simply to strengthening its fidelity to his novel.   Dickens called for better representation of a detail, or suggested additions or deletions that would improve the illustration.[72] One plate drawn by George Cruikshank displeased him so much that he immediately brought the older man to account:

> With reference to the last plate—Rose Maylie and Oliver. Without entering into the question of great haste or any other cause which may have led to its being what it is—I am quite sure there can be little difference of opinion between us with respect to the result—

and Dickens asked Cruikshank to do the plate "afresh and . . . *at once*,"[73] which is about as imperious as he ever got with any of his illustrators.

Perhaps Dickens came to realize that too much domination of his artists (particularly his less famous ones: he always allowed the established artist more leeway) could hurt their work; he gave them freer reign (though never final say) as the years went by. Professor Cohen says that "as Dickens' instructions to Browne became more suggestive and less imperative, the artist responded with increased creativity."[74] As early as *Martin Chuzzlewit* we find him asking Browne to do the frontispiece of Tom Pinch playing the organ, with "any little indications of his history rising out of it, and floating about it, that you please."[75] In a very few instances, Dickens even solicited the artists' opinions about the nature of an illustration; as time passed, he would on occasion give them the option of selecting details, locations—sometimes even the subject— out of a number of the novel. To the end, though, he would remind them that their work was subject to "correction, alteration, revision, and all other ations and isions connected with the Fine Arts."[76]

The extent to which Dickens' work with his illustrators improved his knowledge of and taste in art cannot be fully assessed, but it seems likely that both were materially improved. If the experience did nothing else, it brought him into intimacy with artists at work, and probably prompted him to undertake the fairly ambitious commentary on some of them which he attempted in later years. If this later commentary is not always superior, some of it is very good, and much of it demonstrates a competence for which he has not often been given credit.

The illustrator-artists upon whom Dickens wrote at length were George Cruikshank, John Leech, Daniel Maclise, and Clarkson Stanfield, all of whom he greatly admired. Cruikshank, in fact, was the only one he criticized, though most of his objection was to the content, not the artistry, of the great caricaturist. His first reference, to an unidentified drawing (perhaps for Matthew Barker's "Nights at Sea" in *Bentley's Miscellany*, No. 6, 12/37, which Dickens was then editing), professed that he was "delighted with the drawing, which is most admirable."[77] A few months later, he was even more enthusiastic

about an illustration for another piece in the *Miscellany*: "I've seen
Cruikshank this morning, and he has left me in transports with his
Mudfog association subject."[78] A Cruikshank book which consisted of
eleven illustrations for the artist's version of the popular poem *Lord
Bateman* earned high praise from Dickens.   "You never did anything
like those etchings ever."[79] A subsequent work brought less enthusiastic approval: of *George Cruikshank's Omnibus*, edited by Laman
Blanchard and illustrated by Cruikshank, Dickens wrote to Harrison
Ainsworth that "there seems to me to be too much whisker for a
shilling, but that's a matter of taste."[80] Cruikshank, of course, was
bearded.   The *Omnibus* was successful for a time, but perhaps the
public also at last found it too hairy: the publication expired with its
ninth number.

Characteristically, Dickens' letter to Cruikshank about the "Buss"
carried no hint of adverse criticism: "It is wery light, wery easy on
the springs, well horsed, driv in a slap up style, and altogether an
uncommon spicy con-sarn," he said.   The same kindness appears in
his next comment on and to Cruikshank: writing to him about his
Cruikshank's Almanac for 1844, he said, "You are prodigious,"[81]
though actually he may not have liked the work.

Despite his customary refusal to criticize the productions of his
friends, Dickens could not refrain from adverse comment on several of
Cruikshank's later works—not of their artistry, but of their ideas.   The
first of these was a collection of eight plates entitled *The Bottle*, concerning which Dickens wrote to Forster:

> I think it very powerful indeed; the two last plates most ad-
> mirable, except that the boy and girl in the very last are too
> young, and the girl more like a circus-phenomenon than that
> no-phenomenon she is intended to represent.   I question,
> however, whether anybody else living could have done it so
> well.   There is a woman in the last plate but one, garrulous
> about the murder, with a child in her arms, that is as good
> as Hogarth.   Also the man who is stooping down, looking at

the body.[82]

Elsewhere Forster records Dickens' praise of a similar work, *The Drunkard's Children*:

> I think the power of that closing scene quite extraordinary. It haunts the remembrance like an awful reality. It is full of passion and terror, and I doubt very much whether any hand but his could so have rendered it. There are other fine things too. The death-bed scene on board the hulks; the convict who is composing the face, and the other who is drawing the screen round the bed's head; seem to me masterpieces worthy of the greatest painter. The reality of the place, and the fidelity with which every minute object illustrative of it is presented, are surprising. . . . In the trial scene at the Old Bailey, the eye may wander round the court, and observe everything that is a part of the place. The very light and atmosphere are faithfully reproduced. So, in the gin-shop and the barber-shop. An inferior hand would indicate a fragment of the fact, and slur it over; but here every shred is honestly made out. The man behind the bar in the gin-shop, is as real as the convicts at the hulks, or the barristers round the table in the Old Bailey. . . . [83]

But though he admired the artistry of such works, Dickens did not like their philosophy. He followed his praise of *The Bottle* with this: "But it only makes more exasperating to me the one-sidedness of the thing,"[84] and added, "the drinking should have begun in sorrow, or poverty, or ignorance—the three things in which, in its awful aspect, it *does* begin."[85] Hogarth, he said, did not undertake a "Drunkard's Progress" because he knew there were too many causes of drunkenness to depict. Cruikshank, who in earlier years had been a hard drinker but had now become a teetotaler, thought drinking produced misery; Dickens saw it the other way around. But though he disliked the message of Cruikshank's art (and was on occasion angered by his rude objections to drinking at private parties), Dickens could appreciate his artistry. If we cannot base upon this single instance an argument against those who claim that Dickens' emphasis upon content influenced his artistic judgment, at least we can note that there were exceptions.

Upon two other occasions Dickens was to render homage to Cruikshank's art while raising objection to its content. One of these was in connection with *The Drunkard's Children*. "Few men have a better right to erect themselves into teachers of the people than Mr. George Cruikshank," Dickens wrote in his commentary upon the work. "Few men have observed the people as he has done, or known them better; . . . and there are very, very few artists, in England or abroad, who can approach him in his peculiar and remarkable power."[86] But then Dickens objected again to the idea that social ills can be so easily attributed to drink.

But Dickens' most important disagreement with Cruikshank, one which widened the already perceptible gap between them as friends, came in response to the artist's work entitled *Hop-o'-my-Thumb*. Here Cruikshank had coupled the kind of literature Dickens loved most—fairy tales, children's literature—and the kind he most hated: dry moral tales aimed at improving children. Dickens had already written a tract against such stories in his *The Uncommercial Traveller*: the title of the piece, "Mr. Barlow," was taken from a character in the novel *Sandford and Merton* (1713), by Thomas Day. Mr. Barlow relentlessly draws a moral from every event in the lives of the two young protagonists of the story, and in his article Dickens recorded his distaste for such stuff. Now, in a piece entitled "Frauds on the Fairies," he enters the same objection against Cruikshank's moral pictures. "It was just the kind of pervasive didacticism that Dickens had always regarded as dreary and deadening," Harry Stone says, "the antithesis of fancy and imagination."

. . . The child would enter the storybook world only to find that it contained the same prosing precepts that nagged at him from the pages of his insufferable copy books or his improving moral tracts. To Dickens, Cruikshank's text was a fraud. It would turn children away from the fount of fancy and imagination at the very source.[87]

In a letter to his subeditor Wills, Dickens said "I mean to protest most strongly against alteration, for any purpose, of the beautiful little stories which are so tenderly and humanly useful to us in these times, when the world is too much with us, early and late. . . ."[88] Cruikshank is a "great artist," but he must be criticized for misusing fancy, a fault that is hard to understand in him because "in his own art he understands it so perfectly, and illustrates it so beautifully, so humorously, so wisely. . . ."[89] Dickens did not believe in criticizing his friends in print, but Cruikshank in *Hop-o'-my-Thumb* was striking at one of his fundamental aesthetic principles, and though he worded his criticism as gently as he could, he could not let even a friend get away with it. (It is also interesting to notice this attack upon a kind of morality in a work of art by the man many have accused of placing morality above art, though of course here it is fancy, not art itself, that he elevates.)

Dickens also commented at length upon the work of John Leech, another close friend and illustrator of his novels. Leech was one of the best-known artists of his day, and Dickens found several occasions to praise him. In a speech at the Newsvendor's Benevolent Institution in January of 1852, he referred to "the great popular artist of the time, whose humour was so delicate, so nice, and so discriminating, and whose pencil like his observation was so graceful and so informed with the sense of beauty that it was mere disparagement to call his works 'caricatures'. . . ." According to Lady Russell Dickens paid Leech the highest compliment possible: "Leech, he thought was truer to life than even Hogarth."[90]

Dickens' longest and most careful criticism of Leech extended this consideration of him as a new kind of caricaturist. Forster asked

him to write for the *Examiner* a review of a series of twelve drawings
on stone called *The Rising Generation*, taken by Leech from his
designs done for "Mr. Punch's Gallery" in *Punch* magazine. Dickens
called the work "a careful reproduction by Mr. Leech, in a very
graceful and cheerful manner, of one of his best series of designs,"
and said that "it shows to infinitely greater advantage in the present
enlarged and separate form of publication." He called Leech

> the very first English caricaturist (we use the word for want
> of a better) who has considered beauty as being perfectly
> compatible with his art. He almost always introduces into
> his graphic sketches some beautiful forms or agreeable
> forms; and in striking out this course and setting this
> example, we really believe he does a great deal to refine and
> elevate that popular branch of art. . . .

In the works of such caricaturists as Rowlandson or Gilray, Dickens
said, the great humor displayed was often

> rendered wearisome and unpleasant by a vast amount of per-
> sonal ugliness. Now, besides that it is a poor device to
> represent what is satirised as being necessarily ugly—which is
> but the resource of an angry child or a jealous woman—it
> serves no purpose but to produce a disagreeable result.
> There is no reason why the farmer's daughter in the old
> caricature who is squalling at the harpsichord (to the intense
> delight, by the by, of her worthy father, whom it is her duty
> to please) should be squat and hideous. The satire on the
> manner of her education, if there be any in the thing at all,
> would be just as good if she were pretty. Mr. Leech
> would have made her so. The average of farmer's daughters
> in England are not impossible lumps of fat. One is quite as
> likely to find a pretty girl in a farmhouse, as to find an ugly
> one; and we think, with Mr. Leech, that the business of
> this style of art is with the pretty one. She is not only a

pleasanter object in our portfolio, but we have more interest in her. We care more about what does become her, and does not become her.

Dickens cites another illustration by Leech

representing certain delicate creatures with bewitching coun- tenances, encased in several varieties of that amazing garment, the ladies' paletot. Formerly these fair creatures would have been made as ugly and ungainly as possible, and there the point would have been lost, and the spectator, with a laugh at the absurdity of the whole group, would not have cared one farthing how such uncouth creatures disguised themselves, or how ridiculous they became.

But to represent female beauty as Mr. Leech represents it, an artist must have a most delicate perception of it; and the gift of being able to realize it to us with two or three slight, sure touches of his pencil. This power Mr. Leech possesses in an extraordinary degree.

After registering his "protest against those of the 'Rising Generation' who are precociously in love, being made the subject of merriment by a pitiless and unsympathetic world," Dickens commented on the ac- curate observation and depiction in the twelve drawings, concluding:

In all his drawings, whatever Mr. Leech desires to do, he does. The expression indicated, though indicated by the simplest means, is exactly the natural expression, and is recognised as such immediately. His wit is good-natured, and always the wit of a true gentleman. He has a becoming sense of responsiblity and self-restraint; he delights in pleasant things; he imparts some pleasant air of his own to things not pleasant in themselves; he is suggestive and full of matter; and he is always improving. Into the tone, as well as into the execution of what he does, he has brought a certain elegance which is altogether new, without involving any compromise of what is true. This is an acquisition to popular art in England. . . .[91]

Here are several of the major tenets of the Dickensian canon of art. Where it reasonably can, art should be beautiful; it should find a way of lending pleasantness to "things not pleasant in themselves." It should tell a story, offering characters who can be read, and whose expressions are natural. The work should improve its viewer. Art, in short, should be as close as possible to Dickens' kind of story-telling, though "slight, sure touches of [the] pencil" must replace the written word. Dickens is aware that there are differences between the two disciplines, but he is little interested in them except as they offer means of telling a story beyond the limitations of the word.

The only other artist among Dickens' illustrators upon whom he commented at any length was his close friend, Daniel Maclise, the Scotch-Irish painter. Maclise and the Landseer brothers were the only artist members of the famous Portwiners, a group that included Dickens, Forster, Thackeray, and the actor Macready. If Maclise did relatively little as illustrator for Dickens, it was not for want of respect, as Dickens' comments on Maclise's own work indicate. But curiously, in an exchange of letters with his American friend Felton, Dickens showed a surprising reluctance to characterize Maclise's art: Maclise was, he said, "'such a discursive devil,' (as he says of himself) and flies off at such odd tangents that I feel it difficult to convey . . . any general notion of his purpose."[92] Apparently Felton asked again for a description of the character of Maclise's work, for a few months later Dickens wrote him again, in almost the same words:

He is such a discursive fellow, and so eccentric in his might, that on a mental review of his pictures I can hardly tell you of them as leading to any one strong purpose. But the Annual Exhibition at the Royal Academy comes off in

May, and then I will endeavor to give you some notion of
him. He is a tremendous creature, and might do anything.
But like all tremendous creatures, he takes his own way, and
flies off at unexpected breaches in the conventional wall.[93]

If Dickens kept his promise to give Felton a "notion," it has not been
preserved. His reluctance to describe his friend's art, with which he
must have been as familiar as with the work of any other man, is
perhaps partly understandable: Maclise was eclectic in his selection of
subjects, as Professor Cohen notes,[94] and Felton seems to have been
asking rather about content than form. But one would think Dickens
could at least have called attention to his friend's partiality for
dramatic subjects, which was his main attraction for Dickens, rather
than settling for the description "tremendous creature." "Maclise is
painting wonderful pictures,"[95] he had written to another correspondent
shortly before his first response to Felton; but now, with an opportunity to explain in detail just what was so wonderful about paintings
like *A Girl in a Waterfall* and perhaps *The Actor's Reception of the
Author* and *Scene from Gil Blas*, Dickens is found with very little to
say. Still once more, in September of 1843, he had the opportunity
of describing Maclise to Felton, but once again evaded the task: "He
is such a wayward fellow in his subject, that it would be next to impossible to write such an article as you were thinking of, about
him. . . ."[96]

On all other occasions, though, Dickens showed no reluctance to
speak about his friend's art. His comments indicate that, of all the
painters who worked for him, Maclise was the most admired. Their
close friendship was no doubt part of the reason for his preference: a
cool objectivity was rarely part of Dickens' character. But there were
other important reasons. Maclise was famed for two qualities which
are at the heart of the Dickens aesthetic: beauty and story. Dickens
also liked, Kate Perugini tells us, "the extraordinary facility of his
work. He painted rapidly. . . ."[97] The speed with which Dickens
himself wrote has been greatly exaggerated, but a writer capable of the

amazing amount of work he produced would obviously admire an artist who could do a great deal in a short time. Dickens seems also to have approved of the ability of Maclise to visualize his subject. "What an eye you have," he wrote him in 1842, and though there is some reason to believe this was part of an old joke between them,[98] subsequent letters in the same year offer ample evidence that he meant it. "Nothing is to be said of [Maclise's painting] Hamlet, but wonderful. You know what I honestly think of your extraordinary powers; and how much in earnest I am when I say that it amazed, even me."[99] To Charles Sumner, Dickens wrote, "Maclise's picture from Hamlet is a tremendous production. There are things in it, which in their powerful thought, exceed anything I ever beheld in painting."[100]

Before the end of the year, Dickens wrote to Maclise that his *A Girl at a Waterfall*, a work in progress, was "charming";[101] he later acquired this painting by means of the "pious fraud" we have mentioned. And he wrote to Mrs. De La Rue that Maclise's *Superstition of the Ordeal by Touch* was "very fine indeed."[102] Thackeray liked the painting, too, calling it "perhaps the best and greatest of the artist's works. . . .)"[103] Dickens and Thackeray also liked Maclise's portrait of Dickens, but George Eliot called it "that keepsaking, impossible face."[104] She probably would have thought little of Dickens' advice to Maclise to put "dreaming expressions" on the faces of figures in his *The Sleeping Beauty*, saying that they would be "Beautiful! Very beautiful."[105] Maclise did not use the suggestion.

An incident between Maclise and the Fine Arts Commission elicited from Dickens that volcanic indignation with which he reacted to any fancied or real slight to the Arts. In July, the Commission had named subjects for frescoes to be done in the six arched compartments of the new House of Lords, and had invited six artists to submit, for exhibition in 1845, cartoons, colored sketches, and specimens of fresco. The six were Richard Redgrave, W. C. Thomas, C. W. Cope, J. C. Horley, William Dyer, and Maclise—in that order. In addition, other artists were allowed to compete, and no guarantees were given to the six named painters. "I am disgusted with the Fine Arts Commission," Dickens wrote D'Orsay,

> . . . and think their putting Maclise anywhere but at the very head and front of the Competition, abominable. And I think the terms on which their designs are to be sent in, are disgraceful to the Comissioners as gentlemen—disgraceful to the selected artists, as men of talent—and disgraceful to the country in which the paltry huckstering piece of power is exercised.

D'Orsay agreed: "It is an insult to a man of [Maclise's] talent to be put in competition with such wretched daubers."[106]

But it is in his written review of Maclise's *The Spirit of Chivalry* that Dickens finally gave the thorough description of his friend's art that shows he could indeed say something. The review is too long to be quoted in full, but much of it is worthy of careful attention. Dickens called the painting

> a composition of such marvellous beauty, of such infinite variety, of such masterly design, of such vigorous and skilful drawing, of such thought and fancy, of such surprising and delicate accuracy of detail, subserving one grand harmony, and one plain purpose, that it may be questioned whether the Fine Arts in any period of their history, have know a more remarkable performance.

He commented upon the difficulty of the work: its size, proportion, subject, even title all ordered by the Fine Arts Commission. The subject he thought particularly challenging:

> That the treatment of such an abstraction, for the purposes of Art, involved great and peculiar difficulties, no one who considers the subject for a moment can doubt. That nothing

is easier [than] to render it absurd and monstrous, is a position as little capable of dispute by anybody who has beheld
another cartoon on the same subject in the same hall,
representing a Ghoule in a state of raving madness, dancing
on a body in a very high wind, to the great astonishment of
John the Baptist's head, which is looking on from a corner.

Maclise's handling of the subject had been studied by all kinds of
people, Dickens said: students of art, those accustomed to viewing the
great paintings of the world, and "ignorant, unlettered, drudging men,
mere hewers and drawers, [who] have gathered in a knot about it
. . . and read it, in their homely language, as it were a Book. In
minds, the roughest and the most refined, it has alike found quick
response. . . ." Reading it himself, Dickens found in it the inspiration which comes from love of woman, of glory, of poetry, both in
the "spirit" and in other figures of the painting. There was an
appeal to the aged in the older figures clustering around the spirit,
which were "of the very highest order of Art, and wonderfully serve
the purpose of the picture. There is not one among its three and
twenty heads of which the same remark might not be made."
Dickens mentioned "the prodigious force and *colour* which so separate
this work from all the rest exhibited . . ." and defended it against
the charge that it was "too elaborately finished: too complete in its
several parts" by pointing out that it "is a design, intended to be afterwards copied and painted in fresco," and therefore had to be more
finished than the usual cartoon.

> Great misapprehension on this head seems to have been en-
> gendered in the minds of some observers, by the famous
> cartoons of Raphael; but they forget that these were never in-
> tended as designs for fresco painting. They were designed
> for tapestry-work, which is susceptible of only certain broad
> and general effects, as no one better knew than the Great
> Master. Utterly detestable and vile as the tapestry is, com-

pared with the immortal Cartoons from which it is worked, it is impossible for any man who casts his eyes upon it where it hangs at Rome, not to see, immediately, the special adaptation of the drawings to that end, and for that purpose. The aim of these Cartoons being wholly different, Mr. Maclise's object, if we understand it, was to show precisely what he meant to do, and knew he could perform, in fresco, on a wall. And here his meaning is; worked out; without a compromise of any difficulty; without the avoidance of any disconcerting truth; expressed in all its beauty, strength, and power.[107]

Though the review is something less than a finished piece of art criticism, it is rather better than most published comments on Dickens' ability to judge art would lead us to expect. True, we have in it again the Dickens who wants story in his paintings, to be read "as it were a Book." True, much of the comment is upon content rather than form. But Dickens does recognize the difficulty the painting offered, does speak of the grouping and general harmony, comments upon the color, and shows some knowledge of technical aspects of painting in his distinction between cartoons designed for fresco and those for tapestry, "which is susceptible of only certain broad and general effects. . . ." And some knowledge of Raphael is demonstrated. The opening effusion is embarrassing, but the rest supports Professor Cohen's assertion that Dickens' criticism was "often judicious."

Dickens seems to have had but two reservations concerning Maclise's artistry; of these the first was not in regard to the quality of his work but to the energy of the worker. "If he has a care, he will leave his mark,"[108] he had written to Felton in 1843, and again in 1845 he voiced the concern: "if he will only give his magnificent Genius fair play, there is not enough of Cant and Dulness . . . to keep the Giant down, an hour."[109] Dickens' daughter Kate wrote that Maclise was "incorrigibly idle," and that her father "would gently remonstrate or more often merely joke and tease" in an effort "to rouse him from a kind of moral apathy. . . ." It is characteristic of Dickens that even in his private correspondence he made but these two slightly veiled references to the laziness of his friend, whom he knew to be given to severe seizures of depression. As for Maclise's art, Kate says that her father often found his paintings displeasingly hard and emphatic, owing to his seeing objects from a distance only: "it deprived any distant object he looked at of the mystery and charm which often add so much beauty to a world seen through more short-sighted eyes."[110]

Dickens had much less to say about his remaining illustrators. Among these was another close friend, Clarkson Stanfield. Also a painter of established reputation, Stanfield was one of several whose talents Dickens managed to enlist not only for his books but also for the amateur dramatic productions of which he was so fond. Stanfield and others painted scenes for Dickens (one of which decorated his home for years), and sometimes acted in his plays. Early in their acquaintance Stanfield seems to have sent Dickens pieces of his work: one of Dickens' first letters to him thanks him for two, probably the watercolors *Land's End* and *The Logan Rock*, done during their trip into Cornwall with Maclise and Forster. "Most beautiful," Dickens called them, and wrote to his American friend Felton that on the trip the two artists "made such sketches . . . that you would have sworn we had the Spirit of Beauty with us, as well as the Spirit of Fun." Just a few months later he wrote to Stanfield praising "your immortal scenery," and in a letter from Albaro told him that "the approach to Genoa, by sea from Marseilles, constitutes a picture which you ought to paint, for nobody else can ever do it!" During this same European trip, after seeing Venice, Dickens wrote that Stanfield and Canaletto were "miraculous in their truth"[111] in painting that city.

Subsequent comments continued to express admiration. Stanfield's *Victory* was a "noble painting"; his paintings at the Royal Academy exhibit were (by anticipation) his "latest triumphs." Of his painting of the bridge at Avignon Dickens said, "Beautiful as it undoubtedly is, you made it fifty times better."[112] At Stanfield's death, Dickens described him as a "great marine painter" with "wonderful gifts" whose "grand pictures proclaim his powers . . ."[113]—though the eulogy typically concentrated upon the noble nature of the artist rather than upon his artistic gifts.   Only in the letter to Forster about the Paris Exhibit of 1855, one of the very few places in all his writing about painters in which Dickens let go, did he comment adversely upon Stanfield, saying that his piece in the exhibit "is too much like a set scene."[114]

The strong control Dickens exercised over such artists as these as they illustrated his novels—mitigated here and there among the most famous, but never entirely absent—supports the conclusion that, however limited his artistic training might be, he had considerable confidence in his ability to work in the world of painting and drawing.   And though his work with them reveals flaws in his understanding of art, there are strengths to balance the weaknesses.   Good, careful, and—considering their context—relatively thorough judgments are rendered about several artists, especially Cruikshank, Leech, and Maclise.   In at least one instance—the discussion with Leech about the colors of the illustrations for *A Christmas Carol*—Dickens' judgment proved better than the artist's.   If he does not often comment on color, arrangement, composition, light and shade, he shows that he is capable of doing so.   His essay on Leech's *The Rising Generation* makes a valid distinction between the ugliness of early caricature and the new style of beauty—showing in the process a knowledge of recent art history—and demonstrates considerable ability to read a painting and represent what is there.   And in his long study of Maclise's *The Spirit of Chivalry* he at last dispels our doubts about his ability to comment on the art of his friend; he shows an understanding of the difficulties a subject can offer an artist (we remember the criticism that he never seemed to think from the artist's point of view), comments upon the figures and the use of color, and again demonstrates some knowledge of art history.   There is enough in all this to support

Professor Cohen's summary of Dickens's ability in art:

> The author had no pretension about his ability as an art
> critic. Yet it must be recalled that he not only reflected the
> tastes of his time, but often helped to mould them. Today,
> many still share Dickens's assessment of his own illustrators
> and other artist friends.[115]

But the strongest impression one carries away from a reading of
Dickens' correspondence with and about his illustrators is the tremendous sense of what his ruling passion in art, as in most other things,
was. Dickens loved a good dramatic tale; though other things about
painting certainly attracted him, it was to the story the picture told
that he was inevitably drawn—if it did not tell a story, he was rarely
drawn at all. Nothing else in his aesthetic world ever came close to
his interest in people and what happened to them; his most discriminating criticism of art is of this kind. One of his most revealing
comments is to be found in a little-quoted speech made at the
ceremony of a presentation to him at Birmingham:

> . . . It is not now the province of art in painting to hold
> itself in monastic seclusion. . . . It cannot hope to rest on
> a single foundation for its great temple—on the mere classic
> pose of a figure, or the folds of a drapery—but . . . it must
> be imbued with human passions and action, informed with
> human right and wrong. . . .[116]

This is the heart of Dickens' ethic of art, and though it includes
the moral sense, its larger concern is drama.

True And Faithful Representation

Dickens' comments upon other and lesser artists are not often
helpful: too frequently he merely expresses approval or dislike, without

explaining why. But patient reading of them does demonstrate how constantly—and confidently—the author offered opinions about artists. He assured a correspondent that the reputable painter Robert Benjamin Haydon was "most unquestionably . . . a very bad painter. . . . There was one picture—Nero entertaining himself with a Musical Performance while Rome was burning—quite marvelous in its badness. It was difficult to look at it with a composed and decent face. There is no doubt, on the other hand, that in the theory of his art, he was very clever. . . ."[117] And here and there clues to his aesthetic convictions are to be glimpsed. His simple eulogy on Sir David Wilkie, for example, contains several of his favorite aesthetic words—*true, beautiful, elevating, nature*—and offers another of his fundamental beliefs about art: it has an obligation to all, including the poor.[118] Even in his commentary on so humble an artist as John Banvard, an American painter who is remembered, if at all, only for his three-mile-long painting of the Mississippi River (rolled from one large cylinder to another in an exhibition at the Egyptian Hall, Picadilly), Dickens revealed his taste, commenting on the painting's defects in accuracy, color, subtlety of light and shade, and delicacy, but admiring its "plain and simple truthfulness. . . ."[119]

Dickens reveals himself far more, however, in his remarks on Hogarth, in a study which John Forster called "a masterly criticism of that great Englishman."[120] Unlike Cruikshank, Hogarth never tried a "Drunkard's Progress" because he knew he could not properly show all the causes as well as effects of such a life. "It was never in his plan," Dickens says,

> to be content with only showing the effect. In the death of the miser-follower, his shoes new-soled with the binding of his Bible, before the young Rake begins his career; in the worldly father, listless daughter, impoverished young lord, and crafty lawyer, of the first plate of Marriage-a-la-mode; in the detestable advances through the stages of cruelty; and in the progress downward of Thomas Idle; you see the effects

indeed, but also the causes.   [In the Rake's] immortal
journey down Gin Lane, [he] exhibits drunkenness in the
most appalling forms, [but] also forces on attention a most
neglected wretched neighborhood, and an unwholesome, in-
decent abject condition of life. . . .   I have always myself
thought the purpose of this fine piece to be not adequately
stated even by Charles Lamb.   'The very houses seem absolutely reeling'; it is true; but beside that wonderful picture
of what follows intoxication, we have indication quite as
powerful of what leads to it among the neglected classes.
There is no evidence that any of the actors in the dreary
scene have ever been much better than we see them there.
The best are pawning the commonest necessaries, and tools
of their trades; and the worst are homeless vagrants who give
us no clue to their having been otherwise in bygone days.
All are living and dying miserably.   Nobody is interfering
for prevention or cure, in the generation going out before
us, or the generation coming in.   The beadle is the only
sober man in the composition except the pawnbroker, and he
is mightily indifferent to the orphan-child crying beside its
parent's coffin.   The little children are not so well taught or
looked after, but that they can take to dram-drinking already.
The church indeed is very prominent and handsome; but as,
quite passive in the picture, it coldly surveys these things in
progress under shadow of its tower, . . .   I am confirmed
in my suspicion that Hogarth had many meanings which have
not grown absolute in a century.[121]

Here we see Dickens in his own critical wheelhouse, whether in
painting or any other art: reading the story and idea with keen
penetration, with a clear and exact understanding of what is before
him.   If the work to be examined has even the slightest dramatic
aspect, Dickens will seize upon it and devote most of his attention to
it; the greater that aspect in the work, the surer and more valuable

will be his criticism. In the commentary on Hogarth, the reader must be impressed not only with Dickens' seeing all there is to see, but with his ability to note and interpret what there is not to see. If Dickens could not see understand everything in art, he could understand this; those who would slight him because of his concentration upon the dramatic in art may be interested in a comment attributed to Picasso: "Abstract art is only painting. What about drama?"

Hint Of Heresy

The only other body of Dickensian commentary on artists and their work consists of his well-known pronouncements on Italian painting, found in his letters and in *Pictures from Italy.* If Dickens saw the United States as a place where money ruled, and so entitled his book on it *American Notes for Circulation*, obviously he felt Italy to be best approached through art, both that which he found there and that which he would use to describe it. Though, as Forster has reminded us, Dickens came to Italy with no formal training in painting, it is also true that he did bring with him a certain amount of informal experience, acquired in the manner we have seen. But little that Dickens learned from Stanfield, Maclise, or Cruikshank (especially up to 1844) could have prepared him for the experiences of Raphael or Da Vinci; it took those experiences and ten more years of contact with English painters to lead him to the realization of the smallness of English art, of its insular conviction that anything in art not done in the English way could not be very good.

Dickens had been exposed to a certain amount of Continental art before his trip to Italy: as early as the late 1830's he had seen European (though not Italian) artists in the gallery at Dulwich College, and he saw the private collection of Samuel Rogers (whom he met in 1839), which included works by Rubens, Raphael, Guido Reni, Giorgione, and Titian. Still, the Dickens of 1844 must have brought something of the British narrowness with him to Italy; it is difficult to

see how he could have avoided it. Though he would appear to have
been familiar with such guidebooks to Italy as those by Eustace and
Forsythe, he apparently had but one guide in his tour of Italian art:
Louis Simond's "charming book on Italy," *A Tour in Italy and Sicily*
(1828), which, he said,

> charms me more and more by its boldness, and its frank ex-
> hibition of that rare and admirable quality which enables a
> man to form opinions for himself without a miserable and
> slavish reference to the pretended opinions of other people.
> His notices of the leading pictures enchant me. They are so
> perfectly just and faithful, and so whimsically shrewd.[122]

Instead of opening Dickens' narrowed Anglican view and preparing
him for the greater art world he was about to enter, Simond seems to
have encouraged him only to exercise the judgment he brought with
him: his disclaimer in *Pictures from Italy* from commenting about
Italian art echoes a statement by Simond.

Another source of weakness in Dickens' criticism of Italian art
was his strong prejudice against Roman Catholicism, probably exacer-
bated, as Leonee Ormond suggests, by his disgust with the dirt and
poverty he found in Italy. For all his fairness in *Barnaby Rudge*
about persecuted Catholics in England, Dickens shared his country's
prejudice against the "Romish" European church, and felt that it had
a baleful influence upon Italian art. He complains of the Italian
masters that

> these great men, who were of necessity very much in the
> hands of the monks and priests, painted monks and priests a
> vast deal too often. I constantly see, in pictures of tremen-
> dous power, heads quite below the story and the painter; and
> I invariably observe that those heads are of the convent
> stamp, and have their counterparts, exactly, in the convent
> inmates of this hour.[123]

Elsewhere in a letter to Forster, he protests against "legions of whining friars and waxy holy families, whole orchestras of earthly angels, and whole groves of St. Sebastians stuck as full of arrows according to pattern as a lying-in pin cushion is stuck with pins."[124] Here, though, one may notice that it is not Catholicism Dickens objects to, but the conventionalizing of art. It is the business of art, Dickens feels, as it is the business of the play, to hold the mirror up to nature, and the mirror has no business—not for religion or for anything else—to show arrows carefully arranged in a corpse, as though the archers had as much design as death in their aim.

Dickens' first mention of art in his letters from Italy, even before he has entered a museum, reflects his determination to make independent and unawed judgment. "Ask me a question or two about fresco, will you be so good?" he wrote to Daniel Maclise from Genoa. "All the houses are painted in fresco, hereabout—the outside walls I mean. . . . Sometimes (but not often) I can make out a Virgin with a mildewed Glory round her head; holding nothing, in an indiscernible lap, with invisible arms; and occasionally the leg, or arm, or what Marryat would call the arthe of a cherub. But it is very melancholy and dim."[125] That was written in July of 1844; it was not until November that comments on art began to appear in his letters, which suggests either that he was slow to get to see the great art, or not quite so prepared to speak about it as his first letter, inviting an artist to solicit his opinion about art, seems to indicate. In any case, by November the comments began to flow. After seeing Venice, he called "Canaletto and Stanny [Stanfield] miraculous in their truth" (in their paintings of the city), and spoke of "those silent speaking faces of Titian and Tintoretto. . . ." This was quickly followed by a longer and more ambitious criticism:

> I have never seen any praise of Titian's great picture of the Assumption of the Virgin at Venice, which soared half as high as the beautiful and amazing reality. It is perfection. Tintoretto's picture too, of the Assembly of the Blest at

Venice also, with all the lines in it (it is of immense size
and the figures are countless) tending majestically and dutifully to Almighty God in the centre, is grand and noble in
the extreme.   There are some wonderful portraits there,
besides; and some confused and hurried, and slaughterous
battle pieces, in which the surprising art that presents the
generals to your eye, so that it is almost impossible you can
miss them in a crowd though they are in the thick of it, is
very pleasant to dwell upon.   I have seen some delightful
pictures; and some (at Verona and Mantua) really too absurd
and ridiculous even to laugh at. . . .[126]

Since we are not told what the absurd and ridiculous paintings
are, or what makes them so, we cannot judge Dickens' judgment in
the last sentence; it is tempting to think that he tacked it on just to
show that he was not indiscriminately praising everything. But as his
first lengthy comment upon Italian art, the rest of this makes no bad
start. It deals in part with the qualities of line and grouping, the
absence of which Johnson laments in other Dickensian commentary,
and it shows sound and independent judgment. Titian's *Assumption*
was generally regarded as a masterpiece in Dickens' time, but Dickens
anticipated Ruskin in praising Tintoretto's *Assembly of the Blessed*
(though neither was the first Englishman publicly to admire it). On a
trip to Italy nine years later, he praised the painting even more
highly, in a letter to Forster:

There are pictures by Tintoretto in Venice more delightful
and masterly than it is possible sufficiently to express. His
Assembly of the Blest I do believe to be, take it all in all,
the most wonderful and charming picture ever painted. Your
guide-book writer, representing the general swarming of
humbugs, rather patronizes Tintoretto as a man of some sort
of merit; and (bound to follow Eustace, Forsyth, and all the
rest of them) directs you, on pain of being broke for want

of gentility in appreciation, to go into ecstacies with things that have neither imagination, nature, proportion, possibility, nor anything else in them.[127]

Writing to Forster in March of 1845, Dickens echoed something of Simond's criticism of Raphael, and added his own liking for the Master's pupil, Marco-Antonio Raimondi:

The most famous of the oil paintings in the Vatican you know through the medium of the finest line-engravings in the world; and as to some of them I much doubt, if you had seen them with me, whether you might not think you had lost little in having only known them hitherto in that translation. Where the drawing is poor and meagre, or alloyed by time—it is so, and it must be, often: though no doubt it is a heresy to hint at such a thing,—the engraving presents the forms and the idea to you, in a simple majesty which such defects impair. Where this is not the case, and all is stately and harmonious, still it is somehow in the very grain and nature of a delicate engraving to suggest to you (I think) the utmost delicacy, finish, and refinement, as belonging to the original. Therefore, though the Picture in this latter case will greatly charm and interest you, it does not take you by surprise. You are quite prepared beforehand for the fullest excellence of which it is capable.

According to Forster, this view had at the time of Dickens' writing "Eloquent reinforcement from critics of undeniable authority."[128] Later in the same letter Dickens offered his opinion of other artists:

There are portraits innumerable by Titian, Rubens, Rembrandt and Vandyke; heads by Guido, and Domenichino, and Carlo Dolci; subjects by Raphael, and Correggio, and Murillo, and Paul Veronese, and Salvator; which it would be difficult indeed to praise too highly or to praise enough. It is a happiness to me to think that they cannot be felt, as they should be felt, by the profound connoisseurs who fall into fits upon the longest notice and the most unreasonable terms.   Such tenderness and grace, such noble elevation, purity, and beauty, so shine upon me from some well-remembered spots in the walls of these galleries, as to relieve my tortured memory from legions of whining friars and waxy holy families.   I forgive, from the bottom of my soul, whole orchestras of earthy angels, . . . and I am in no humour to quarrel even with that priestly infatuation, or priestly doggedness of purpose, which persists in reducing every mystery of our religion to some literal development in paint and canvas, equally repugnant to the reason and sentiment of any thinking man.[129]

Elsewhere in *Pictures from Italy* he criticized Correggio's fresco in the cupola of the cathedral at Parma, a criticism for which he himself has been criticized, but Leonee Ormond supports him: the fresco has since been restored, but when he saw it it was so damaged that its design was a "labyrinth of arms and legs. . . ." But after this, Dickens confined his letters to brief statements of like and dislike, with very little indication of what had helped to form his opinions.   Thus *Il Putto Bianca* in the Durazzo Palace is "a noble painting," and "the Venuses . . . [are] all bad . . . and like anything but women. . . ."[130] Nor do we find much more in *Pictures from Italy* than such statements as that, in the palaces of Genoa, he found "masterpieces by Vandyke. . . ."[131]

The materials of the Italian experience, however, are less important as a record of Dickens' unformed critical judgment than they are as a means whereby we may learn about other aspects of his experience of art.   A brief humorous incident in Mantua demonstrates again his desire to think independently, and also shows familiarity with an important treatise on art.   Going into a picture gallery, he was surrounded by geese whose quacking he interpreted as advice not to go in. Having seen the paintings, he said of the geese, "I would take their opinion on a question of art, in preference to the discourses of Sir Joshua Reynolds."[132] Another comment, on the art found in the cathedral at Parma, suggests that he was capable of looking on painting, if not "with the eyes of an artist," then at least with the eyes of a fellow-artist: "The decayed and mutilated paintings with which this church is covered, have, to my thinking, a remarkably mournful and depressing influence. It is miserable to see great works of art—something of the Souls of Painters—perishing and fading away, like human forms."[133]

Dickens' comments on Italian art tend to be frustratingly incomplete. Only in a few instances is there enough to help us understand at least a little. A section of *Pictures from Italy* on art in Rome begins with the usual generalization: in the Vatican "many most noble statues, and wonderful pictures, are there; nor is it heresy to say that there is a considerable amount of rubbish there, too." But a few pages later Dickens gets down to specific judgment:

> The portrait of Beatrice di Cenci, in the Palazzo Berebini, is a picture almost impossible to be forgotten. Through the transcendent sweetness and beauty of the face, there is a something shining out, that haunts me. . . . She has turned suddenly toward you; and there is an expression in the eyes—although they are very tender and gentle—as if the wildness of a momentary terror or distraction, had been struggled with and overcome, that instant; and nothing but a celestial hope, and a beautiful sorrow, and a desolate earthly helplessness remained. . . . The history of her unhappy life, is written in the Painting; written in the dying girl's face, by Nature's own hand![134]

No one who remembers Little Nell will miss what attracts Dickens here, in addition to the usual dramatic interest: a young female dying, a situation including wildness and terror, the overcoming of earthly ills, and the finding of comfort in the expectation of a better world. But there is also appreciation of the artistry: Dickens' sense that the figure "has turned suddenly" indicates that the painting has conveyed motion to him, just as he wanted some of his illustrations to do. And the reading of the expression of the eyes is sensitive and perceptive; we note too the appreciation for anything that seems natural.

A comment on Giulio Romano is also interesting. The Palazzo Te is singular for those

> unaccountable nightmares with which its interior had been decorated by Giulio Romano. There . . . are . . . Giants . . . so so inconceivably ugly and grotesque, that it is marvellous how   any   man   can   have   imagined   such creatures. . . .   The figures are immensely large, and exaggerated to the utmost pitch of uncouthness; the coloring is harsh and disagreeable; and the whole effect more like (I should imagine) a violent rush of blood to the head of the spectator, than any real picture set before him by the hand of an artist.[135]

The passage reflects, I believe, the difficulty Dickens had before art which intentionally violated his favorite precept of beauty. The greatest imaginer in the English language cannot understand how any one could imagine such things, and though the paintings undoubtedly get to Dickens, he can hardly attribute their effect to human effort; such works are like manifestations of physical illness rather than like art. A similar feeling can be sensed in his reaction to the paintings on the walls of St. Stefano Rotondo, a church on the outskirts of Rome. The pictures there of martyred saints he found

> hideous. . . .   Such a panorama of horror and butchery no man could imagine in his sleep, though he were to eat a whole pig raw, for supper. Gray-bearded men being boiled, fried, grilled, crimped, singed, eaten by wild beasts, worried by dogs, buried alive, torn asunder by horses, chopped up

small with hatchets: women having their breasts torn with iron pincers, their tongues cut out, their ears screwed off, their jaws broken, their bodies stretched upon the rack, or skinned upon the stake, or cracked up and melted in the fire. . . ."[136]

Dickens seems unable to conceive of why anybody would want to paint such things.

My Own Path

Not everyone has decided that Dickens' comments on Italian art mark him as aesthetic ignoramus. Harvey Sucksmith, recognizing that he wanted "to form independent and honest judgments," thought that his opinions on Italian painting "are by no means those of a silly or uncultured man." Still, no great case for Dickens as critic can be made from his reactions to Italian art. Nor can it be claimed that any sudden upsurge in critical acumen occurs upon his return to England: the letters reveal no immediate enlargement of understanding nor deepening of judgment, and in some things Dickens remained limited to the end. But eventually there are, as Johnson says, "strides in his development,"[137] and it is not far-fetched to believe that in part these strides are owing to his exposure to the greatness of Italian art. Some of the effects of that exposure are certainly doubtful, or mixed, in their value, it is true. The determination to walk apart, with a developing concurrent inclination to view as "cant" all pronouncements that smacked of the common path, probably both helped and hurt him. This inclination developed early in his Italian trip. "I am already brim-full of cant about pictures," he wrote in 1844, and the following year wrote to D'Orsay that

there is such an extensive amount of humbug afloat on these matters; and people are so strangely disposed to take what they have heard or read for granted and not use their own

intellects and sense, that whenever I go into a Gallery I
hang out 'No Trust' in legible white letters on a black
ground—like an English Turnpike.

That same year he spoke in a letter of "the Criticism of Art; from
which Sterne prayed kind Heaven to defend him, as 'the worst of all
the Cants continuously canted in this Canting world . . .'" and asked,
"is not our motto Truth for ever, and Cant be damned?"[138]
     When he returned to Italy in 1853, Dickens wrote to Forster
about what he considered to be canting praise of the famous.

Egg's honest amazement and consternation when he saw
some of the most trumpeted things was what the Americans
call a "caution." In the very same hour and minute there
were scores of people falling into conventional raptures with
that very poor Apollo, and passing over the most beautiful
little figures and heads in the whole Vatican because they
were not expressly set up to be worshipped.

An earlier part of the same letter reads almost like a credo:

I am more than ever confirmed in my conviction that one of
the great uses of travelling is to encourage a man to think
for himself, to be bold enough always to declare without
offense that he does think for himself, and to overcome the
villainous meanness of professing what other people have
professed when he knows (if he has capacity to originate an
opinion) that his profession is untrue. The intolerable nonsense against which genteel taste and subserviency are afraid
to rise, in connection with art, is astounding.[139]

     Certainly Dickens' desire not to mouth accepted judgments is
laudable, but he seems to have developed along with this desire the
conviction that almost any discussion of art which employed terminol-
ogy, such as color or line, was equally culpable, as another letter

from Italy in 1853, while travelling with Collins and Egg, suggests:

> The Fine Arts afford a subject which I never approach;
> always appearing to fall into a profound reverie when it is
> discussed. Neither do I ever go into any gallery with them.
> To hear Collins learnedly holding forth to Egg (who has as
> little of that gammon as an artist *can* have) about reds, and
> greens, and things "coming well" with other things, and
> lines being wrong, and lines being right, is far beyond the
> bounds of all caricature. I shall never forget it.[140]

Of course Dickens may be responding to pretentiousness on the part
of Collins here, but similar criticisms of others suggest that Dickens
was beginning to think of all technical discussion as affectation. If
this is true, we have another reason for the widely-cited scarcity of
such discussion in Dickens' writing: perhaps it was owing not so
much to inability as to his desire to avoid what he considered to be
cant. Kate Perugini, herself an artist, wrote of her father that "the
talk of 'vehicles,' 'flat tones,' 'ciaro-scuro,' 'carnations,' and other
mysteries about which artists are apt to grow eloquent, became sometimes a little wearisome to one who was extremely reticent concerning
his own work, and who seldom . . . allowed himself to talk
'shop.'"[141] Dickens' letters show that he found such talk more than a
little wearisome; "I keep out of the way when pictures are in question
and go my own path,"[142] he wrote his wife, and kept to that path for
much of the rest of his life.

    In painting as in his own art, Dickens felt that a work should
speak for itself, and that any discussion of its method, technique, or
message by the artist or anybody else was better left unsaid. Artists,
he told his daughter Kate, should have "the art to hide the art," and
he found little profit or pleasure, and much pretentiousness, in labor-
ing to expose what they had worked to conceal. A number of his
letters show him declining to be drawn into long disquisitions on color
and composition.[143] His refusal to engage in technical discussion is

obviously no proof that he could have if he had wanted to, but it does suggest a reason other than ignorance for his frequent silences.

Dickens' rejection of cantish admiration of painting, and of appreciation according to rules, was accompanied by a distaste for artists who, in his judgment, painted by rule. Again, it is his experience in Italy that seems to have developed this dislike; at least it is then that he begins to write that

> the rules of art are too much slavishly followed; making it a pain to you, when you go into galleries day after day, to be so very precisely sure where this figure will be turning round, and that figure will be lying down, and that other will have a great lot of drapery twined about him, and so forth. This becomes a perfect nightmare.[144]

This dislike of the predictable may be seen as one more facet of Dickens' love of the dramatic in art. We find the same dislike in his reaction to drama and to prose fiction: as a story or play loses its appeal when its action is easily anticipated, so a painting must be poor if one knows beforehand what the position of a figure or the nature of his apparel will be. In any art form, he enjoyed that which could evoke a fresh and untrammeled emotional response; among his favorite words are *striking*, *brilliancy*, and *interest*. His daughter Kate said he called this quality force: "He admired more than any other quality great breadth and force in the conception and treatment of a subject, but looked for a certain delicacy and refinement of finish. . . ." And he rejected anything that tended toward uninspiring formula, such as conventional poses or situations, hackneyed props, and the repeated use of the same models. For a while there was a craze for armor in paintings: Frith spoke of Dickens' reaction to one such by Marcus Stone, entitled *Rest*:

> "A capital picture," said Dickens, in his hearty way. "I am delighted to see it. Armour beautifully done. Apples too— only I think the old boy [the subject of the painting was an

ancient knight collapsed in an orchard] was too far gone for apples. It would require burnt brandy and a good deal of it, to bring him to."[145]

He made fun of conventional backgrounds in portraits: a piece in *Sketches by Boz* speaks of one in which a figure is represented "with a curtain over his head, six large books in the background, and an open country in the distance. . . ."[146] In a piece for *Household Words* entitled "The Ghost of Art," he made serious fun of the conventional in art, first criticizing such standard props as "a high backed chair with a red cushion, and a table with twisted legs," and (in the words of the model in the piece) "warses of flowers, and any number of table-kivers, and antique cabinets, and warious gammon." He also suggested that Royal Academy artists made "monsters" by joining parts of different models to each other. The Ghost of Art is one such model who links Dickens' feelings about models and about rules by stating, "I revere the Royal Academy. I stand by its forty Academical articles almost as firmly as I stand by the thirty-nine Articles of the Church of England." The model has grown a beard in order to meet the "German taste," and has managed, simply by changing its length or shape, to represent "Society!," "Benevolence," "death!," "Adoration, or a vow of vengeance," and "Romantic character," among others. "The beard did everything." The beard haunts the author of the article "from the walls of the Royal Academy (except when Maclise subdues it with his genius) . . . eternally working the passions in hair."[147] If Dickens never actually suffered from such a protean beard, he certainly did endure the stultifying use by artists of stock casts of models, each all too effortlessly representing a standard character, quality, or emotion. It was not that he objected to models: as some of his correspondence with his own illustrators shows,[148] he realized the value to an artist of a living form. But professional models troubled him: when Mark Lemon suggested that actors serve as models for illustrations in his novels, he was horrified.

In a letter to Coutts, Dickens wrote from Rome laughing at

Italian artists for using professional models who gathered each day on the Spanish Steps, and lamented that "men should go on copying these people elaborately time after time, and find nothing fresh or suggestive in the actual world about them." To his friend Count Alfred D'Orsay, he wrote a longer version of the same experience, claiming that "it is a good illustration of the Student system that young men should go on, batch after batch, reproducing these people: and finding nothing fresh or stirring in the active real world about them."[149] So impassioned was he about the subject that he wrote it out a third time in *Pictures from Italy*,[150] and repeated it in 1856 in his article "Insularities," in which he connects his distaste for models with his ruling passion, the use of art for dramatic purposes.   The reason for getting rid of all models, he says, is to "reduce our men of genius, who paint pictures, to the shameful necessity of wresting their great art to the telling of stories and conveying of ideas. . . ."[151] In another article, "His Brown Paper Parcel," he even poked fun at the need for artists to look like artists.   Van Gogh may have been the first to credit Dickens for disliking slavish imitation.   He wrote that "Dickens tells a few good things about the painters of his time and their wrong working methods, namely, their following the model servilely, yet only half way.   He says, 'Fellows, try to understand that your model is not your final aim, but the means of giving form and strength to your thought and inspiration.'"[152]

Despite his admiration for painters like Frith, Dickens at his best repudiated the art of setting and costume, and looked for the evocation of emotion by a fresh perception of the actions, passions, and suffering of men and women.   To confine oneself to no more than this in art is to miss much, and Dickens did, but his concentration upon the dramatic in painting was not as most have assumed owing to a mere taste for the theatrical: it was the consequence of his belief that art should penetrate to an inner truth, as seen by the artist.

It has been thought that by *truth* Dickens meant little more than fidelity to nature.   Certainly this is part of what he did mean in certain moods or in relation to certain kinds of art—though even then the possibility exists of his meaning something more. In portraiture, for example, Dickens has been described as exclusively concerned with the accurate, photograph-like reproduction of the subject's face: Count D'Orsay's sketch of Daniel Maclise is "excellent" because "I should have recognized it instantly, though I had seen it pasted on the wooden leg of a Greenwich Pensioner or in any other equally unexpected place."[153] But even in portraiture Dickens seems at times uncomfortable with the mere "likeness" of a face, as though a painter could do no more than a camera. Leonee Ormond points out that in *Bleak House* and *Little Dorrit* he "closely related the potentially dishonest art of portraiture to hypocricy." This dislike is as much moral as aesthetic, but it is cousin to the distaste for the slavish copying of models, and suggests that for Dickens good portraiture neither flattered nor merely delineated its subject, but did something more. A series of comments upon Ary Scheffer's portrait of him shows Dickens uneasily attempting to reconcile his respect for the painter with his feeling that the picture lacked this something. The first of his reactions, written to Forster, sets the pattern:

> Scheffer finished yesterday, and [Wilkie] Collins, who has a good eye for pictures, says that there is no man living who could do the painting about the eyes. As a work of art I see in it spirit combined with perfect ease, and yet I don't see myself. So I come to the conclusion that I never do see myself.[154]

In another comment on the portrait, Dickens said that Scheffer "is a great painter, and of course it has great merit," but added, "I doubt if I should know it, myself . . . ," and concluded, "it is always possible that I may know other people's faces pretty well, without knowing my own."[155] And still again, to Forster, he wrote, "It is a fine spirited head, painted at his very best, and with a very easy and natural appearance in it. But it does not look to me at all like, nor does it strike me that if I saw it in a gallery I should suppose myself to be the original."[156]

When Scheffer later confessed to Dickens that *he* was not satisfied with the portrait, Dickens crowed in relief to Forster, "My own impression of it, you remember?"[157] Still, a feeling that the failure was somehow not Scheffer's but his own seems to have persisted: five years later, writing to a photographer who had experienced difficulty in getting a good picture of him, Dickens said

> I feel I owe you an apology for being (innocently) a difficult subject. When I once excused myself to Ary Scheffer while sitting to him, he received the apology as strictly his due, and said with a vexed air: "at the moment, mon cher Dickens, you look more like a Dutch admiral than anything else;" for which I apologized again.[158]

Kate agreed that her father "was exceedingly difficult to represent adequately upon canvas . . . for the features which in repose looked at times so grave and preoccupied completely changed in expression when he was interested or aroused. . . ." The Dickens of one mood, that is, might change in mid-painting to become the Dickens of another, leaving the painter in doubt which he was to attempt to catch. Charlie, in speaking of the failure of all portraits of his father but Maclise's, mentioned "the ever-changing expressions, grave or gay, humorous or pathetic, which were reflected in that singularly handsome face." Certainly his depictors never caught him in a gay mood: Philip Collins points out that no existing sketch, painting, or photograph shows Dickens smiling. Several others comment on the ever-changing face of Dickens: Eleanor E. Christian said that his eyes were "Nondescript in colour, though inclining to warm grey in repose; but lighting up suddenly into a luminous depth of hue. . . ." And several comment on the difficulty of catching his face. The American journalist C. Edwards Lester thought that "The portraits of him do him little justice, nor are the artists particularly to blame, for it is not very easy to paint or engrave the expression of his face, while he is engaged in an interesting conversation." Frith called all portraits of him between Maclise's and his own absolute failures. People seem to have seen him differently: of middle height, or short; with a regular, or almost a Roman nose; eyes hazel, grey, or black, dark, or clear blue; hair fine, or waxy, dark brown, or auburn. When Americans first saw him in 1842, a newspaper declared that ". . . We must discard all the prints that have been issued professing to the likeness of 'Boz'. There is not one of them that does not give an entirely incorrect impression of his appearance. . . . In none are the lines, nerves, or muscles of the face delineated with any truth to nature." Many others who knew him concurred.[159]

Aware as he was of the difficulty of representing the quality of his own face, Dickens must have realized that portraiture was not simply capturing a likeness—for a face might have more than one likeness to catch—but of representing something in the subject that was deeper than the moment's mood. There is no letter in which Dickens expresses such a thought, but there are several which suggest he may have had it. His final comment upon the Scheffer portrait, written to his wife, admitted "that nobody could mistake whom it was meant for," but still objected "that it has something disappointing in it. . . ."[160] The painting, he was at last ready to concede, did look like him, yet there was something missing. Simple likeness, it seemed, was not enough.

Even in portraiture, then, where all have agreed that Dickens was concerned only with a recognizable representation of the subject, it is possible that he may have looked for something more, a something which in other kinds of painting I believe he called *truth*. For Dickens, says Leonee Ormond, "it referred as much [to] the spiritual essence of the subject as to its visual appearance. . . ." There is another comment on a portrait which conveys a similar sense. Writing to Lewis Gaylord Clark about a picture of him which he had seen in *Knickerbocker* (No. XXIV, facing page one), Dickens started with his usual criterion—"I think [it] . . . might be more like," but then tried to say what was wrong with it, only to end by confessing that it was a good likeness: "It looks to me the likeness of a testy, contradictory fellow—which I am sure you are not. It is still like the original, too, which is an aggravating kind of merit."[161] It is aggravating, obviously, because it meets what Dickens thought of as a sufficient standard for portraiture, yet does not produce a good portrait: something is missing.[162]

Perhaps we cannot know what the "something" was that Dickens missed in such paintings; if he himself ever knew, he never expressed it in writing. But some things his daughter tells us about him help us to take an informed guess. First, she says that her father "was naturally an excellent judge of a portrait," though "generally very modest in expressing an opinion." We may be grateful that she was not equally modest, and in view of her own abililty as portrait painter we may lend some credence to the opinion she offers, while noting Dickens' modesty as a further possible restraint upon his commentary upon art. But if Dickens was an excellent or even a merely good judge of portraiture, why did he have trouble deciding what he did not like about some portraits? Kate provides a possible answer, though she is talking about all painting, not just portraits. Dickens did not like some paintings, she says, because of the "excessive realism of his mental vision": "he always saw what he had read or heard about. . . . Thus the picture in his own mind of any subject which attracted him was often so vivid as to preclude the possibility of its being conceived in any other way. . . ."[163] "Realism of mental vision" exactly describes the overriding concern Dickens had for his illustrations—that they should be not merely good drawings, but should convey what he meant.

But how may this mental vision apply to portraits, in which the faces are real, not imagined? The answer, I believe, is that Dickens "saw" in human faces much more than surface likeness; like a true Wordsworthian, he half-perceived and half-created, and it was the "excessive realism" of his creative "mental vision" that missed something in the portraits of Clark and of himself, despite their accurate rendering of mere faces.   The object of his mental vision could be called the soul or inner nature of the subject, the something that passeth show, that makes the character what he or she is, in any mood or expression—that which we all know to be within ourselves that the physical cannot convey.   Again, Dickens' word for this, in faces or in anything he saw, was, I believe, *truth*, and it was this that he thought art should try to capture.

Granted, he did not always use the word with such deep meaning; often he simply meant fidelity to nature, as in his comment upon the "rubbish" he found in the Vatican:

> I unreservedly confess, for myself, that I cannot leave my natural perception of what is natural and true, at a palace door, in Italy or elsewhere, as I should leave my shoes if I were travelling in the East.   I cannot forget that there are certain expressions of face, natural to certain passions, and as unchangeable in their nature as the gait of a lion, or the flight of an eagle.   I cannot dismiss from my certain knowledge, such commonplace facts as the ordinary proportion of man's arms, and legs, and heads; and when I meet with performances that do violence to these experiences and recollections, no matter where they may be, I cannot honestly admire them, and think it best to say so.[164]

Here *truth* and *nature* are identical, but elsewhere a certain distinction is to be found.   Kate remarks that

> he was intuitively an excellent judge of a portrait, remembering with distinctiveness any face he may have seen for however short a time, and although always insisting on the slightest peculiarity of individual character or on the little difference in symmetry of features which sometimes occur and upon which so much of the expression of a head depends, he was quick to note the smallest exaggeration into which the artist might have been tempted to fall in order to enforce the

likeness.[165]

This suggests that likeness was not enough for Dickens, at least not a likeness that depended upon such tricks as exaggeration. The true artist must capture not only the "symmetry of features" but "the slightest peculiarity of individual character."

It seems possible that truth in portraiture and in painting in general was for Dickens comparable to what he strove for in the illustrations of his fictional characters: he looked in pictures for what he saw in his mind's eye, and it did not matter whether there was a real or an imagined face to begin with. Dickens was not so much concerned with what was there as with what he saw. Perhaps he felt portraiture to have the same magical power over real people that he felt it did over his fictional characters. When W. P. Frith asked him about a portrait of him begun some time ago, Dickens answered, "Well, the truth is, I sat for it a great many times. At first the picture bore a striking resemblance to Ben Carent, then it changed into somebody else, and at last I thought it was time to give it up. I had sat there and looked at the thing till I felt I was growing like it."[166] Dickens' insistence upon "truth" in portraiture may have been something more than a mere liking of likeness, may even have been more than a search for the truth of the inner eye: it may have been akin to the savage's refusal to have his picture taken.

In any case, there is no doubt that, in other kinds of painting, he looked, as Jane R. Cohen puts it, for "The kind of truth that elevated a subject and its associations."[167] This almost Emersonian desire to thrust through the appearance of an object to some higher meaning he found within it provides a far better explanation than is given by Angus Wilson of why Dickens, the lover of verisimilitude, could attack the Pre-Raphaelite painters, especially Millais, as fiercely as he did. Assuming that Dickens uniformly insisted upon surface reality in painting, Wilson finds it "surprising" that Dickens objected to "everyday models in sacred subjects," and quotes from a Dickens letter:

You know all the Pictures and Statues I have seen—and how many of them are really good, and how many really bad. I am guilty of all sorts of heresies in these respects; and when I see a Jolly Young Waterman representing a cherubim, or a Barclay and Perkins's Drayman depicted as an Evangelist, am obliged to confess that it is not exactly my idea of either character. Neither am I partial to angels who play on Genuine Cremonas and brazen bassoons, for the edification of sprawling monks apparently in liquor—nor to Josephs surveying Nativities, from shiny backgrounds, in a state of considerable mystification—nor to Saint Sebastians, of whom I wouldn't have a specimen on any terms, notwithstanding the extreme rarity of the subject. All this kind of High Art is out of my reach, I acknowledge. Not the less so, because I have the purest and most enduring delight in those achievements of the pencil which are truly great and grand, and worthy of their theme.[168]

But Dickens' distaste for models is not limited to religious subjects, as Wilson suggests; his assumption that Dickens would like them anywhere else shows he does not fully understand Dickens' idea that reality, slavishly copied, destroys creativity. Though at his least Dickens insisted that art be little more than mimetic, at his best he instinctively sought in it what Calvin Tompkins has called it: "not a mirror held up to nature but a talisman of changing life." Wilson concludes that it is Dickens' insistence upon the "elevated" in art that made him frown on commonplace models in religious paintings and that set him against the Pre-Raphaelites. But it is Dickens' belief that *all* painting, of whatever subject, should seek to elevate its material, that caused him to object to such a painting as Millais's *Christ in the Carpenter's Shop*. Dickens was indeed a devout Christian, but his objection to Millais's painting is not on sacred grounds—at least not on those grounds alone. He disliked any painting that did not attempt to move through surface realism to a deeper truth—the truth, I believe, that he missed in the accurate portraits which he criticized. As Dolores Lehr points out, "Dickens had long complained of the absence of idealized beauty in pictures"[169]; it is the absence of this beauty, and the ugliness substituted for it, that he laments in "Old Lamps for New," his review of *Christ in the Carpenter's Shop* in *Household Words*. First, in a passage that compensates for any slight he gave to Raphael in his Italian letters, Dickens offers that painter as the originator of beauty in painting (since the article is satirical, his admiration is couched in the negative):

> Raphael . . . [was a painter] with a ridiculous power of etherealizing, and exalting to the very Heavens, what was most sublime and lovely in the expression of the human face divine on Earth—with the truly contemptible conceit of finding in poor humanity the fallen likeness of the angels of God, and raising it up again to their pure spiritual condition. This very fantastic whim effected a low revolution in Art, in this wise, that Beauty came to be regarded as one of its indispensable elements.   In this very poor delusion, Artists have continued until this present nineteenth century, when it was reserved for some bold aspirants to "put it down."

The "bold aspirants" are, of course, the Pre-Raphaelites, whom Dickens attacks in a long description of *Christ in the Carpenter's Shop*:

> You behold the interior of a carpenter's shop.   In the foreground of that carpenter's shop is a hideous, wry-necked, blubbering, red-headed boy, in a bed-gown; who appears to have received a poke in the hand, from the stick of another boy with whom he has been playing in an adjacent gutter, and to be holding it for the contemplation of a kneeling woman, so horrible in her ugliness, that (supposing it were possible for any human creature to exist for a moment with that dislocated throat) she would stand out from the rest of the company a monster, in the vilest cabaret in France, or

the lowest gin-shop in England. Two almost naked carpenters, master and journeyman, worthy companions of this
agreeable female, are working at their trade; a boy, with
some small flavor of humanity in him, is entering with a
vessel of water; and nobody is paying any attention to a
snuffy old woman who seems to have mistaken that shop for
the tobacconists's next door, and to be hopelessly waiting at
the counter to be served with half an ounce of her favourite
mixture. Wherever it is possible to express ugliness of
feature, limb, or attitude, you have it expressed. Such men
as the carpenters might be undressed in any hospital where
dirty drunkards, in a high state of varicose veins, are
received. Their very toes have walked out of St. Giles's.[170]

This is probably one of the passages Humphrey House had in
mind when he said that Dickens "recoiled in almost neurotic horror
from all the most vigorous and original work that aimed to bring
colour and form back into art and religion"; in the same paragraph,
House specifically mentions the Pre-Raphaelites as "targets for his
scorn."[171] At the least, this is overstated. In "Old Lamps for New,"
Dickens does recoil, but it is aesthetic principle rather than neurosis
that makes him do so (as well as, perhaps, as Holman Hunt and
others guessed, his affection for his painter-friends of the old style,
held up to scorn by the new movement). And it is not the originality
of the painting to which he objects, but, as his title indicates, his
belief that the Pre-Raphaelites have taken art backward to mere reality
instead of forward to greater inner beauty. Dickens, if he had a
neurotic horror, had it of the past; his objection to Millais and his
school was that he thought, along with most of the people of his time,
that they intended to abandon all of the advantages of modern art, and
return painting to the qualities it had before Raphael. For Dickens
and for many others the greatest virtue of Raphael and those who followed him was that they attempted, as Ruskin put it, "to paint fair
pictures"[172]—that is, to elevate their subject above the realistic level

into a higher beauty.   It is the refusal of Millais to do this that
Dickens finds most objectionable in his review—just as the *Times*
reviewer, who found the painting "disgusting" and "revolting," did.
But in another article upon the Pre-Raphaelites in 1851, the *Times*
also argued that they lacked "truth" in their work, speaking of their
"strange disorder of the mind or the eyes," and arguing that they had
"an absolute contempt for perspective and the known laws of light and
shade. . . ."[173] Except for the woman with the "dislocated throat"
and one other brief comment later in his article, Dickens does not
attack Millais on this ground—a ground which Ruskin refuted in his
letter to the *Times*.[174] Dickens is not interested in fidelity but in what
he considers another kind of truth: the "fair picture" of the
carpenter's shop as a holy place (or, to put it less devoutly but no
less accurately, the representation of the carpenter's shop which would
enable the viewer to see it with the inner eye).   And, just as we have
seen in some of his animadversions on Italian art, he feels that the
painting has failed to capture that fair picture because it has held too
closely to a low (one could almost say a distorting) reality—has made
its figures as real as those in a French cabaret, an English gin-shop,
or a London hospital.   For the *Times* "truth" may consist of perspective and light and shade, of fidelity to nature, but for Dickens it
seems to require something more.

Ruskin's letter presents the Pre-Raphaelites in terms that, were
Dickens the mere advocate of superficial verisimilitude he is often
thought of as being, would have made them most congenial to him.
Ruskin says that Millais and his colleagues "draw either what they
see, or what they suppose might have been the actual facts of the
scene they desire to represent. . . ."   They intend, he says, not to
return to "archaic *art*" but to "archaic *honesty*," which may rescue art
from the "acknowledged decadence"[175] it has been in ever since
Raphael.   If Dickens' "truth" is mere external realism, how much all
this ought to have made him admire the Pre-Raphaelte School.   But
clearly his definition of truth extends beyond such a conception to a
higher, inner truth which he thought Millais missed.   His response to

Millais may have been, as it has been called, "unfortunate," but it is consistent with the most fundamental principle of his art. And if it was unfortunate, it was understandable. Harvey Sucksmith says,

> Millais' painting was one of the earliest Pre-Raphaelite canvases to be exhibited and Dickens would not be the first intelligent and sensitive man to have made a fool of himself over a new revolutionary school of art, which invariably requires some time for adjustment. . . .[176]

But Dickens was by no means an inveterate enemy of the Pre-Raphaelite painters. As Edgar Johnson has pointed out, he "later became an admiring friend of Millais and of Holman Hunt."[177] Johnson could have added that Millais used Kate Perugini as a model for his *The Black Brunswicker*; indeed, he became a close friend of Mrs. and Mrs. Perugini—a "dear fellow" to them. In her article on her father and art, Kate speaks of his judgment on *Christ in the Carpenter's Shop* as "a criticism that I have reason to believe he regretted having published in later years."[178] Does this mean Dickens came to accept the Pre-Raphaelite principles? Kate does not say, but I think it more likely that it was the publication rather than the criticism that Dickens came to regret; once again he probably found friendship more important than criticism, and wished that he had held his tongue. In any case, the friendship between Dickens and Millais seems to have survived the criticism. It was Millais, apparently, who recommended Luke Fildes to Dickens as an illustrator for *The Mystery of Edwin Drood*.[179] By that time, it should be noted, Millais had abandoned his pre-Raphaelite work, and had turned to more conventional painting.

A Vigorous And Bold Idea

In 1855, in his comments upon the Paris Exhibition and in related reflections on English art, Dickens demonstrated his ability to speak perceptively about painting. It is significant that his criticism here was directed against that same English art which in earlier years had been a part of his own training, and that several of the English artists he criticized are those whom he had admired before. English art "seemed to him small, shrunken, insignificant, 'niggling,'" Forster tells us. "He thought the general absence of ideas horribly apparent." "And even when one comes to Mulready," Dickens wrote,

> and sees two old men talking over a much-too-prominent table-cloth, and reads the French explanation of their proceedings, "La discussion sur les principes de Docteur Whiston," one is dissatisfied. Somehow or other they don't tell. Even Leslie's Sancho wants go, and Stanny is too much like a set scene. It is of no use disguising the fact that what we know to be wanting in the men is wanting in their works—character, fire, purpose, and the power of using the vehicle and the model as mere means to an end. There is a horrid respectability about most of the best of them—a little, finite, systematic routine in them, strangely expressive to me of the state of England itself. . . . There are no end of bad pictures among the French, but Lord! the goodness also!—the fearlessness of them; the bold drawing; the dashing conception; the passion and action in them! The Belgian department is full of merit. It has the best landscape in it, the best portrait, and the best scene of homely life, to be found in the building. Don't think it a part of my despondency about public affairs, and my fear that our national glory is on the decline, when I say that mere form and conventionalities usurp, in English art, as in English government and social relations, the place of living force and truth.

This is Dickens' finest moment. It is more than an attitude toward painting; it is his attitude toward life. Worse than the violent villains in his novels—the Bill Sykes's and the Daniel Quilp's—are the villains

of form and convention: the Bradley Headstones. That which drains
the blood of life, freezes it, regulates it until it loses force and truth,
is the enemy not only of art but of all that exists. Dickens could
now see that much in English art did this. Forster summarizes
Dickens' conversation with English artists about the French:

> French nature is all wrong, said the English artists whom
> Dickens talked to; but surely not because it is French, was
> his reply. The English point of view is not the only one to
> take men and women from. The French pictures are
> "theatrical" was the rejoinder. But the French themselves
> are a demonstrative and gesticulating people, was Dickens's
> retort; and what thus is rendered by their artists is the truth
> through an immense part of the world.[180]

It was in the year after the Paris Exhibition that Dickens wrote
the article entitled "Insularities," in which he more fully described the
way in which English narrowness inhibited the English perception of
art:

> One of our most remarkable Insularities is a tendency to be
> firmly persuaded that what is not English is not natural. In
> the Fine Arts department of the French Exhibition, recently
> closed, we repeatedly hear, even from the more educated and
> reflective of our countrymen, that certain pictures which ap-
> peared to possess great merit—of which not the lowest item
> was, that they possessed the merit of a vigorous and bold
> Idea—were all very well, but were "theatrical." Conceiving
> the difference between a dramatic picture and a theatrical
> picture, to be, that in the former case a story is strikingly
> told, without apparent consciousness of a spectator, and that
> in the latter case the groups are obtrusively conscious of a
> spectator, and are obviously dressed up, and doing (or not
> doing) certain things with an eye to the spectator, and not
> for the sake of the story, we sought in vain for this defect.

Taking further pains then, to find out what was meant by the term theatrical, we found that the actions and gestures of the figures were not English. That is to say,—the figures expressing themselves in the vivacious manner natural in a greater or less degree to the whole great continent of Europe, were overcharged and out of the truth, because they did not express themselves in the manner of our little Island—which is so very exceptional, that it always places an Englishman at a disadvantage, out of his own country, until his fine sterling qualities shine through his external formality and constraint. Surely nothing can be more unreasonable, say, than that we should require a Frenchman of the days of Robespierre, to be taken out of his jail to the guillotine with the calmness of Clapham or the respectability of Richmond Hill, after a trial at the Central Criminal Court in eighteen hundred and fifty-six. And yet this exactly illustrates the requirement of the particular insularity under consideration.[181]

Perhaps the public reaction to his criticism of art in *Pictures from Italy* deterred Dickens from further criticism of art in his later years. Perhaps his own illustrators escaped criticism on the principle that, as he wrote to Forster, "friendship is better than criticism, and I shall steadily hold my tongue."[182] But, as we have seen, in his lifetime he said more than a little. If he was not a skilled student of the discipline, he was by no means ordinary. Though he admitted that he had no training in the fundamentals of art, he was too modest to add that through active and intelligent observation, and through extended and close work with some of the best artists of his time and place, he had learned a great deal, and had come to hold definite ideas, about painting. He believed that it should be useful, and that the best way for it to convey a moral to its viewer was to offer a dramatic situation, presented in as lifelike a manner as possible. If his comments show relatively little skill in judging form and color, they also record his awareness of the importance of such things, and suggest that he might have spoken more astutely about them but for his modesty and dogged desire to avoid shop talk and the appearance of speaking cant.   But he said enough to show how much he valued that art which moved the viewer—which was striking, which evoked powerful emotion, which elevated the subject by seeing in it something more than its outward appearance.   By 1855, his judgment had sharpened to the point that he was capable of repudiating the lifeless art of his own English friends in favor of the depth and vigor of European painting.   As his father said of him, he had indeed "educated himself," and had acquired an understanding of the visual arts which not only distinguished him from his formally-educated contemporaries but contributed to the practice of his own art as well.

2

Architecture and Sculpture

Architecture: Gorgeous Work

Virtually nothing has been written about Dickens and architecture, for the good reason that he had little to say about it. The debates about styles and methods of construction in which many men of his century engaged seem to have touched him not at all. Yet it is not quite right to speak, as Delores Lehr does, of his "indifference to the artistic quality of architecture." She is right in stressing his interest in architecture which would benefit the masses, but she herself quotes some of the critical comments he made about the beauty or lack of it in certain buildings. And she has missed a number of comments in the letters which show that in his response to architecture Dickens demonstrated the same striving for independent judgment, the same delight in aroused emotion and in beauty that he exhibited in his reaction to other arts forms. One of these comments most intriguingly suggests that when Dickens traveled he sometimes looked around for confirmation of what his imagination had anticipated. When he visited Rome in 1845, Dickens wrote his wife that "The ancient part of Rome, and a portion of the Campagna, are what I meant when I came here. . . . The Coliseum by daylight, moonlight, and every sort of light, most stupendous and awful."[1] It is analogous to Dickens' feelings about the illustrations of his novels: as in them he sought external realization of his imagination, so here he would use Rome as confirmation of it.

Dickens observed architecture with the same attention to detail that he gave to painting. In Albaro in 1844, he wrote Maclise that

> There is a church here—the Church of the Annunciation— which they are . . . restoring at a vast expense, as a work of piety. It is a large church, with a great many little chapels in it, and a very high dome. Every inch of this edifice is painted, and every design is set in a great gold frame or border elaborately wrought. You can imagine nothing so splendid. It is worth coming the whole distance to see.

As always, the positive effect of such details lay in the ability of their beauty to stir his imagination. To another correspondent he wrote that the redecoration of the portico "is the most gorgeous work imaginable. Standing on a bright day before the Great Altar, and looking up into the Three Domes, one is made giddy by the flash and glory of the place." In *Pictures from Italy* he wrote of a cathedral in Venice, "gorgeous in the wild luxurient fancies of the East," and of another "grand and dreamy structure, of immense proportions. . . ." From Venice he wrote that "The wildest visions of the Arabian Nights are nothing to the piazza of Saint Mark, and the first impression of the inside of the church. The gorgeous and wonderful reality of Venice is beyond the fancy of the wildest dreamer. Opium wouldn't build such a palace, and enchantment couldn't shadow it forth in a vision. . . . Venice is above . . . the imagination of man."[2] Architecture must have impressed him greatly to have called forth such a statement.

Wherever he went—in Venice, Milan, Pisa, Geneva—Dickens commented on such things as "a glorious structure," "beautiful arches," or a cathedral which had "the loveliest font I ever saw. . . ." He liked too the Baptistry at Parma, and thought that in Pisa "the group of buildings . . . comprising the Tower, the

Baptistry, the Cathedral, and the Church of the Campo-Santo is perhaps the most remarkable and beautiful in the whole world. . . . It is the architectural essence of a rich old city. . . ." He seems to have been struck by the quality that antiquity could give to such places: in Verona, he commented on the city's "rich architecture," and said that "The Roman amphitheatre . . . delighted me beyond expression. I never saw anything so full of such a solemn interest. There are the Four and forty rows of seats, as fresh and perfect as if their Roman occupants had vacated them but yesterday—the entrances, passages, dens, rooms, corridors; the very numbers over the arches." But the enrichment afforded by history did not manifest itself for him in St. Peter's Cathedral, possibly because of the same anti-Catholicism that turned him against some Italian paintings, possibly because he felt he was expected to like it, and possibly because he did not find in it the mood of reverence he expected in a Christian church. The building "looked immense in the distance, but distinctly and decidedly small, by comparison, on a near approach." Though the Piazza was hardly to be exaggerated in its beauty, he was disappointed in the interior which, though beautiful, was at the time decorated for a festival and lacking in the sense of veneration he had anticipated. "It is an immense edifice," he said, "with no one point for the mind to rest upon; amd it tires itself with wandering round and round. The very purpose of the place, is not expressed in anything you see there. . . ."[3] A church should be a church.

He preferred the solemn and decaying grandeur of the Coliseum. Writing from Rome he said that St. Peter's "struck me of course, immensely. But the latter is the great sensation. And I never *can* forget it."[4] He returned to the Coliseum several times, and wrote of it repeatedly; it was "awful and tremendous," and "enchanted" him: "I went there continually, and never could see enough of it." In *Pictures from Italy* he wrote that "Its solitude, its awful beauty, and its utter desolation, strike upon the stranger . . . like a softened sorrow," and concluded that he "could never get through a day without going back to it. . . ." Eight years after this trip he wrote Sir James

Tenant from Rome that "The Coliseum, in its magnificent old decay, is as grand as ever, and with the electric telegraph darting through one of its ruined arches like a sunbeam and piercing direct through its cruel old heart, is even grander."[5] In *Pictures from Italy* he commented on balconies, platforms, vestibules, staircases, pillars, arches, and chambers in the Genoa palaces. And from Florence he wrote that "There are some places here—oh Heavens how fine! I wish you could see the tower of the Palazzo Vecchio. . . ."[6] Similar comments fill other letters from Italy and, in 1846, from Germany, Switzerland, and France.

By contrast, there is relatively little comment on buildings in England. Dickens occasionally describes a theater in which he is to act or read, and sometimes calls a theater he has attended "beautiful" or otherwise, but he does not appear to study the architecture. Forster said that Dickens thought that Stanfield Hall "had nothing attractive about it . . ."; that is about as much comment on English architecture as we get. His tours of America, however, though brief and concentrating on things other than art, produced some reactions to architecture, as well as to city planning. In New York, he found the First Bank of the United States to be handsome but "dreary to behold. . . . The building looked as if the marble statue of Don Guzman could alone have any business to transact within its gloomy walls." The architectural style of Broadway struck him as making it "a sort of elongated New Cut." Philadelphia was "a handsome city, but distractingly regular. After walking about it for an hour or two, I felt that I would have given the world for an irregular street." (Elsewhere he boasted about the irregularities he had built into his own house at Gad's Hill.) In Washington he thought the Capitol "a fine building of the Corinthian order, placed upon a noble and commanding eminence."[7] With the same attention to detail he had shown in Italy, he gave the measurements of the rotunda, described its compartments and pictures, and called it "fine." The House of Representatives was "a beautiful and spacious hall, of semicircular shape, supported by handsome pillars. It is an elegant chamber to

look at, but a singularly bad one for all purposes of hearing.   The
Senate, which is smaller, is free from this objection, and is exceedingly well adapted to the uses for which it is designed." He also
liked the "President's Mansion," which he described as "like an
English clubhouse," and thought its garden walks "pretty, and agreeable to the eye," but missed in them that sense of the past which he
had liked in Italian scenes: "they have that uncomfortable air of
having been made yesterday, which is far from favorable to the display
of such beauties."   Other buildings he disliked: the Goverment House
was "neither elegant nor commodious," and a building he saw from
his hotel room in Washington was "an odd, lop-sided, one-eyed kind
of wooden building . . . with a flag-staff as long as itself sticking out
of a steeple something larger than a tea-chest."[8]

Dickens' interest in architecture apparently extended to the
reading of only a few works on the subject: from Italy he wrote that
"Gwilt's Architecture [possibly Joseph Gwilt's *Notizia Architectoria
Italiano*, 1818] looms large and grim from a table in the Sala."
Forster reported that he read Ruskin's *Lamp of Architecture*.   This is
not much; still, he had enough knowledge of architecture to advise
Miss Coutts, when she planned to build homes in the slum area of
London known as Nova Scotia (in the East End), to consult with
knowledgeable people like Dr. Sunderland Smith and Henry Austin
(Dickens' brother-in-law, a professional architect) before approving the
plans of her architect, Philip Hardwick.   "I should not lke to say this
to Mr. Hardwick," he wrote, "(knowing what tender corns architects
usually have) but I have no doubt that your noble design would
benefit by such a course.   They know little (but most important)
things, beforehand, which an architect would only find out, probably,
by your experiencing the worst of them when the building was done."
He also knew enough to engage in a long debate about the size of
houses for cities, arguing that large houses kept cities smaller and
gave more access to the countryside and to work locations, and were
usually better constructed and afforded better sanitation.[9] But Dickens'
own tender corns made it with architecture as with painting: he did

not care to read the opinions of others. In *Pictures from Italy* he wrote of a cathedral in Lyons that "If you would know all about the architecture of this church, or any other, . . . it is not written in Mr. Murray's Guide Book, and may you not read it there, with thanks to him, as I did!"[10]

Dickens oversaw the remodeling of his own house at Gad's Hill, demonstrating if not great knowledge of architectural styles certainly sufficient ability to get what he wanted in a house. In two letters to Henry Austin he "materially altered the plans for the house," removing a conservatory and balcony, changing a painting-room into a drawing-room in order to leave space for a hall from the front entrance "right through the house to a back door leading to the garden"; he also expressed his wishes about drains, a supporting pillar, the cutting of a doorway, and the installation of a brass ventilator. Seven years later he wrote that he had "added to and stuck bits upon" the house, "so that it is as pleasantly irregular, and as violently opposed to all architectural ideas, as the most hopeful man could possibly desire."[11] Again, independence in architecture was apparently as precious to him as it was in judging painting.

Dickens seems to have known a good deal about acoustics. One of his early newspaper pieces, "Report of Lord Grey's Reception in Edinburgh," noted that the Pavilion in which the banquet was to be held was "very ill adapted for hearing. . . ." He made several comments on the acoustics of theaters in which he played. He wrote Wills that he had "a notion . . . for improving the acoustics of St. James's Hall." From Torquay, he described the place from which he was to read:

It is something between a theatre, a circus, a riding school, a Methodist chapel, and a cow-house. I was so disgusted with its acoustic properties on going to look at it, that the whole unfortunate staff have been all day, and now are, sticking up baize and carpets in it to prevent echoes.

Of the hall in Liverpool where a dinner was to be held in his honor, he wrote that the acoustics were "as bad as bad can be," and said that he "had been this morning to look at St.   George's Hall, and suggest what can be done to improve its acoustics."   George Dolby said that "he alone seemed to know" the way to improve acoustics in the halls in which he read, and recorded that the testing of acoustics of a building was "a process that was always gone through in every new room in which he read."[12]

Dickens also noticed and commented on landscape architecture. From the house in Boulogne which he made a summering place, he wrote in 1853 a careful description of the house and grounds.   To de Cerjat he wrote that "The Thames embankment is (faults of ugliness in detail apart) the finest public work yet done.   From Westminster Bridge to near Waterloo it is now lighted up at night, and has a fine effect."[13]

When this much has been said, the fact remains that Dickens' contact with architecture is scantier than with any other art form.   His brother-in-law may have been the only architect he knew well, he was not active in the organizations of architects, and of course he did not work with architects (except in the renovations of Gad's Hill) as he had with his illustrators.   Still, he was interested in the aesthetics of buildings, knew as always what he liked, and would seem to have had some knowledge of architecture in general.   A few allusions in his fiction to the structure of buildings add slightly to our sense of his interest in the art, but, as Dolores Lehr, says, not much.[14]

Sculpture: Exquisite Shapes

We learn little about Dickens' aesthetic from his commentary upon sculpture, but it is worth noting that he did enjoy and occasionally comment on this form of art. At least one friend, Angus Fletcher, was a sculptor for a time, and Dickens demonstrated a fair knowledge of several other sculptors of his age. He would seem to have visited sculptors' studios, as he did those of other artists: Gladys Storey says that he met her father, as a boy, in the studio of W. Behnes.[15]

He passed judgment on numerous statues and monuments, like the one in honor of Scott in Edinburgh, which he thought "a failure. It is like the spire of a Gothic church taken off and stuck in the ground." "The Wellington Statue," he wrote, "seemed to me worse than Punch's wildest exaggeration of it." More frequently, he commented on busts of himself and of his friends. According to G. W. Putnam, he thought Henry Dexter's bust of him was "a very successful work of art. . . ."[16] Of one made of him by Angus Fletcher he said, "The Bust . . . is considered by everybody . . . *much more like* in the Marble than in the cast," in accordance with his custom of judging all representation first by its fidelity to its model. A similar comment on Samuel Joseph's bust of Basil Hall sounds much like his reaction to portraiture: "likeness *amazing*— recognizable instantly if encountered on the summit of the Great Pyramid. . . ." Such comments are fairly early, and suggest that the young Dickens did indeed consider that art had done its job when it approximated its original. He thought that Christopher Moore's bust of David Colden was "certainly not a striking success. I don't think I should have recognized it in a room, but certainly did not in the [Royal] Academy [Exhibition] without referring to the catalog; though I was looking hard in its face. . . . [Still,] it has good points."[17]

In later years, his comments on statuary extended beyond mere similarity, especially when he traveled. In the United States (though again *American Notes* is not intended to assess the art of that country), he said of Horatio Greenough's statue of Washington that "It has great merits of course, but it struck me as being rather strained and violent for its subject. I could wish, however, to have seen it in a better light than it can ever be viewed in, where it stands."[18] As with other art, Dickens was aware of the extent to which the placing of a statue could affect its reception.

Pictures from Italy offers more on statues.   In a courtyard in Genoa he saw "a melancholy statue, so piebald in its decay, that it looked exactly as if it had been covered with sticking-plaster, and afterwards powdered. . . ."   He stood in one of the workshops in Carrara, and looked at "beautifully finished copies in marble, of almost every figure, and bust, we know," but he was impressed less with "these exquisite shapes, replete with grace, and thought, and delicate repose," than with the realization of the toil and death which produced the marble, and drew the moral that "every good thing . . . has its birth in sorrow and distress."[19]   Given the choice in the famous story of saving either the paintings or the cat in a burning Louvre, Dickens would have saved the cat.

In Rome, he commented on several sculptors, including Canova and Bernini:

> The exquisite grace and beauty of Canova's statues; the wonderful gravity and repose of many of the ancient works in sculpture, both in the Capitol and the Vatican; and the strength and fire of many others; are, in their different ways, beyond all reach of words.   They are especially impressive and delightful, after the works of Bernini and his disciples, in which the churches of Rome, from St. Peter's downward, abound; and which are, I verily believe, the most detestable class of productions in the wide world.   I would infinitely rather (as mere works of art) look upon the three deities of the Past, the Present, and the Future, in the Chinese Collection, than upon the best of these breezy maniacs; whose every fold of drapery is blown inside-out; whose smallest vein, or artery, is as big as an ordinary forefinger; whose hair is like a nest of lively snakes; and whose attitudes put all other extravagances to shame.   Insomuch that I do honestly believe, there can be no place in the world,

where such intolerable abortions, begotten of the sculptor's chisel, are to be found in such profusion, as in Rome.

It is surprising that Dickens did not like the energy and pictorial quality of Bernini, but his comment suggests that the former was too extravagant, too Baroque for him; perhaps too he did not like the refusal of Bernini to confine his picture to the natural. In St. Peter's Cathedral, he liked the fact that the statue of St. Peter was "larger than life," but thought that it did "not heighten the effect of the temple, as a work of art; and it is not expressive—to me at least—of its high purpose." He thought the statue of Pompey in the Palazzo Spada "A stern, tremendous figure!" but called the statues on the bridge approaching the Castle of St. Angelo "execrable works."[20]

Like all others kinds of artists, sculptors appealed to Dickens for assistance, if not often for aesthetic advice. Samuel Joseph, perhaps encouraged by Dickens' praise of his bust of Basil Hall, informed him that he had done a bust of him, and asked if he knew anyone who would like to buy it. Dickens replied that he did not, and that he was "not rich enough, just now, to secure it to myself." According to Samuel Haydon, the clay bust was destroyed because no commission to cast it was ever received. One sculptor, a Mr. Adams, apparently did ask Dickens for advice concerning his work, which appears to have been a bust of Wellington; acting on Dickens' opinion, he

made some alteration in . . . the face—*I* think . . . greatly to its improvement. I also found, according to my eye, the mouth much too tight, and a general want there about of a suggestion of flexibility. This the sculptor also worked upon. It seemed to me that the best and most hopeful thing that can possibly be done now, is to let the sculptor alone. The bust is far more like than any I have seen, and strikes me as possessing very great merit.[21]

The decision to "let the sculptor alone" may be further evidence that Dickens had learned from his experience with his illustrators that some amount of freedom improves the artist's work.

He was inclined to think that public statuary was both poor and too prevalent. In a satire in which an aging gentleman predicts that the English are raising their children to be dwarfs, the speaker says, "I will not expatiate upon the number of dwarfs who will be found representing Grecian statues in all parts of the metropolis; because I am inclined to think that this will be a change for the better; and that the engagement of two or three in Trafalgar Square will tend to the improvement of the public taste." In an article titled "Raven in the Happy Family," Dickens had the raven make a proposal "for erecting an equestrian statue to the Hippopotamus." In a later article, he took up his own fictional suggestion, telling of the plans of one "Mr. Hamet Safi-Cannana, the Arabian gentleman," to erect it, and offering a long description of the plans, all mocking the way in which statues were raised to honor prominent and unworthy figures. In another article he said that the English had "choked our towns with bad statues," especially of Wellington; in still another he offered as evidence that the English are not as "eminently practical" as someone has suggested the "monstrous statues" they insisted on erecting.[22] On leaving the United States, Dickens is reputed to have said, in response to a proposal to erect a statue in his honor, "No, don't; take down one of the old ones instead!"

3

Drama: The Fanciful Reality

Dickens' fascination with the stage has probably received more attention than anything else about him except his novels. Every aspect of his interest and participation in the world of drama has been mentioned—his constant attending of stage events, from a Macready production of *King Lear* to the humblest puppet show; his attempts to write plays on his own and with others; his assistance to both amateur and professional playwrights; his early thoughts about acting as a career; his acting in and directing and producing amateur performances, ranging from those in which his children played roles for family entertainment to that offered before the Queen; his involvement with dramatizations of his own stories, and his public readings from them; his own critical commentary. With drama we are at the very heart of Dickens' interest in the arts; as James Payne said, "The subject . . . which most interested him . . . was the dramatic—nay, even the melodramatic—side of human nature."[1]

No one who reads of Dickens' activities in and related to the theater can fail to be impressed with the tremendous amount of experience he had, the great knowledge of the theater of his time that he acquired, and the deep love he possessed for drama. His experience included virtually all phases of amateur dramatic effort, from actor to director to manager, to designer of stages, selector of costumes—the list is almost endless. He was undisputed master of his time in his knowledge of its theaters, plays, and actors, not only in London but throughout England, and to some extent in other countries

as well. His command of the drama of other times is less extensive,
but is still impressive, especially his familiarity with and critical
acumen concerning Shakespeare. But clearly for Dickens the play was
a thing not so much to be read as to be seen; the striking thing
about him is his sense of the living stage. He was keenly aware of
what would work upon it, and what would not—of what an actor could
or could not accomplish with a role, of what a line or prop or scene
setting or piece of business might do to help or hinder a performance.
He could anticipate how an audience would react to anything; in such
matters his judgment, if sometimes tainted by his fascination with
melodrama and tricks, or restrained by his ever-present sense of
propriety, is nevertheless most impressive. And always the true
artist's painstaking attention to the most minute detail, and to each
detail's necessary contribution to the whole, is in evidence.

Among the strongest impressions to emerge in this and the following chapter will be Dickens' insistence upon realistic presentation.
He thought this essential in every art, but in particular he did not
believe that a play could work its magic if the audience could not take
what it saw as reality, as life occurring before its eyes. Therefore he
hated pretensiousness, artificiality, exaggeration, the trite and repetitive,
and the merely sensational (though sometimes he was helplessly attracted to the last). He liked freshness, vigor, and what he called
"generosity of spirit," by which he usually meant that which could
call forth the best in human nature. He admired characterization
which was real and distinct, each role marked with individuality. And
he liked roles in which effective contrast could be seen, just as he
liked contrasts of mood and tone. Above all, he loved "truth" in a
play, as we have defined the term: the penetration through mere appearance (especially when it was cynical and negative) to essential affirmation of life and of humanity.

As with most of his adult interests, Dickens' attraction to the
theater began at an early age—indeed, Santayana has said that Dickens
was born into it: "Dickens entered the theatre of this world by the
stage door. . . ." If so, one of his first ushers was James Lamert,

"a sort of cousin by marriage," who, like the youthful Dickens, "had a turn for private theatricals"; according to Forster it was by him that Dickens "was first taken to the theatre at the very tenderest age." Perhaps it was Lamert who took Dickens at age six to see *Richard III*, or to see at age eight the famous clown Joseph Grimaldi, whose *Memoirs* he edited years later; defending himself against a charge that he had no business doing so because he had been too young to see Grimaldi, Dickens said, "I was brought up from remote country parts in the dark ages of 1819 and 1820 to behold the splendour of Christmas pantomimes and the humour of Joe, in whose honour I am informed I clapped my hands with great precocity. . . . I even saw him act in the remote times of 1823. . . ." Later, when the family had moved to London, it was Lamert, ironically, who as chief manager of a blacking warehouse got young Dickens the job that scarred him for the rest of his life. But Lamert may have sensed Dickens' misery at that time more fully than the child's own parents did: Forster tells us that, pitying his solitary life in the slums of Camden town, Lamert "painted a little theatre for him. It was the only fanciful reality of his present life."[2] Twenty years later, when his son Charlie got his toy theater, Dickens set about to produce in it a spectacle called the *Elephent [sic] of Siam*, with every bit as much energy and pleasure as he had expended upon his own childhood playhouse.

By the time of the blacking warehouse, the theater had already begun to shape Dickens' way of seeing, and had become what it would always be for him, and what he came to believe it was for everyone: a correction to the increasing ugliness of the real world (one wonders why David Copperfield, when he began to find life sloppier than he had expected, was not given a play or two in London by way of compensation). While his father languished in prison, Dickens was, he said, "seduced more than once . . . by a show-van at a corner, and have gone in, with a very motley assemblage, to see the Fat Pig, the Wild Indian, and the Little Lady." One day when he lost his way in the London streets he would eventually know as well as any man, he went into a theater; the incident was prophetic.   If anything was needed to strengthen Dickens' interest in drama, its function as a miraculous escape from his own prison of humiliation, disappointment, and parental indifference during this unhappy London period must have provided it.   When the dark experience of the warehouse world was ended, and Dickens was safely back in the middle-class environment of the Wellington Academy, he immediately became involved in schoolboy theatrical experiences there.   A former school chum wrote that the Academy was "very strong . . . in theatricals.   We mounted small theatres, and got up gorgeous scenery. . . .   Dickens was always a leader at these plays. . . ." Apparently he was also active outside the school: he told a fellow student that at age fourteen he took parts at a small playhouse in Catherine Street, where amateurs could assume leading roles for a small sum.[3]

A year later, Dickens left school and began the study of law as a clerk at Gray's Inn.   George Lear, a fellow-clerk, said he was an excellent mimic, imitating street people and popular singers.   His employer, Edward Blackmore, noted that "His taste for theatricals was much promoted by a fellow-clerk named Potter," and added that "They took every opportunity . . . of going together to a minor theatre, where (I afterwards heard) they not infrequently engaged in parts"— again, probably, by purchasing the roles.   Dickens later spoke harshly of these "private theatres" and of those who participated in them—"the donkeys who are prevailed upon to pay for permission to exhibit their lamentable ignorance and boobyism on the stage. . . ."   Dickens played the part of Flexible in *Love, Law, and Physic* during this period.[4]

Only a few years later, when he had become a Doctor's Commons reporter, Dickens made a serious though fortunately abortive attempt to become a professional actor.

> I went to some theatre every night, with a very few excep-
> tions, for at least three years; really studying the bills first,

and going to where there was the best acting: and always going to see [Charles] Mathews whenever he played. I practised immensely (even such things as walking in and out, and sitting down in a chair): often four, five, six hours a day: shut up in my own room, or walking about in the fields. I prescribed to myself, too, a sort of Hamiltonian system for learning parts; and learnt a great number.

Forster says that Dickens "finally wrote to make offer of himself to Covent Garden." An appointment was actually made, but when the time came Dickens was too sick to go, and wrote to say that he would apply again next season. By that time, though, he had become a Parliamentary reporter, and nineteenth-century London had lost an actor while the world was about to gain one of its greatest novelists. But the profession of acting retained its appeal, both as a thing he loved to do and as a possible means of bringing its own wealth and fame. In 1833 he participated in the production of *Clari; or, The Maid of Milan*, as well as an opera, *The Married Bachelor*, by P. P. O'Callaghan, and *Amateurs and Actors*, a farce by R. Brinsley Peake; he played roles in all three works. The theater became the subject of some of his early writing: several of the first pieces which would be collected as *Sketches by Boz* are devoted to the stage, and references to the theater occur throughout the book. Though years later Dickens told Forster that he "had never thought of the stage but as a means of getting"[5] money, his heart remained always with the stage; not even his great success as a novelist prevented twinges of regret in later years that he had not made the theater his profession.

Curiously, the weakest attraction to drama for Dickens seems to have been the writing of it. The libretto and the few farces he produced on his own reveal nothing of his genius, and very little of that intense commitment he made everywhere else to doing everything he did as well as he could do it. If he ever thought seriously of writing for the stage, critical reaction to his first efforts must have discouraged him; there is no evidence that he found the predominantly negative response unjust, and much that indicates he agreed with it. When his farce *The Lamplighter* (adapted for Macready, then managing the Drury Lane Theater, from a piece printed in *The Pic-nic Papers*) was rejected, he wrote, "I am quite satisfied with the opinions of those who must know so much better than myself what would tell upon the stage. . . ." *The Village Coquettes*, a comic opera written two years earlier, was produced, and the comic actor John Harley predicted that it would run fifty nights, but it lasted only nineteen before taking the road to Edinburgh. In his preface Dickens sounds self-conscious and defensive: "the libretto of an opera must be, to a certain extent, a mere vehicle for the music," and "it is scarcely fair or reasonable to judge it by those strict rules of criticism which would be justly applicable to a five-act tragedy or a finished comedy." It was an accurate prediction: the only real value of *The Village Coquettes* was that a copy of it brought about the first meeting between Dickens and Forster. When, a year before Dickens' death, Frederick Locker-Lampson asked him if he had a copy of it, he replied, "No; and if I knew it was in my house, and if I could not get rid of it in any other way, I would burn the wing of the house where it was!"[6]

He did not suffer as did Henry James from such failure, and might have reversed something the American said about his experience with plays: "I may have been meant for the Drama—God knows!—but I certainly wasn't meant for the Theater." Dickens was not meant to write drama, but spent much of his life doing virtually everything else connected with the stage. It is possible that, at the beginning of his career, Dickens thought of playwriting as a refreshing sideline and additional source of income. In 1836, when his first literary successes had released him from the pressures of Parliamentary reporting, "he was led to take much interest in Mr. Braham's enterprise at the St. James Theatre . . ." and wrote a farce, *The Strange Gentleman*, as well as the story and lyrics for *The Village Coquettes*. But later ventures were usually undertaken as much for some special interest as for any hope of earning money, and with no thought at all of adding to his reputation as writer. Forster says that he co-authored (with Wilkie Collins) *No Thoroughfare*, for example, in the hope of "being able to contribute some such achievement in aid of Macready's gallant efforts at the Covent Garden, to bring back to the stage its higher associations of good literature, and intellectual enjoyment." (Produced and acted in by Charles Fechter, it enjoyed considerable popular success, in New York and Paris as well as London.) He also worked so closely with Collins on *The Frozen Deep* that he may be said to have co-authored the play. But he was careful in later years to make it clear that he had no ambition to be a dramatist; in 1847 he wrote Samuel Phelps, actor and manager of Saddler's Wells, asking him to send over his copyist "so I can give him a play (not mine—Heaven forbid!). . . ."[7]

Much time has been spent, none too fruitfully, in speculating why Dickens was not successful in what he wrote for the stage, and why he did not try to write more. T. E. Pemberton offered five reasons: 1) Such effort was precluded by the success of the novels; 2) the novelist finds it easier both to write and to get published; 3) there is no need for the novelist to subject his work to interpretation and performance by another; 4) the novel is not as subject as is the play to "hastily-written criticisms"; 5) the quality of dramatic performance in Dickens' day was not good.[8] Of these the first four seem to me either wrong, specious, or only marginally useful: 1) The novels did not prevent Dickens from trying his hand at drama, nor within a few years from undertaking other labors, such as editing a journal. 2) Much that Dickens said to young writers shows how hard he thought it was to publish fiction; when he tried plays, he had no trouble obtaining good and impartial consideration: if the plays had been anywhere near as good as his novels, they would have succeeded. 3) Dickens did not mind, but rather enjoyed seeing his novels dramatized upon the stage—so long as they were done well. 4) Dickens' novels were frequently subjected to hasty criticism, often far less just and competent than that afforded the few plays he had performed.

Only the fifth reason has some substance. Angus Wilson agreed that Dickens did not write plays because "the conventions of the day were too strong and too bad." T. E. Pemberton supports the idea by arguing that the failure of stage adaptations of Dickens' novels was owing to the attempts of stage managers to force them into the conventional slots of most plays of the time:

> As plays [the adaptations] are altogether different from their predecessors. The *dramatis personae* cannot, as that of the sentimental comedy and heavy melodrama, be summarily and arbitrarily put into the various conventional classes amongst which stage managers distribute the "parts." One cannot be safely given out at once to the "heavy father" of the company; another to the "smart servant"; a third to the "low comedian"; a fourth to the "juvenile tragedian"; a fifth to the "chambermaid" or a sixth to the "sentimental young lady." Dickens's characters are too much like nature for that.[9]

There is something to this argument, but no one ought to pretend that it is a sufficient explanation for Dickens' failure to write great or even good plays. Greatness may not always succeed in forcing its way through the conventions of its age, but it has a pretty good record of doing so, sooner or later. For all his command of the stage as critic, manager, actor, and reader, Dickens never wrote anything that gives much indication of a playwright's ability. Even in the farce, which one would think he could have tossed off with his left hand, he was uncomfortable: trying to write one for the benefit of the Guild of Literature and Art, he finally begged off, pleading his other work as manager of a play, and adding that he was

> constantly striving, for my reputations's sake, to get into a meaning that is impossible in a farce; constantly thinking of it, therefore, against the grain; and constantly impressed with the conviction that I could never act in it myself with that wild abandonment which can alone carry a farce off.[10]

Why did he not try some more substantial form of drama? Perhaps, with such modest success as he had in the things he first tried, he simply realized that the play was not for him. Dickens did so many things so well, and loved the stage so much, that one is reluctant to suggest that his failure as a dramatist is owing to inner rather than outer limitations, but that is probably the case. At least two such limitations thrust themselves upon the attention of the reader. First, Dickens needed the narrative voice, that ever-present third person which enabled him to see, order, unify, and give perspective to his story. Deprived of that voice, his plays lack stance, vision, the poetic density of his novels. Only three times in his major fiction did he depart from such a voice (and in his minor works he departed with little success): in one of these three (*Bleak House*), he carefully alternated it with a first-person narration; in the other two, the first-person narrators (David and Pip) were alter egos.

Dickens' second limitation was his difficulty in working within the restricted space of the play. His inability to get meaning into a farce was symptomatic of his difficulty in getting enough of what he wanted into any dramatic form—one reason, surely, why some writers write novels and not plays. With the single exception of the inspired *A Christmas Carol*, Dickens was not successful in a little space (F. R. Leavis made a case for *Hard Times*, but did so by showing that it was not a typical Dickens novel). Even in his readings from his works, Dickens preferred elbow room: having in 1855 read from his Christmas books in Birmingham, he said, "I should like to get out of the restriction, and have a swim in the broader waters of one of my long books."[11] No apology need be made for the fact that Dickens did not succeed in drama: he was simply a novelist. But it is a fascinating footnote to human creativity that this man who triumphed in almost everything else to which he put his hand, could not write within that genre which he loved the most.

At The Theatre

Dickens did not suffer from his failure to write plays, for he enjoyed drama in many other ways. A complete record of Dickens' activity in drama—as spectator (definitely an activity, as he undertook it), writer, critic, reader, performer, director, producer, stage designer, even carpenter, apparently at times even best boy—would make a heavy book. A full chapter could be devoted to his attending performances: again and again his letters mention a theater he has visited, a play he has seen—in London, the provinces, the Continent, America, wherever he happened to be. The plays mentioned in the letters must have been but a fraction of those he saw, yet even these are impressive. "We were at the theatre last night," he wrote his wife from Bradford, Yorkshire, "—much better than usual." To his actor friend Macready he wrote, "I am going to take Drury Lane—the Strand—the Olympic— the Victoria—Sadlers Wells—and the Marylebone. I don't mention the Haymarket, because (though I am going to take that too) it's a mere fleabite." Even a fleabite, if it was dramatic, was worth a look. He proposed to his artist friend John Leech that they go to see *Antony and Cleopatra*; to another artist, Frank Stone, he wrote that he would see Dion Boucicault and Charles Kenney's *The Willow Copse* that night, and hoped to see Macready in *Macbeth* the following week. He informed Wilkie Collins that "If you should be disposed to revel in the glories of the eccentric British Drayma [*sic*], on Saturday evening, I am the man to join in so great a movement." In 1860 he wrote Mary Boyle that he was "taking a stall at a theatre every night."[12] And so the letters go on. Forster tells us that during his stay in Italy, "With the theatres he soon became acquainted," and that the same was true of France. Visiting the birthplace of Robespierre, he came upon a

> Theâtre Religieux—"donnant six fois par jour, l'histoire de la
> Croix en tableaux vivants, depuis la naissance de notre

Seigneur jusqu'à son sepultre. Aussi l'immolation de Isaac,
par son père Abrahman." It was just before nightfall when
I came upon it; and one of the three wise men was up to
his eyes in lamp oil, hanging the moderators. A woman in
blue and fleshing (whether an angel or Joseph's wife I don't
know) was addressing the crowd through an enormous
speaking-trumpet; and a very small boy with a property lamb
(I leave you to guess who *he* was) was standing on his head
on a barrel-organ.[13]

Perhaps remembering what Lamert had done for him, Dickens
made sure that his children also saw theatrical performances; in 1852
he recorded that he was to take Sydney to a play that night for the
first time, availing himself of the box Miss Coutts offered.[14] Needless
to say, virtually every member of the Dickens circle accompanied him
at one time or another to the theater (but there are few instances
mentioned in which he took his wife).

No writer can convey the sense of fascination and delight with
the stage that comes from a reading of Dickens' letters. As a young
man, he apparently talked so much about the theater that new friends
like G. H. Lewes at first thought him capable of little else: it was
only when he met him again two years after the publication of
Pickwick Papers, that Lewes found Dickens able to speak of "graver
subjects than theatres and actors. . . ."[15] Dickens did not simply go
to plays of an evening; he sometimes spent nearly the whole night
there. Writing to Georgy from Paris he said that he and Collins
"dine at five, in a different restaurant every day, and at seven or so
go to the theatre—sometimes to two theatres, sometimes to
three. . . ." This, despite the fact that "the theatres are not particularly good. . . ." More than entertainment, more than escape,
the play was an elixir: urging Macready to come to Paris, he said,
"It will renew your youth to visit a theatre. . . ." I have found only
one instance in which Dickens turned down a theatrical evening
(except when other commitments prevented him from attending):

writing to Georgy from Dublin, he said, "We walked out last night, with the intention of going to the theatre; but the Piccolomini establishment (where they were doing the "Lucia") looked so horribly like a very bad jail, and the Queen's looked so blackguardly, that we came back again, and went to bed." That night Thespis must have shuddered. There were also a few instances in which, once inside a theater, Dickens wished himself outside; one of these occurred in Paris, when he "went to the Chatelot (a beautiful theatre!) the other night to see 'Rothomago,' but was so mortally gené with the poor nature of the piece and of the acting, that I came out again when there was a week or two (I mean an hour or two, but the hours seemed weeks) yet to get through." Another occurred when he and Percy Fitzgerald attended a revival of Pocock's *The Miller and His Men*, which he had seen in his youth and for which he felt all the nostalgia of his first taste of the theater. But the performance was disappointing; by the second act Dickens said "he could stand it no longer," and the two left.[16] The experience must have been for Dickens much like his encounter in his middle years with the aging, fat, chattering married version of the young Maria Beadnell, whom in his youth he had loved.

Some non-dramatic performances he did decline to attend because he saw that such things threatened to crowd the play off the stage. In 1861 he wrote to Macready that "What with Blondin at the Crystal Palace and Leotard at Leicester Square, we seem to be going back to barbaric entertainments. I have not seen, and don't intend to see, the Hero of Niagara (as the posters call him) . . ." but he admitted that he had seen Leotard, "and it is at once the most fearful and most graceful thing I have ever seen done." Not even the danger such performances posed to legitimate drama could keep him away from such things for long, and virtually nothing could keep him from seeing plays. When the choice must be made, he denied himself some other duty or pleasure in favor of the theater. In 1862 he told Mary Boyle that he was supposed to go to a party, but his legs carried him "to the Olympic, where I saw a very good play. . . ." He kept on seeing plays, good and not good, until a week before his death, when he attended a private performance in which his two daughters acted, at the house of Mr. and Mrs. Freake.[17]

The letters demonstrate not only frequency of attendance, but considerable knowledge of contemporary theater. Modest to a fault about most of his abilities, Dickens permitted himself a boast or two about his acquaintance with the play. He was, he said in a speech, an "old stager"; in another about Samuel Phelps' Sadler's Wells Theatre he said, "I have as accurate a knowledge of that theatre as any man in the kingdom." Yet even here he kept his perspective: he did not like those who made a show of their familiarity with the current stage, and laughed when they puffed themselves by demonstrating their knowledge of the social lives of stage people (by using the last names of actresses and the nicknames of actors, for example), or of London theaters by adopting pet names for them: "Covent Garden is the garden, Drury-lane the lane, the Victoria the vic, and the Olympic the pic." But without ostentation, Dickens' letters show that he knew virtually everything about the stage, from its argot to its audiences. He told Herman Merrivale that "He fancied he knew the name of every new play that had been acted for years. . . ."[18] He knew when to catch the best plays and performances: in the winter of 1838-39 he wrote to George Cruikshank to suggest postponing their visit to the Adelphi Theater for one week: "In so doing we shall see better pieces." He knew and frequently used theatrical terms: a dull pantomime was "worked"; his son Walter was sent "away over what they call, in Green Bush melodrama, 'the Big Drink'"; a letter to the actor Macready about a stage referred to the "O. P." (opposite prompter); in a speech an actor was described as having made "one of those little mistakes which we call 'missing his tip,'" and another was mentioned with "features unprepared by the hare's foot"—i.e., not made up; two bars of quick music used in a play are "technically called a 'hurry.'" As the sketch "Mrs. Joseph Porter" shows, he knew all the stage props: "floats, flies, wings, lamps, bridges, clouds, thunder and lightning, festoons and flowers, daggers and foil, and various other messes in theatrical slang."[19]

Dickens used theatrical terms when writing about other matters, often illustrating his points by allusions to the stage. Employing the word "suppose" as it was used at rehearsals—action was "supposed" so that rehearsal could go on to later parts of the play—Dickens, when he omitted an expression from a letter, asked his correspondent to "suppose the term." Street scenes in Boston were so bright and fresh that they "looked exactly like a scene in a pantomime." A letter to Mark Lemon, who was ill, noted that he had "stated times" for chills, "like the demons in the melodramas"; a watch lent Dickens while his own was being repaired was described as going "like the Clown's in a Pantomime." On occasion, he used the form of a play in his letters, as when he expressed to Mary Boyle how much he missed their acting together. Some of these allusions demonstrate Dickens' knowledge of the dramatists of his time: from the Parker House in Boston he wrote, "Down below in this hotel are the bar loungers, dram drinkers, drunkards, swaggerers, loafers, that one might find in a Boucicault play."[20]

If theatrical terms invaded the language of Dickens, they found a country congenial to their nature. Everything about the man appears to have been dramatic, from his parents to his appearance to his writing to his speech to his life.[21] Even getting into a cab could be, for him, "essentially melodramatic." Angus Wilson says that "The chief features of Dickens's parents as they are transformed into his fiction is [sic] dramatization," and mentions the father's stagey phrasing and the mother's dress—in sables, once, Dickens said, "like a female Hamlet." Alexander Woolcott speaks of "his gallant and undeniably Thespian appearance and his flamboyant raiment, geranium in the buttonhole, brilliantine on the hair, rings on the fingers. . . ."[22] Dickens would seem to have adopted this mode of dress when he became a parliamentary reporter; he suddenly appeared before his friends with a new hat, "a very handsome blue cloak, with black velvet facings, the corner of which he threw over his shoulder a l'

Espagnol." Edgar and Eleanor Johnson say that "In a way, the complete works of Dickens, with the entire story of his life thrown in as
well, might constitute one extended and monumental theatrical Reader.
His imagination and personality were steeped in the stage; the world
in which his spirit dwelt was a world brilliant in theatrical hue and
violent in theatrical movement. . . . Life itself glared in a circle of
stage fire." Dickens' contemporaries agreed. ". . . He had in an
extraordinary degree the dramatic element in his character," Charles
Kent said. "It colored his whole temperament or idiosyncracy.
Unconsciously he described himself, to a T, in *Nicholas Nickleby.*
'There's genteel comedy in your walk and manner, juvenile tragedy in
your eye, and touch-and-go farce in your laugh.'. . ."[23]

Best Of Critics

Some of Dickens' friends were disturbed by his theatrical appearance (as well as by his appearance in theatricals), but all of them
shared his love of the stage. Only his illustrator Hablôt Knight
Browne, Jane R. Cohen tells us, "rarely joined Dickens's theater
parties and never participated in his amateur theatricals."[24] But even
Browne loved the drama; he simply preferred reading plays to seeing
or acting in them. If there were not as many men of the theater in
Dickens' inner circle as there were artists, certainly there were
several: one of his best and most admired friends was the great
Shakespearian actor William Charles Macready (who mentions Dickens
in his diary 199 times, making him third behind only Macready's wife
Catherine, and John Forster); a later friend was the French-English
actor Charles Fechter; and novelist friends like Ainsworth, Collins,
and Bulwer also wrote plays. When he visited France, Dickens apparently immersed himself in dramatic society. He spent much of his
time in Paris attending plays, but "great as was the pleasure . . .
derived" from that, Forster says, "he was, in the matter of social in-
tercourse, even more indebted to distinguish [*sic*] men connected with

it by authorship or acting."[25] Among several, Forster mentions Scribe, Auber, Pichot, and Legouvet.

Many of these knowledgeable friends testified to Dickens' extraordinary command of the world of drama. Mrs. Cowden Clarke, the compiler of a Shakespeare concordance, praised "the feeling and understanding with which he spoke of the theatre" at a testimonial for Macready. We hear of "the high opinion that Douglas Jerrold had of his dramatic judgment. . . ." T. Edgar Pemberton speaks of "his keen interest in the theatre and his vivid knowledge of it and its surroundings from every point of view . . ."; these, he said, "were nowhere better shown than in his public speeches." Lord Mulgrave, Forster says, applied to Dickens for information about places of amusement in the country, "which Dickens knew better than any man; small theatre, saloon, and gardens in city or borough. . . ." Kate Field, a perceptive American who wrote about the English theater, called him "that best of dramatic critics." But perhaps the strongest testimony to Dickens' knowledge of the theater—at least of its technical aspects—comes to us from a stage carpenter. Writing to Mrs. Richard Watson to say that he would send her carpenter some ideas about developing a small stage for amateur performances at her residence, Dickens added, "I developed these wonderful ideas to the master carpenter at one of the theatres, and he shook his head with an intensely mournful air, and said, 'Ah, sir, it's a universal observation in the profession, sir, that it was a great loss to the public when you took to writing books!'"[26] Modern scholars have not gone quite so far, but all have praised Dickens as a dramatic authority. Angus Wilson called him "that Englishman who wrote of the theatre oftener and with more insight than any one else of his century or ours," and said that he wrote "some of the best dramatic criticism in the language." Edgar and Eleanor Johnson said that in his critical comments "repeatedly Dickens gleams a rich response or a sharp twist of analysis, an amused insight, a glimpse of histrionic absurdity, or a deeply moved awareness of some revelation of truth and beauty." But it was

Forster who spoke first and most forcefully in urging that Dickensian dramatic criticism be preserved:

> . . . This perishable employment has only so much as may survive out of such recollections [as are found in Dickens' letters] to witness for itself to another generation; and an unusually high place may be challenged for the subtlety and delicacy of what is said in these letters of things theatrical, when the writer was especially attracted by a performance or a play.[27]

The praise of Forster and the Johnsons is merited, but Wilson's assertion of Dickensian supremacy seems somewhat overstated: Dickens wrote very well indeed about drama, but others in his and our times have written quite as well. What Dickens may have done better *"than anyone else in his century or ours"* was to know the theater of his time, inside and out, upside and down, in London, in the provinces, on the continent, in its most professional and its most amateurish states, its very best and its very worst forms. He did not merely love good or great drama; he loved *all* drama, loved anything that remotely resembled drama, and seems to have enjoyed himself almost as much at a puppet show or a circus melodrama as he did at the finest production at the Strand. Like a lover, he took delight in the faults and weaknesses of his inamorata: rarely do we hear of anything done so badly that he could not find something in it to enjoy; as Angus Wilson says, he was *"almost as happy to be entertained by what was bad"* as by what was good (and not only in plays, it should be noted: Dickens always hugely enjoyed any form of kitsch). His American friend, the publisher James T. Fields, put it best:

> He was passionately fond of the theatre, loved the lights and music and flowers, and the happy faces of the audience. He was accustomed to say that his love of the theatre never failed, and, no matter how dull the play, he was always careful while he sat in the box to make no sound which

could hurt the feelings of the actors, or show any lack of attention.[28]

In some cases, it must have required an heroic effort. After watching a performance of Talfourd's *The Athenian Captive*, he wrote Forster that he must come and see it too:

> . . . oh! if you had but been with us! Young Betty, doing what the mind of man without my help never *can* conceive, with his legs like padded boot-trees wrapped up in faded yellows drawers, was the hero. The comic man of the company enveloped in a white sheet, with his head tied with red tape like a brief and greeted with yells of laughter when he appeared, was the venerable priest. A poor toothless old idiot at whom the very gallery roared with contempt when he was called a tyrant, was the remorseless and aged Creon. And Ismene, being arranged in spangled muslin trowsers very loose in the legs and very tight in the ankles, such as Fatima would wear in *Blue Beard*, was at her appearance immediately called upon for a song.[29]

It is in his thorough knowledge of and love of the stage of his time, more than in his critical commentary upon it, that Dickens surpasses every man of his, and perhaps of our, generation.

Dickens' knowledge of drama extended well beyond his own time. It had blank spots—he cared nothing for French classical drama, for example, and there is little to indicate familiarity with Roman or Greek plays—but in certain areas he demonstrated considerable command of the history of drama. In a review of Charles Macready's production of *King Lear* he commented on the destruction Nahum Tate ("a notorious poet-laureate") had wreaked upon the play in the seventeenth century: Tate

> omitted the grandest things, the Fool among them; polished all that remained into commonplace; interlarded love scenes;

sent Cordelia into a comfortable cave with her lover, to dry her clothes and get warm, while her distracted and homeless old father was still left wandering without, . . . and finally, rewarded the poor old man in his turn, and repaid him for his suffering, by giving him back his gilt robe and tinsel sceptre!

. . . Betterton was the last great actor who played Lear before the commission of this outrage. His performance of it between the years 1663 and 1671 are recorded to have been the greatest efforts of his genius. Ten years after the latter date, Mr. Tate published his disgusting version, and this was adopted successively by Boheme, Quin, Booth, Barry, Garrick, Henderson, Kemble, Kean.[30]

Further evidence that Dickens' knowledge of drama was not limited to his own time is found in his familiarity with English playwrights ranging back to the Elizabethan Age. He spoke with authority on the plays of Goldsmith, Sheridan, Massinger, Fletcher, Jonson, and, of course, Shakespeare. It will surprise no one that he knew his Shakespeare, but not everyone may be aware of how well he knew him, and could write about him. Casual quotations and paraphrases of the Master so fill the pages of his letters—many of them not at all the standard lines one is accustomed to hearing—that he seems almost to have known Shakespeare by heart. Indeed, he would seem to have known him thus since his days as law clerk when, according to a fellow employee, "he could give us Shakespeare by the ten minutes, and imitate all the leading actors of that time." Both his own journals took their titles from the Bard; both phrases are used in his writing well before he employed them as titles, "household words" appearing in an article on Scott as early as 1839. The characters and actions of Shakespeare's plays are echoed throughout Dickens' writing. But characteristically, Dickens showed no pride in his apparent total recall of Shakespeare, and even mocked the ability to quote him as a "parrot-like accomplishment."[31]

Astonishing Success

As everyone knows, Dickens was content neither to sit behind the lights nor to demonstrate his knowledge of what went on in front of them. From his childhood he had in one way or another trod the boards; the family servant Mary Weller tells us that the Dickenses "would sing, recite, and perform parts of plays," and that "A rather favourite piece for recitation by Charles at this time was 'The Voice of the Sluggard' from Dr. Watts, and the little boy used to give it with great effect, and with *such* action and *such* attitudes. . . ."[32] The action and attitudes kept up until his death (which, it has been said, was hastened by his exhausting dramatic readings from his works), reaching their first peak when, in 1845, he undertook almost single-handedly the private production of Jonson's *Every Man in his Humour*. He directed, of course, and of course he was not satisfied with his actors: he wrote Macready that he thought "the company 'damned bad'—no other phrase will express the sentiment, at present." A month later things were not quite so terrible: it was only, "The actors rather disappoint me so far." He took responsibility for many other details of the production, as well: he wrote to John Wilmot, stage manager at the Lyceum, for "stage cudgels," adding that some of his actors "begin to feel like used-up cab horses—going perceptibly at the knees." He involved himself in everything, though the actors seemed to give him the most trouble:

> I am half dead with Managerial work—and with actual work in shirt sleeves; with a dirty face, a hammer, and a bag of nails. I never in my life saw a place in such a state, or had to do with such an utterly careless and unbusiness-like set of dogs (with the exception of Stanfield and Brainworm) as my fellow actors.[33]

Needless to say, there was nothing careless or unbusinesslike in his preparation for his own role, that of Bobadil. He wrote a letter to the tailor about details of his costume, and sought Macready's advice about acting the role: "Do you think Bobadil is *humble* before the Justice, or still carrying it off in his swaggering way?" The response did not please him:

> I am going to adopt your reading of the fifth act with the worst grace in the world. It seems to me that you don't allow enough for Bobadil having been frequently beaten before as I have no doubt he had been. The part goes down hideously on this construction, and the end is mere lees.

The greatest actor of his time might persuade Dickens, but he could not convince him. (Certainly Macready's judgment could be faulty: he once lectured at length to Dickens and Forster concerning "the utter impractibility of *Oliver Twist* for any dramatic purpose.") He also consulted Maclise about his costume, and said that he had been reading books about the dress of the period. At the same time, he kept up with his other duties: a week before the play was to be performed, he described himself as "in Managerial agonies . . . all day. . . ." Forster says that Dickens did everything:

> He was the life and soul of the entire affair. . . . He took everything on himself, and did the whole of it without an effort. He was stage-director, very often stage-carpenter, scene-arranger, property-man, prompter, and bandmaster. . . . He adjusted scenes, assisted carpenters, invented costumes, devised playbills, wrote out calls, and enforced as well as exhibited in his proper person everything of which he urged the necessity on others.

The outcome appears to have been worth the effort. "It really was a brilliant sight. . . . As to the acting, modesty forbids me to say more than that it has been the town talk ever since. I have known nothing short of a Murder, to make such a noise before."[34] If there was ever any doubt that he would continue to be active in the theater, this performance ended it: Dickens was, in the old sense of the word as well as the new, enchanted. Trying to write a letter to Mme. De la Rue on several topics, he kept drifting back into details about the performance, such as his costume and his beard, which was put on "singly, by the individual hair!" and at last had to confess that "I am constantly returning to this Play, I find."[35]

Every Man in his Humour was repeated twice, as benefit performances for the Sanitorium and for the actress-manager Miss Kelly, in whose theater the first performance had been given. Dickens kept on top of things to the end, writing to Clarkson Stanfield about scenery, and to Miss Kelly about the final performance and tickets for his friends, and reminding her about such details as lighting, music, props, costumes, and even the callboy. His last words to Miss Kelly were, "I want everything to be *well done*. . . ."[36]

These last letters were written on Christmas Day, 1845; three days later, he was writing a letter about the prologue he had supplied for a production of Fletcher's *The Elder Brother*, of which there was to be another performance, with Dickens playing the role of Eustace. Forster also had a role, and apparently all did not go well between the two friends as they rehearsed. "When I am bullied through those four acts," Dickens wrote another friend, "—always regard me as being ready (in serious earnest) to stab Forster to the heart. It makes me so damned savage that I could rend him limb from limb." Perhaps part of the savagery was owing to Dickens' immersion in his role, but Forster could be a hard man to live with, and apparently some real animosity did develop between them: Macready, who visited Forster while he and Dickens were trying on costumes, wrote in his diary that he "was sorry to hear of intemperate language between them, which should neither have been given nor received, as it was."[37]

By June of 1847, Dickens was busy preparing for performances of other plays; a letter to Forster shows the kind of things with which he had to deal:

Good Heaven! I find that A. hasn't twelve words, and
I am in hourly expectation of rebellion!

You were right about the green baize, that it would
certainly muffle the voices; and some of our actors, by Jove,
haven't too much of that commodity at the best.

B. shocked me so much the other night by a restless,
stupid movement of his hands in his first scene with you,
that I took a turn of an hour with him yesterday morning,
and I hope quieted his nerves a little.

I made a desperate effort to get C. to give up his part.
Yet in spite of all the trouble he gives me I am sorry for
him, he is so evidently hurt by his own sense of not doing
well. He clutched the part, however, tenaciously; and three
weary times we dragged through it last night.

That infernal E. forgets everything.

I plainly see that F. when nervous, which he is sure
to be, loses his memory. Moreover his asides are inaudible,
even at Miss Kelly's; and as regularly as I stop him to say
them again, he explains (with a face of agony) that "he'll
speak loud on the night", as if anybody ever did without
doing it always!

G. not born for it at all, and too innately conceited, I
much fear, to do anything well. I thought him better last
night, but I would as soon laugh at a kitchen poker.

Fancy H, ten days after the casting of that farce,
wanting F.'s part therein! Having himself an excellent old
man in it already, and a quite admirable part in the other
farce.[38]

Such worries and doubts naturally meant that the plays went
well: Dickens called the tour to Liverpool and Manchester "a most
brilliant and successful trip," and wrote to R. B. Peake that "The
country performances went off with astonishing success." Early in
1848, his letters show him active again in the preparation of more

amateur offerings, this time for the benefit of the new Guild of Literature and Art, in which Dickens was active. He tried hard, as usual, to bring the plays off; we find him writing to Miss Kelly, promising information about a suitable actress (as well as discussing circulars, probably not for the plays but for Miss Kelly's Shakespeare readings, concerning which she apparently had asked to be allowed to quote his good opinion), and to Mark Lemon about details of the performance. But just a few days later, he wrote to Miss Kelly that this time the actors really had failed him: "I have decided to relinquish the Amateur Performances—not having the least hope, as you know, of some of the parties concerned." Only a few months later, though, the project was revived: Dickens wrote to Lewes considering possible farces to be used along with the newly-selected plays.[39]

Soon the post was filled with Dickens' letters about the coming performances. He offered Mrs. Cowden Clarke the roles of Mistress Quickly in *Merry Wives* and Mrs. Hillary in the Kenney farce, and added that they were now not playing "to purchase the [Shakespeare] house (which may be positively considered as paid for) but towards endorsing a perpetual curatorship of it, for some eminent literary veteran" (who turned out to be James Sheridan Knowles). He informed Anne Romer, actress and cousin of Ellen Lemon, that they would play "twice in London, and twice in the country," and asked her to undertake Anne Page in *Merry Wives* and Constance in *Animal Magnetism*; a third part was also available if she was interested.[40] The flood of letters continued—far too many even for summary—until September; I count a total of one hundred and thirteen more that at least mention the project (including the Shakespeare House). The majority are working letters, arranging dinners for the performers, deciding what edition of *Merry Wives* would be used, offering parts to prospective actors, getting out announcements, advertisements, and posters, setting dates for rehearsals and performances, locating theaters, settling details about tickets, arranging for music, urging actors to memorize their parts, settling details of business, deciding which plays would be acted in which cities, getting railroad passes for actors, declining offers to appear in other cities, getting playbooks, making last-minute changes, and even arranging for "the luggage."[41]

Working as he was all this time at his own profession, as well as on numerous projects such as the charitable work in which he was often engaged with Miss Coutts, Dickens' only concession to time seems to have been, as he wrote to Macready, to cut back on social engagements: "I must keep myself free for some part or other of this play." The pace told, even upon him. He wrote to the Reverend Edward Tagart to say that he was "living, like Falstaff, in a state of continual dissolution and thaw, with the protracted agonies of management." "When I find myself at the Haymarket all day," he wrote his sister Fanny, "and at Miss Kelly's half the night, I begin to wonder why one does such things for nothing."[42] Certainly no one could have labored harder for any amount of money. The work on amateur performances continued for several years, all of them, as he had written in his prospectus about plays which were to have been offered by the projected Provident Union of Literature, Science, and Art, "presented with the utmost care, and the most scrupulous attention to accuracy, fidelity and completeness in all respects. . . ."[43]

Prominent among the projects were the three nights of performances put on at Knebworth, Bulwer's estate, in 1850. These inspired Bulwer to propose what came to be called "The Guild of Literature and Art," an endowment to be used for deserving and needy artists and men of letters. Bulwer donated some property for the site of the Guild, and wrote a comedy, *Not So Bad as We Seem*, to be acted by Dickens' amateur group for its benefit. "I propose," Dickens wrote to Bulwer, "(for cheapness and many other considerations) to make a theatre expressly for the purpose, which we can put up and take down . . . and move into the country." The play was performed twice, on May 16 and 27, 1851, at the Duke of Devonshire's palatial residence in Picadilly, before a distinguished audience which included the Queen and the Prince Consort; tickets went at five guineas. It was through this performance that Dickens met Wilkie Collins: he wrote his artist friend Augustus Egg to offer

Collins the part of Valet—"a small part, but, what there is of it, decidedly good. . . ." (He sounds like a manager, talking an actor into taking a minor role.) "I knew his father," Dickens added, "and should be very glad to know him." Dickens urged an old friend, Miss Coutts, decidely not to act in but to attend the performance (like some other friends, she held what he called a "mysterious objection" to his dramatic activities), urging the benefit to the Guild, and defending his participation by declaring that

> there is no one else whom these men would allow to hold them together, or to whose direction they would good-humouredly and with perfect confidence yield themselves.
>   . . . You will not find it like any other amateur Plays, I think. You will be impressed by the general intelligence and good sense. And you will find a certain neatness in it which I should compare with the French stage, if you were not so profoundly English!

Dickens played a vigorous role (naturally) in the planning and development of the Guild of Literature and Art, and did his best to produce other plays for it. But despite his usual energy, he could save neither the performances nor the Guild, which eventually was disbanded.[44]

In 1852 Dickens added another managerial activity: Christmas theatricals in his own home. "These began," Forster tells us,

> with the first Twelfth Night at Tavistock House, and were renewed until the principal actors [the children of Dickens and his friends] ceased to be children. The best of the performances were *Tom Thumb* and *Fortunio*, in '54 and '55; Dickens now joining first in the revel, and Mr. Mark Lemon bringing into it his own clever children and a very mountain of child-pleasing fun in himself.

The first performance in 1852 was of Albert Smith's burletta *Guy*

Fawkes; in 1853, Robert Brough's extravaganza *William Tell* was done. Edgar Johnson neatly summarizes the offering of *Tom Thumb* in 1854:

> Dickens, playing the Ghost of Gaffer Thumb, billed himself as "the Modern Garrick," and stout Mark Lemon, playing the Giantess Glumdalca, was listed as "the Infant Phenomenon." Little Betty and Lally Lemon, his daughters, were gravely irresistible as Huncamunca and Dollalolla. A small boy named Alfred Ainger (later Canon Ainger, Master of the Temple and biographer of Charles Lamb) played Lord Grizzle so drolly that Thackeray, who was among the guests, fell off his chair in a helpless fit of laughter. The supreme hit of the evening, however, was the small, helmeted hero, Tom Thumb, acted with solemn conviction by four-year-old Henry Fielding Dickens.

The performance of *Fortunio* in 1855 was distinguised by the "First appearance on any stage of Mr. Plornishmaroontigoonter [Dickens' youngest son, Edward]—age 2 (who has been kept out of bed at a vast expense)." With Mark Lemon as the dragon, "—with a practical head and tail,"[45] it must have approached the previous production in hilarity.

In the summer of 1855 a "*grown-up Play*" was undertaken: Dickens "threw open to many friends his Tavistock House Theatre . . ." and Collins' *The Lighthouse* was given, with Dickens, Collins, Lemon, Egg, Georgina, and Mamie taking parts. The accompanying farce was *Mr. Nightingale's Diary*, for which Frank Stone and young Kate joined the company. By Christmas of that year things had become more serious; the schoolroom at Tavistock House was turned into a theater, with "sawing and hammering worthy of Babel"; it was dubbed "the theatre Royal, Tavistock House," described on the playbill as "the smallest theatre in the world," with "Mr. Vincent Crummles" as manager.[46] Clarkson Stanfield now lent his art to the creation of scenery, and Mr. Cooke of Astley's was engaged to find more space for the audience and actors (but apparently found none). Such was the demand for seats that additional performances were scheduled, and workmen did not get the theater back to its schoolroom form until January 20.

In 1856 Dickens actually declined to get up a play—for Colonel Waugh of Campden House, where *The Lighhouse* had been performed: Dickens' meager excuse was that he was working on *Little Dorrit*. But he got up several plays elsewhere, and undertook other dramatic activities including "a day reading by me; a night reading by me," for the benefit of the family of Douglas Jerrold. Forster says that Dickens accomplished all this with "an amount of labour in acting and travelling that might have appalled an experienced comedian. . . ."[47]

The Twelfth Night performances ended in 1857—not simply, as Forster said, because the children were growing up, but because by 1858 Dickens had begun his break with his wife, moving first out of their bedroom, and eventually out of the house. Reality, once again, had beaten imagination; Dickens might have thought of Keats' statement in "Ode to a Nightingale" that "the fancy cannot cheat so well / As she is fam'd to do." Dickens must have abandoned the holiday plays with a deep sense of loss, for they had been a special part of his enjoyment of theater, at the season of year he had all but made his own, and had in his judgment been an important part of his children's education—"about the best training in Art and respect for Art, that my young people could receive."[48]

As manager of amateur productions, Dickens was superb. Forster said that "Without offending anyone, he kept everyone in order. For all he had useful suggestions, and the dullest of clays under his potter's hand were transformed into little bits of porcelain." "Never in the world of theatres," said R. H. Horne, "was a better manager than Charles Dickens."[49]

A Piece Of Genius

Not everyone was equally enthusiastic about Dickens' acting; as Angus Wilson puts it, "accounts differ." Though Forster is unqualified in his praise of Dickens as manager, he finds limitations in his acting ability. ". . . He was always greater in quickness of assumption than in steadiness of delineation . . ."; "though Dickens had the title to be called a born comedian, the turn for it being in his very nature, his strength was rather in the vividness and variety of his assumptions, than in the completeness, finish, or ideality he could give to any part of them." Remembering that tension between Dickens and Forster as actors to which Macready referred, we may wonder whether such judgment is entirely objective, but perhaps it is well to resist the temptation to find reasons for discounting negative judgments; we do not question Forster when he may have had reason to over-praise his friend. Suffice to say that others disagreed with Forster. Thackeray, seeing Dickens in *The Frozen Deep* (not a comedy), said, "If that man would now go upon the stage he would make his Ł20,000 a-year."[50] Wilkie Collins said that as Richard Wardour in *The Frozen Deep* Dickens "literally electrified the audience." (Let us hope not.) Charles Kent claimed that as an amateur, he was "simply unapproachable. He passed, in fact, beyond the range of mere amateurs, and was brought into contrast by right, with the most gifted professionals among his contemporaries." Mrs. Cowden-Clark said of his Justice Shallow in *Merry Wives* that "His impersonation was perfect," and that his Bobadil in *Every Man* "was a veritable piece of genius. . . ." And in contrast to Forster's emphasis upon comedy, Kent found Dickens, at least in one of his readings, to have had considerable dramatic range: the climax of his performance of the murder of Nancy from *Oliver Twist* "was as splendid a piece of tragic acting as had for many years been witnessed."[51] It was indeed in his readings from his own works that Dickens achieved his greatest triumphs upon the stage, triumphs so important that they must be studied in a separate chapter.

Like To Serve

In addition to attending dramatic performances, directing them, and appearing in them, Dickens was active in the theatrical world in several other ways. He lent assistance to many theatrical people, with no thought but to improve a performance or aid a needy member of the profession. He gave the actress Fanny Kelly advice about her Shakespeare readings, suggesting the best time of year to begin (after Easter), kinds of audiences to avoid (seaside), and the most advantageous way to make engagements (through the prestige she would get by appearances in cities such as Manchester).[52] We have noted in passing some of Dickens' efforts on behalf of the Shakespeare House, the committee of which had in 1848 begun "imploring and beseeching me to call my Amateur Company together, and act for the benefit of the Fund. . . . I am not particulary anxious to take the needful trouble. . . ." It is one of the few moments on record in which even a momentary mood or pretense of one inclined him to express indifference to dramatic activity, but needless to say, he took the trouble, of which we have sampled a portion. That work had begun in earnest in April of 1848; as late as October of the same year Dickens wrote to Miss Coutts to say he had to stay at home for a meeting with the "gentlemen from the Shakespeare Committee . . ."; he was still mentioning details to be attended to in January of the next year.[53] No man could ever have had more energy, or employed it more generously, than Charles Dickens.

Other actors and causes received similar attention. To Walter Savage Landor, who was seeking assistance for the actress Isabel Dickenson, Dickens offered his services. He helped put on a benefit for Mrs. Warner, an actress dying of cancer. Early in 1853 he took, says Forster, "a good natured journey to Walworth to see a youth rehearse who was supposed to have talents for the stage, and he was able to gladden Mr. Toole's friends by thinking favourably of his chances to success. 'I remember what I once myself wanted in that way,' he said, 'and I should like to serve him.'" He asked Charles Knight for a copy of his book, *Shakespeare*, which contained the airs sung by Ophelia, to assist a German actress performing that part. On very few occasions did Dickens refuse to extend his hand; usually, such denials were made when aspiring dramatists sought his help, as when he declined to assist Richard Lee in getting his play produced, or to help Charles Elleman publish his play, *Alphonso Barbo*: "I never communicate with any manager on such a subject," he wrote to the latter, "or with any one, as a Mediator for any purpose. Nor do I ever give an opinion on any such production for the purpose of its being published or used."[54] As with artists and sculptors, so with playwrights: a work of the imagination should make its own way.

In all others ways, his assistance was offered. He was instrumental in getting a pension for Poole, and chaired a fund-raising group for the family of actor Edward Elton, drowned at sea. And he helped in lesser ways, as well; for example, he gave advice to the Reverend Christopher Carey on public speaking (speak more from the throat, address the last bench of the room, don't drop the voice at the end of a sentence), and he wrote a prologue for Dr. Westland Marston's *The Patrician's Daughter*, produced by Macready at Drury Lane in 1842.[55]

To Charles Fechter, the French-English actor and manager whom he much admired, he lent immeasurable assistance, especially during Fechter's leasing of the Lyceum in London; Forster says he was moved to help "quite as much by generous sympathy with the difficulties of such a position to an artist who was not an Englishman, as by genuine admiration of Mr. Fechter's acting. He became his helper in disputes, adviser in literary points, referee in matters of management. . . ."[56] In 1862 he got Bulwer to rewrite his play, *The Sea Captain*, as *The Rightful Heir*, for Fechter to produce. Dickens also had a hand in several of Bulwer's plays, changing for example such details in one as the time of day (so lighting could be more effective), and replacing a letter by dialogue.[57] To less famous playwrights, many more letters offered constructive criticism, encouragement (or compassionate discouragement), and sympathy.

Dickens also participated in the extra-theatrical activities of the dramatic world.   He was a member of the short-lived Shakespeare Club.   He attended innumerable dinners, including one to honor Macready at the end of his three-year management of Covent Garden, in 1839; in 1851 he was a member of the organizing committee for a banquet in honor of Macready's farewell performance as Macbeth.   At a meeting for the Formulation of the Dramatic College in 1858, he offered the resolution for the organization of the Royal General Theatrical Fund, and for the acceptance of five acres upon which it was to be located; he was elected a trustee of the organization, and chaired its first and second anniversary festivals.   In 1864 he chaired a meeting to establish the Shakespeare Foundation Schools in connection with that organization.   The high esteem in which he was held by the theatrical world is evident not only in these several honorary and working posts, but in the number of books of or about drama which were dedicated to him, including Peter Peterson's *Glimpses of Real Life*, Kate Field's *Charles Albert Fechter*, and the Reverend James White's play, *John Saville of Haystead*.   Finally, Dickens helped to shape newspaper reviews of drama to some extent.   When he served for a brief period as editor of the *Daily News*, he "permitted his father-in-law, George Hogarth, to begin a series of gossipy, informal, semi-critical articles on current drama and music.   The critique of the drama and music were nothing new, but it had been formal, stilted, and dull.   Under Dickens' encouragement, Hogarth introduced a popularizing element into his articles such as had not been seen before."[58]

This Honest Opinion

To all these activities relating to drama must be added a lifelong reading of plays. The letters do not provide a great list of readings: Dickens never liked to parade his erudition. But from time to time—almost always for some specific purpose, hardly ever simply to say what he had been reading—he mentioned a play he had read. In 1839 it was a translation of a German play, sent him by "a young Scotch lady"; Dickens sought Macready's opinion of the first act, "and especially the opening, which seems to me quite famous." Most of the plays mentioned in the letters were read for friends and others who sought Dickens' opinion, as John Hollingshead seems to have done for his farce, *The Birthplace of Podgers*:

> Although there is a very droll (and an original) idea in the farce, I doubt if it would do on the stage. I don't think it ends as well as it opens, and I don't see enough for an actor to "make" in it. By far the best part is Mr. Maresnest's, but you could not hold the stage with the piece unless Cranby were done by a good actor; and, as the piece stands, a good Farce-actor would not play the said Cranby, because the character is really not strong enough to win the presence and eye of an audience all that time.

Without the play before us, we cannot judge Dickens' judgment, but one guesses from his success as director that he had a good sense of what would work upon the stage; the letter conveys an awareness of what an actor can and cannot do with a role. Much of his advice to aspiring dramatists centered upon this kind of thing. To Percy Fitzgerald's request for an opinion of a play of his, Dickens responded:

> It goes very gliby and merrily and smoothly, but I make so bold as to say that you can write a much better one. The

most characteristic part in it is much too like Compton in
The Unequal Match.   And the best scene in it (where the
husband urges his wife to go away) is so excessively dangerous, and is so very near passing a delicate line, that I
think the chances would be very many to one against an
audience's acceptance of it.   Because, however drolly the
situation is presented, the fact is not to be got over that the
lady seriously supposes her husband to be in league with
another man, to hand her over to that other man, both these
men being present with her.

Put your sister, mentally, in the situation.

Dickens also read contemporary plays simply for his own
pleasure, as is attested by the letters of praise he often sent to
dramatists; one such was written to James White about *The Earl of
Gowrie*, which Dickens said he read

with a delight which I should in vain endeavor to express to
you.   Considered with reference to its story, or its characters, or its noble poetry, I honestly regard it as a work of
most remarkable genius.   It has impressed me powerfuly and
enduringly.   And if I have to tell you what complete possession it has taken of me—that is, if I *could* tell you—I do
believe you would be glad to know it.[59]

By no means did Dickens limit himself in his letters to comments on plays; as Edgar Johnson says, he also offered opinions on
"cabarets and minstral shows, ballet dances, pantomimes, and
marionettes, even on ventriloquists, magicians, and 'grimaciers.'"
(My own count lists just under forty references to such slight things
in the letters alone.)   Not even a play written by Laman Blanchard's
ten-year-old son was beneath his notice: "I have been amused beyond
all telling with your son's play, in which the rival kings talk a great
deal more common sense than any stage kings I have ever known.   I
suppose its excessive length is an insuperable objection to its represen-

tation at Covent Garden. . . ."   What a happy touch he had in such comments.   He had time, too, for the simple efforts of the working man, John Overs, whose play he could not commend, but whom he praised for the effort: "The production is most honourable and creditable to you. . . ."   Gently, he tried to let Overs down easily: ". . . It would not benefit you, either in pocket or in reputation, if it were printed;—and acted, I do not think it ever could be. . . ."[60]

But of course it is Dickens' comments upon the reputable dramatists of his time, as well as those few he made upon great playwrights, that are of most interest.   He liked Dion Boucicault's *The Long Strike*, which he thought "done with a master's hand.   Its construction is admirable."   But he saw a danger: the "small parts" required the most exacting attention, for they "cannot take the play up, but they can let it down.   I would not leave a hair on the head of one of them to the chance of the first night, but I would see, to the minutest particular, the make-up of every one of them at a night rehearsal."   On the whole, he did not like Boucicault, whom he identified as "one of a school that I utterly detest, abominate, and abjure," apparently because he found a false quality in his plays:

> Shall I ever forget [Madame] Vestris in London Assurance
> [Boucicault's first success] bursting out into certain praises
> (they always elicited three rounds) of a—of a country morning
> I think it was!   The atrocity was perpetrated, I remember,
> on a Lawn before a Villa.   It was led up to by flowerpots.
> The thing was as like any honest sympathy or honest English
> as the rosepink on a Sweep's face on May Day, is to a
> beautiful complexion. . . ."[61]

He commented more frequently on the novels of Wilkie Collins than on his plays, but he thought *Black and White* was "a really clever piece," and was intimately involved in the writing of *The Frozen Deep* and *No Thoroughfare*.   He liked the plays of T. N. Talfourd: he called *Glencoe* "so noble a tragedy," and said *The Athenian Captive*

was, "as an acting piece, . . . admirable; I am . . . surprised . . .
to imagine by what mental process such a very striking and complete
thing can have been forged in so short a time." "The play haunts
me, and did so all night," he wrote to a friend. "I am in raptures
with it." But he did not care for *Ion*: "It never was a popular play,
I say. It derived a certain amount of out-of-door popularity from the
circumstances under which, and the man by whom, it was written.
But I say that it never was a popular play on the stage, and never
made out a case of attraction there."[62]

Despite his affection for Bulwer, Dickens did not like all his
plays, either. With his *The Sea Captain*, he wrote, "I was disappointed . . . Oh! grievously! I can scarcely say how much. . . .
[It was] out-Adelphying the Adelphi. . . ." The critics agreed that
the play was too sensational. Though he wrote a kind review of *The
Lady of Lyons*, his private opinion must have been less enthusiastic: he
invited his friend Mitton to see it, but added that it was "only the
Lady of Lyons. . . ." But he did like the play *Money*: "I told
Macready when he read it to me a few weeks since, that I could not
call to mind any play since the Good Natured man, so full of real,
distinct, genuine character; and now that I am better acquainted with
it, I am only the more strongly confirmed in this honest opinion."
Dickens had said to Macready that he "had not supposed that Bulwer
could do anything so good." He also liked the farce *Used Up*—"a
delightful piece," he wrote the Hon. Col. Phipps, ". . . a very striking picture of the time of George the First. . . ." He thought his
amateur company's performance of it "by far the best thing we have
ever done." He also liked Bulwer's *The Rightful Heir*—the revision of
The Sea Captain—despite some reservations both Bulwer and Fechter
had about it: "It seems to me *exceedingly strong*." Elsewhere he
said that Bulwer had, "in his dramatic genius, enchanted and
enthralled. . . ."[63]

Among other playwrights, Dickens liked Gerald Griffin's
Gisippus, and was "struck" by passages in William Lemaitre's
Caracalla, but found it "very unequal," with verse that "halts

woefully," and characters either not sufficiently contrasted, unfortunate in their probable effect on an audience, tedious in their conversations, or insufficient for their roles.   He expressed appreciation of the fresh-ness and truth in the plot of Douglas Jerrold's *Time Works Wonders*, and he liked Mark Lemon's *The Loving Woman*, though his comments, as so often happened, were as much on the performance of it as on the play itself: "It went admirably—rose as it went on—mounted im-mensely as it went on—and closed in triumph. . . .   I have never seen such a fine, picturesque, splendid piece of melodrama."   Finally, he approved of Marston, calling *Camilla's Husband* "a very good play," and crying at *A Hard Struggle* "till I sobbed again."   In a letter to Marston he compared the play to the popular *La Joie fait Peur*, spoke of the subtlety of development in one of the characters, and concluded, "A touching idea, most delicately conceived and wrought out by a true artist and poet, in a spirit of noble manly generosity, that no one should be able to study without great emotion."   He must have liked the play indeed, for these are some of his most laudatory adjectives.   No doubt the subject impressed him at least as much as the artistry: a child growing into a devoted woman was always a pleasure for him to conceive, and in 1858 probably had especial appeal.   He sent the play to Regnier at the Français in Paris for consideration.[64]

Dickens made far fewer written comments on great dramatists than on his contemporaries, no doubt simply because he had less oc-casion to do so.   He spoke of one dramatic effort by a contemporary with a far greater name than any of his friends—Robert Browning—with enthusiasm.   Of *A Blot in the 'Scutcheon* he said:

> Browning's play has thrown me into a perfect passion of sorrow.   To say that there is anything in its subject save what is lovely, true, deeply affecting, full of the best emotion, the most earnest feeling, and the most true and tender source of interest, is to say that there is no light in the sun, and no heat in blood.   It is full of genius, natural

and great thoughts, profound and yet simple and beautiful in
its vigour. I know of nothing that is so affecting, nothing
in any book I have ever read, as Mildred's recurrence to
that "I was so young—I had no mother." I know no love
like it, no passion like it, no moulding of a splendid thing
after its conception, like it. And I swear it is a tragedy that
must be played. . . . There are some things I would have
changed if I could (they are very slight, mostly broken
lines); and I assuredly would have the old servant [Gerald]
begin his tale upon the scene; and be taken by the throat, or
drawn upon, by his master, in its commencement. . . . I
believe from my soul there is no man living (and not many
dead) who could produce such a work.

Here is the same love of the passionate, the beautiful, the "true" that
we have seen elsewhere, as well as of the simple and the vigorous.
The suggested change in the servant's part is not a good one, but we
can see why Dickens liked it: anything which would affect the
audience, however melodramatically, was worth doing. But it is the
combination of opposite emotions that probably attracted Dickens most
to the play; in a later letter he said that "Browning's Tragedy . . . is
at once the most tender and the most terrible story I ever read. It
made my eyes so red and dim, in the perusal, that I thought they
would never sparkle . . . anymore."[65]

Dickens commented briefly on Sheridan. "The 'Rivals' is more
droll," he said, "as a mere piece of drollery, but the 'School for
Scandal' is a more delightful piece of comedy."[66] The letter does not
explain why, but perhaps the point was one he often made elsewhere:
to truly please, the dramatist must do more than make one laugh; he
must make a coherent whole of the amusing pieces.

Dickens made but one reference to Goethe, calling his *Faust*
"that sad and noble story." He loved Goldsmith's plays, of course.
"Let me recommend you," he wrote to de Cerjat,

as a brother-reader of high distinction, two comedies both Goldsmith's—"She Stoops to Conquer" and "The Good-natured Man." Both are so admirable and so delightfully written that they read wonderfully. A friend of mine, Forster, who wrote "The Life of Goldsmith," was very ill a year or so ago, and begged me to read to him one night as he lay in bed, "something of Goldsmith's." I fell upon "She Stoops to Conquer," and we enjoyed it with that wonderful intensity, that I believe he began to get better in the first scene, and was all right again in the fifth act.[67]

He did not like Massinger's *A New Way to Pay Old Debts*, apparently: he wrote his wife that he "meant to have gone to the Theatre tonight, but I thought better of it when I found Charles Kean was doing Sir Giles Overreach. . . ." It was the character, not the actor, he disliked, as a letter to Forster makes clear: "Charles Kean is playing for his last night to-night. If it had been the 'rig'lar' drama I should have gone, but I was afraid Sir Giles Overreach . . . might upset me so I stayed away."[68] Possibly it was some quality of the character other than its artistry that bothered Dickens, but it is difficult to guess what that might be, though it is equally difficult to understand why Massinger's play is not "rig'lar."

Dickens once spoke disparagingly of Jonson's *Every Man in his Humour*, perhaps more out of frustration in his efforts to get his amateur group to do it well than from considered judgment of its merits. His objection was to the convenient entrances and exits of characters, and to his own character of Bobadil: "I don't think its [*sic*] a very good part, and I think the comedy anything but a very good play. It is such a damned thing to have all the people perpetually coming on to say their part, without any action to bring 'em in or take 'em out, or keep 'em going."[69]

Dickens made little written comment on the plays of Shakespeare, but quotations by friends suggest that he spoke of the great plays frequently. Edmund Yates said that on one occasion he

talked about Falstaff, calling him the "hugest, merriest, wittiest creature that never lived."   At a meeting to celebrate Shakespeare's
birthday, he called the day "the birthday of a vast army of living men
and women, who would live forever with an actuality greater than that
of the men and women whose external forms we saw around us . . .
types of humanity, the inner working of whose souls was open to us,
as were the faces of ordinary men."   On the same occasion, another
member of the meeting recorded, Dickens criticized the conventional
manner in which Hamlet was acted, with "his hair crisply curled
short as if he were going to an everlasting dancing-master's party at
the Danish court," as "most Hamlets since the great Kemble have
been bound to do" (a figure he would later use in an article).   And
he criticized the presentation of Iago as "frowning, sneering diabolically, grinning, and elaborately doing everything else that would
induce Othello to run him through the body very early in the play"
(also used in an article).   The Reverend Whitwell Elwin said that
"Many of the remarks which he let fall in conversation upon
Shakespeare and others were original and true, and, had he cared to
cultivate the faculty, he would have excelled in terse, distinctive
criticism. . . ."[70]

Dickens' written commentary on Shakespeare is confined to
reviews of performances, but much of it is so good that we can see
how well he could have written Shakespearean criticism if he had
wished to do so.   One such was his review of Macready's production
of _King Lear_,[71] which restored the role of the Fool; his dissertation
on the importance of the character demonstrates his capacity for acute
critical reading, as well as judging of a performance.   The Fool, he
argued,

> is one of the most wonderful creations of Shakespeare's
> genius. The picture of his quick and pregnant sarcasm, of
> his loving devotion, of his acute sensibility, of his despairing
> mirth, of his heartbroken silence—contrasted with the rigid
> sublimity of _Lear's_ suffering, with the huge desolation of

Lear's sorrow, with the vast and outraged image of *Lear's* madness—is the noblest thought that ever entered into the heart and mind of man.

Dickens imagined Shakespeare writing the play, and realizing

that its gigantic sorrows could never be presented on the stage without a suffering too frightful, a sublimity too remote, a grandeur too terrible—unless relieved by quiet pathos, and in some way brought home to the apprehensions of the audience by homely and familiar illustrations. . . .

The *Fool* in *Lear* is the solitary instance of such a character, in all the writings of Shakespeare, being identified with the pathos and passion of the scene. He is interwoven with *Lear*, he is the link that still associates him with *Cordelia's* love, and the presence of the regal estate he has surrendered. The rage of the wolf *Goneril* is first stirred by a report that her favourite gentleman had been struck by her father "for chiding of his fool,"—and the first impatient questions we hear from the dethroned old man are: "Where's my knave—my fool? Go you and call my fool hither."— "Where's my fool? Ho! I think the world's asleep."—"But where's my fool? I have not seen him these two days."— "Go you and call hither my fool,"—all which prepare us for that affecting answer stammered forth at last by the knight in attendance: "Since my young lady's going into France, sir, the fool hath much pined away." Mr. Macready's manner of turning off at this emotion—"No more of that, *I have noted it well*"—was inexpressibly touching. We saw him, in the secret corner of his heart, still clinging to the memory of her who was used to be his best object, the argument of his praise, balm of his age, "most best, most dearest." And in the same noble and affecting spirit was his manner of fondling the *Fool* when he sees him first, and asks him with earnest care, "How now, my pretty knave? *How dost thou?*" Can there be a doubt, after this, that his love for the *Fool* is associated with *Cordelia*, who has been kind to the poor boy, and for the loss of whom he pines away? And are we not even then prepared for the sublime pathos of the close, when *Lear*, bending over the dead body of all he had left to love upon the earth, connects with her the memory of that other gentle, faithful, and loving being who had passed from his side—unites, in that moment of final agony, the two hearts that had been broken in his service, and exclaims, "And my poor fool is hanged!"

Mr. Macready's *Lear*, remarkable before for a masterly completeness of conception, is heightened by this introduction of the *Fool* to a surprising degree. It accords exactly with the view he seeks to present of *Lear's* character. The bewildered pause after giving his "father's heart" away— the hurry yet hesitation of his manner as he orders *France* to be called—"Who stirs? Call Burgundy"—had told us at one how much consideration he needed, how much pity, of how little of himself he was indeed the master, how crushing and irrepressible was the strength of his sharp impatience.

Dickens described Macready's power in the "first great scene with Goneril," and the scene in the second act with both undutiful daughters, to the point where Lear

hides his face on the arm of *Goneril* and says

> I'll go with thee;
> Thy fifty yet doth double five and twenty,
> And thou art twice her love

The *Fool's* presence then enabled him to give an effect, unattempted before, to those little words which close the scene, when, in the effort of bewildering passion with which he strives to burst through the phalanx of amazed horrors that have closed him round, he feels that his intellect is shaking, and suddenly exclaims, "O *Fool*! I shall go mad!" This is better than hitting the forehead and ranting out a self-reproach.

But the presence of the *Fool* in the storm-scene! The reader must witness this to judge its power and observe the deep impression with which it affects the audience. Every resource that the art of the painter and the mechanist can afford is called in aid of this scene—every illustration is thrown on it of which the great actor of *Lear* is capable, but these are nothing to that simple presence of the *Fool*! He has changed his character there. So long as hope existed he had sought by his hectic merriment and sarcasms to win *Lear* back to love and reason, but that half of his work is now over, and all that remains for him is to soothe and lessen the certainty of the worst. *Kent* asks who is with *Lear* in the story, and is answered—

> None but the Fool, who labours to outjest
> His heart-struck injuries!

When all his attempts have failed, either to soothe or to outjest these injuries, he sings, in the shivering cold, about the necessity of "going to bed at noon." He leaves the stage to die in his youth, and we hear of him no more till we hear the sublime touch of pathos over the dead body of the hanged *Cordelia*.

Dickens also wrote perceptively of "Mr. Macready's scenes upon the heath," of which he thought the "finest passage" to be

> his remembrance of the "poor naked wretches," wherein a new world seems indeed to have broken upon his mind. Other parts of these scenes wanted more of tumultuous ex-

travagance, more of a preternatural cast of wildness. We should always be made to feel something beyond physical distress predominant here. His colloquy with *Mad Tom*, however, was touching in the last degree, and so were the two last scenes, the recognition of *Cordelia* and the death, which elicited from the audience the truest and best of all pathos. Mr. Macready's representation of the father at the end, broken down to his last despairing struggle, his heart swelling gradually upwards till it bursts in its closing sigh, completed the only perfect picture that we have had of *Lear* since the age of Betterton.[72]

This is a penetrating reading of the use of a character; if we can forget for a moment all the subsequent Shakespearian scholarship at our disposal and remember how very little Dickens seems to have had at his, the commentary becomes all the more impressive. The perception of the Fool's role as a vital part of the whole is masterly, as is the sensitive reading of Lear himself. Particularly impressive is Dickens' recogniton of the use of the Fool's "quiet pathos" and "homely and familiar illustration" to control the grandeur and sub-limity of the presentation of Lear—and in this we note once again Dickens' constant concern for the way in which an audience should be worked upon. The comment upon the line, "My poor fool is hanged," anticipates modern criticism, according to Roger Gard. Noticeable here are favorite aesthetic words: *noble, touching, affecting, completeness of conception* (Macready's, not Shakespeare's), *true, power, beauty, wildness,* and *nature*. Dickens wrote again on the subject on October 27, 1849, but added nothing of note to the above review.[73]

Only in such reviews, and in occasional comments in his letters, did Dickens write anything like literary criticism. He did not believe that Shakespeare needed him to explain the plays, and he wrote about the Fool only because he was reviewing a performance, and because his friend Macready needed support. Criticism for its own sake—or even, it would seem, for the purpose of helping the reader of great plays—is not for him; one can almost hear him say, "Don't read about the play; read the play." Better to read on one's own and miss something than to subject imaginative literature to the ponderous misuse of a Dr. Blimber (in *Dombey & Son*): Dickens never quite put it that way, but much that he said carried the implication.

Dickens made few other comments upon performances of Shakespeare. One such shows understanding of the pace at which the plays did and should progress: he wrote to Macready that he had seen *Macbeth* played "in three hours and fifty minutes, which is quick, I think." One wonders what he would have thought of twentieth-century productions, sometimes well under three hours. In 1854 he wrote to Lemon, "I think we had better postpone the visit to Islington until Richard III comes on which is next week, with an entirely new cast. I've seen the Othello, and oh! what a precious slow nigger he was when I did see him. . . ."[74]

Among French dramatists, Dickens commented on Victor Hugo just once, calling his "Lucreese [*sic*] Borgia . . . a very remarkable and striking play." Forster tells us that in 1844 Dickens "had seen a version of Dumas' preposterous play of Kean." (One assumes Dickens agreed with the adjective.) He thought Scribe's *Irene ou le Magnatisme* "charmingly written. . . . I was quite fascinated by it. . . . The story is beautiful. The whole idea most touchingly and elegantly worked out." And he liked the English version of Latour de St. Ytres's play *Virginie*, which he found "most spirited, scholarly, and elegant"; he noted differences between the English and French handling of the play.[75]

What Dickens disliked most about French drama was not its poor translations into English, but its attempts at classicism. Forster tells us that "at the Porte St. Martin, drawn there doubtless by the attraction of repulsion, he supped full with the horrors of classicality at a performance of *Orestes*, versified by Alexandre Dumas. 'Nothing I have ever seen,' [he quoted Dickens] so weighty and so ridiculous. If I had not already learnt to tremble at the sight of classic drapery on the human form, I should have plumbed the utmost depths of terrified boredom in this achievement. The chorus is not preserved otherwise than that bits of it are taken out for characters to speak. It is really so bad as to be almost good. Some of the Frenchified classical anguish struck me as so unspeakably ridiculous that it puts me on the broad grin as I write.

Dickens despised English condescension to the French; to have used the word "Frenchified" he must have been upset indeed. In 1841 he wrote that he had not been to see the famous actress Rachel (Felix) because he was unable "to believe that anybody or anything could impart an interest to Racine."[76]

Comments on other French plays Dickens saw in 1856 are rather on performances than on the works themselves. He liked the melodrama *Sang Mele*, but said of two traveling ladies in it that "there is something positively vicious in their utter want of truth." He enjoyed *Paradise Lost*, at the Ambigu, but only in its silliness: "some of the controversies between the archangel and the devil, when the celestial power argues with the infernal in conversational French, as 'Eh bien! Satan, crois-tu donc que notre Seigneur t'aurait expose aux tourments que t'endures a present, sans avoir prevu,' etc., are very ridiculous. All the supernatural personages are alarmingly natural (as theatre nature goes), and walk about in the stupidest way." He and Wilkie Collins had speculated with some titilation about the costume of Eve, and he now reported, perhaps a bit disappointedly, that she was dressed "very modestly"; he did not see fit to insist upon reality here. He liked much better a play called *Les Cheveux de ma Femme*, because of "an original comic idea in it" which consisted of a husband seeking knowledge of his wife's romantic past by taking a lock of her hair to a clairvoyant, who tells him "that the owner of this hair has been up to the most frightful dissipations, insomuch that the clairvoyante can't mention half of them. The distracted husband goes home to reproach his wife, and she then reveals that she wears a wig, and takes it off."[77]

Forster tells us that Dickens' favorite plays in France at that time were *Medecin des Enfants* and *Memoires du Diable*, the latter apparently liked because, like *Les Chevaux de ma Femme*, it had an original idea—or, as he put it to Forster, a "tag"— which he described:

A certain M. Robin had got hold of the papers of a deceased lawyer, concerning a certain estate which has been swindled away from its righful owner, a Baron's widow, into other hands. They disclose so much roguery that he binds them up into a volume lettered "Memoires du Diable." The knowledge he derives from these papers not only enables him to unmask the hypocrites all through the piece (in an excellent manner), but induces him to propose to the Baroness that if he restores to her her estate and good name—for even her marriage to the deceaced Baron is denied—she shall give him her daughter in marriage. The daughter herself, on hearing the offer, accepts it; and a part of the plot is, her going to a masked ball, to which he goes as the Devil, to see how she likes him (when she finds, of course, that she likes him very much). The country people about the Chateau in dispute, suppose him to be really the Devil, because of his strange knowledge, and his strange comings and goings; and he, being with this girl in one of its old rooms, in the beginning of the 3rd act, shows her a little coffer on the table with a bell in it. "They suppose," he tells her, "that whenever this bell is rung, I appear and obey the summons. Very ignorant, isn't it? But if *you* ever want me particularly—very particularly—ring the little bell and try." The plot proceeds to its development. The wrong-doers are exposed; the missing document, proving the marriage, is found; everything is finished; they are all on the stage; and

M. Robin hands the paper to the Baroness. "You are reinstated in your rights, Madame; you are happy; I will not hold you to a compact made when you didn't know me; I release you and your fair daughter; the pleasure of doing what I have done, is my sufficient reward; I kiss your hand and take my leave. Farewell!" He backs himself courteously out; the piece seems concluded, everybody wonders, the girl (little Mdlle. Luther) stands amazed; when she suddenly remembers the little bell. In the prettiest way possible, she runs to the coffer on the table, takes out the little bell, rings it, and he comes rushing back and folds her to his heart. I never saw a prettier thing in my life. It makes me laugh in that most delightful of ways, with the tears in my eyes; so that I can never forget it, and must go and see it again.

". . . The thing it celebrates," Forster remarks, "could not have a nicer effect than is produced by this account of it." The triteness and improbability of the play which we surmise from Dickens' account of it are not alluded to by him; he concentrates upon the emotional impact of the device upon the audience. The play may have had other attractions: Dickens wrote to the Duke of Devonshire that it was "Admirably constructed," and to Forster that he liked a role in it "in which a man says merely 'Yes' or 'no' all through the piece, until the last scene." But it is the artfully contrived emotional twist at the end from disappointment to joy—"upon which we all cry with pleasure, and then laugh heartily," as he said to the Duke, that most attracted him. Such comments appear to support the criticism made of his reading performances—that he was more concerned with the effect of a performance than with its intrinsic quality. Anything in a play that produced an unusual, powerful, emotional reaction was for him, if not always good art, almost always enjoyable; only occasionally did he criticize anything for being overdone. Of a melodrama called *The French Revolution*, he wrote that "in the first act . . . there is the most tremendous representative of *a people* that can be well imagined.   There are wonderful battles and so forth in the piece, but there is a power and massiveness in the mob which is positively awful. "[78] But it is significant that such expressions of delight in contrived scenes are confined to the letters; one does not find them in Dickens' published dramatic criticism.   His review of Macready's *Lear* is concerned solely with acting and production; there is no mention of gimmickry.   In his casually scribbled notes to his friends, it is the offhand pleasant little thing that he likes to mention, but he never confused such things with serious art.   Still, the fact remains that Dickens was drawn most frequently to that which elicited emotional response, often through an unusual device such as original character, twist in plot, or striking scene.   He wrote to Mark Lemon from Paris about a scene in *Rentree a Paris* that used the telegraph: "There is nothing in the piece, but it was impossible not to be moved and excited by the telegraph part of it. "[79] The task of the play was to make the audience respond, and even implausible tricks and cheap devices were better than a scene with no power to move the viewer.

Another of the very few performances Dickens walked out on was a French version by George Sand of *As You Like It*.   He was prepared for the play by an account of it brought to him by Macready which made it seem "absolutely stunning.   The speech of the Seven Ages delivered as a light comedy joke; Jacques at the Court of the Reigning Duke instead of the banished one, and winding up the thing by *marrying Celia!*   Everything as wide of Shakespeare as possible, and confirming my impression that she knew just nothing at all about it. "   Nine days later, he saw the play himself, and called it "a kind of Theatrical Representation that I think might be got up, with great completeness, by the Patients in the asylum for Idiots.   Dreariness is no word for it, vacancy is no word for it, gammon is no word for it, there is no word for it.   In *Comme il vous Plaira* nobody has anything to do but to sit down as often as possible on as many trunks of trees as possible.   When I had seen Jacques seat himself on 17 roots of trees, and 25 grey stones, which was at the end of the second act,

I came away."[80]

Among other French playwrights upon whom Dickens commented are Legouvet, whom he seems to have disliked, and Mme. E. de Giradin, whose "*La Joie fait Peur*, at the Français, delighted me."[81]

As is readily apparent, Dickens did not often comment on plays; he commented on performances. His letters on drama are filled with judgments of theaters, producers, performances, and actors, but he said very little more of plays as artistic compositions than has been recorded. The exceptions to this are, as Harry Stone points out, the early reviews of plays in the *Morning Chronicle*, the *Examiner*, and the *Daily News*, an examination of which Stone urges upon scholarship as "invaluable" evidence of "Dickens' critical values and judgments." Some of these early reviews remain to be identified, and perhaps the story of Dickens and drama will not be complete until they are found and studied. It is a curious omission from Dickensian scholarship: William J. Carlton points out that as early as 1883 Edward Dutton Cook called attention to the value of his dramatic criticism, and we have noted Forster's praise of it even earlier (it is not quite true, as Carlton says, that Forster ignored the subject completely), but from Forster to Edgar Johnson no biographer has studied it. Johnson only noted that "sometimes Dickens had to write a notice of a new play."[82]

But with all this said, the reviews reproduced by Stone and Carlton are, when read, not of as great importance as we might hope. They do their job: Dickens was twenty-two when he wrote the first one, which was of Buckstone's adaptation of his own "The Bloomsbury Christening"; it and subsequent reviews are competent, but not particularly revealing of the writer's critical strengths. Little can be learned that is not available in the later critical comments. In one, for example, Dickens criticizes acting, finds a plot interesting but not worked out as well as it might have been, says a good actress saved a piece by her performance, and states that the Queen's Theatre shows promise. Comments on the lover in another play reveal a little more:

> The character of the lover is a failure.   In trying to
> make him gay and careless, the author had made him
> frivolous, vulgar-minded, and unworthy of the devoted attach-
> ment of a high-minded woman.   Of such a part no actor
> could make anything.   There is nothing remarkable in the
> other parts, which are of the ordinary melo-dramatic kind.

This shows us something: Dickens finds fault with the writing, not the
performance, and gives early evidence of distaste for conventional
melodrama.   But if no more than this is to be found, one wonders if
the early reviews, when they are all identified and studied, will add
much to our understanding of Dickens' dramatic criticism.   They do
attest to the confidence with which the young Dickens spoke of the
stage: in one review, at age twenty-three, he called a play, as spectacle, "altogether one of the most gay and animated pictures we have
ever seen on the stage."[83] If we remember that Dickens began attending plays at age six, however, perhaps this is not so much youthful
pretense to years of experience as it at first seems.

Later critical comment, most of it private judgment rendered in
the letters, offers more insight into Dickens' aesthetic judgment.
Much of this consists of responses to dramatists who have solicited his
opinion.   The following is typical: he liked John Saunders' play
Love's Martyrdom, but undertook to point out what he considered "very
dangerous portions . . . *for presentation on the stage"*; these consist
of a plot part of which was much like a famous contemporary play,
an incident which if poorly acted would be ludicrous and if well acted
would be disagreeable, and a scene so long that the emotion it should
arouse was lost; the scene also would "set the sympathy of an
audience in the wrong direction, and turn it from the man you make
happy to the man you leave unhappy."   There were still more
problems:

I would on no account allow the artist to appear, attended by

that picture, more than once.   All the most sudden incon-
stancy of Clarence I would soften down.   Margaret must act
much better than any actress I have ever seen, if all her
lines fall in pleasant places; therefore, I think she needs
compression too.

All this applies solely to the theatre.   If you ever revise the
sheets for readers, will you note in the margin the broken
laughter and the appeals to the Deity?   If, on summing them
up, you find you want them all, I woud leave them as they
stand by all means.   If not, I would blot accordingly.[84]

Such comments are of value because they treat the play itself,
not just its performance; on the other hand, they concern inferior
works, ones that we do not know.   Enough can be understood from
them, however, to reveal the acuteness and perceptiveness of Dickens
as reader of a play.

A Great Desideratum

Dickens knew and assessed all of the London theaters of his
time, as well as many other theaters in England, France, Italy, and
the United States.   The first such opinion ventured (that I have found)
was in 1835 when, in one of his first reviews for the *Morning
Chronicle*, he wrote that, "with a little attention," Mrs. Nisbett's
management of the Queen's Theatre might provide London with "a
great *desideratum*. . . ."   Later that year, he found *The Rival Pages*,
performed there, to be "a miserable failure," and when Mrs. Nisbett
reopened the Adelphi in November, he criticized the acting as suffering under "petticoat management," and urged change, "or there is no
telling where all this will end."[85] He made no other specific comment
on the Queen's theater, but did speak well of a play he saw there.
Among other theaters he disliked were Cranmer's, with Braham in
charge, which "has by many degrees the worst company in London,

[and] charges the highest prices," the Adelphi, which was oversen-
sational, and the Haymarket, that "mere fleabite" whose offerings were
"very trash." Noting that the August performances of 1848 at the
Theater consisted merely of a burletta and a farce, he wrote
T. J. Serle that "all sorts of commerce and enterprise" had recently
gone to the dogs, adding, "I understand that the British Drayma [*sic*]
is kenneled somewhere near the Haymarket, where the dogs are very
busy with it indeed."[86] But under Benjamin Webster the Haymarket
improved: in 1850 Dickens called him the "manager of two admirably
conducted theatres. . . ." Dickens in an early review had criticized
Webster for imitating Buckstone; by now, apparently, Webster had
forged beyond his model. But in 1854 Dickens had a humorously
unpleasant evening in the Haymarket:

I went there to see the Easter piece last night, and I
never beheld anything so dreary. The agonies of Mrs.
Fitzwilliam and Buckstone were positively most distressing to
see. Everything went wrong, and was bad if it had gone
right. Once, before a pair of flats (clouds), Mrs. F. waved
a golden patent hearthbroom about five and twenty minutes,
without anything happening. Then she and Miss
Featherstone and Young Farren came down to the Float, and
sang and pattered *all the rest of the piece*—got off it at once—
and after another long interval a carpenter was disclosed in a
celestial place (but swearing awfully) and a man in black,
supposed to be unseen, seized some red fire and wildly
lighted it up. Buckstone meantime, perfectly idiotic and im-
becile with grief, laid his head on Mrs. Fitzwilliam's
Bosom.

J[ohn] F[orster] was there, and perpetually said, "My
dear Dickens, good God, what does this mean?" To which
that eminent man replied, after the manner of Commodore
Trunnion, "Hold your tongue and be damned!" For we
were sitting on the stage.

But Dickens continued to approve of Webster; in 1859 he wrote to assure him of his continuing interest in his theatre, explaining why he had not attended recently, and advising him to "dash at the town with a thorough good melodrama. . . ."[87]

Apparently he did not like the Lyceum, prior to Fechter's taking it over: in 1859, failing to get Regnier to put on a dramatized version of *A Tale of Two Cities*, he had offered it instead to Madame Celeste at the Lyceum, but said, "I fear her company (troupe) is a very poor one." But under the direction of his friend Fechter, the Lyceum improved: "Fechter doing wonders over the way here," he wrote Macready in 1863, "with a picturesque French drama"—probably *The Duke's Motto*.[88] In a review written in 1840 he described the Drury Lane as "very agreeable. . . . The theatre is not a temple of obscenity—which (its old-established character in that respect being remembered) is worthy of remark. . . . Macready took over the Drury Lane shortly thereafter, and did his best to further improve its condition; Dickens wrote him offering "heartiest congratulations" on his performance of Shylock in *The Merchant of Venice* on opening night, but he also criticized the theater's saloon for not yet escaping its earlier reputation. He had nothing but praise for Macready's management of the Covent Garden, writing in his first review of a performance that "What we ventured to anticipate when Mr. Macready assumed the management of Covent Garden Theatre, has been every way realized." When Macready announced his impending resignation, Dickens wrote him that the people would miss "such a theatre as you gave them" and predicted that "for a long and dreary time that exquisite delight has passed away." And he expressed disappointment when, in his judgment, newspapers overpraised the first production of the next manager: "I am astonished at the Papers. There is little hope for [Covent Garden] the next time they produce anything good, when they get such praise for what is so vilely bad."[89]

Among references to other London theaters, I find but one comment on the Oxenford: Dickens in a review of the English version of Latour de St. Ytres' *Virginie* said that "the Oxenford has done

. . . delicate poetical justice. . . ." Later in the review he wrote
that

> It is a pleasant duty to point out the deserts of this theatre
> as it is now conducted, and to recommend it honestly. We
> know what some minor theatres in London are, and we
> know what this was before it became a refuge for the
> proscribed drama. The influence of such a place cannot but
> be beneficial and salutary.

In some of the above, and in several other letters, Dickens expressed
his concern about rowdiness and coarseness among the theater
audiences of his time. He complained in an article in *Household
Words* of the tendency of spectators "to put vile constructions on sufficiently innocent phrases in the play, and then to applaud them in a
satyr-like manner." Of one such "gent" sitting behind him at a play,
a drunken "thing," he said, "it drawls its slang criticisms on the
representation, and inflames [me] with a burning ardour to fling it
into the pit." He invited Benjamin Lumley, Manager of Her
Majesty's Theatre, to dinner, and "gave him some uncompromising
information on the subject of his Pit, and told him that if he didn't
conciliate the middle classes he might depend on being damaged—very
decidedly." Behavior in the pits of theaters was often so bad that respectable people could not sit there; also, tickets were often so expen-
sive that they could not afford to go. (Some things never change.)
In an article Dickens complained of purchasing "a seat at a pantomime; after which . . . a hungry footpad clapped a rolled-up
playbill to our breast, like the muzzle of a pistol, and positively stood
before the door of which he was the keeper, to prevent our access
(without forfeiture of another shilling for his benefit) to the seat we
had purchased."[90] Dickens also praised William Dowton, manager of
Margate Theater, and co-managers Samuel Phelps and Thomas
Greenwood of Sadler's Wells for their respectful treatment both of
plays and audiences. "If ever a theatre [was well conducted]," he

said in 1857, "it is the theatre Sadlers' Wells."[91]

Dickens often visited theaters in the London environs, and his own readings and vacations took him to many country and seaside towns where he visited the theaters. His article, "Two Views of a Cheap Theatre," included in *The Uncommercial Traveller*, greatly praised the Britannia Theatre in Hoxton for providing the lower class with decent drama and environment. But he thought little of an actors' group at Greenwich Fair, "where you have a melodrama (with three murders and a ghost), a pantomime, a comic song, an overture, and some incidental music, all done in five-and-twenty minutes." He gave an account of a country theater he and Lemon visited together:

> Mark and I walked to Dartford from Greenwich, last Monday, and found Mrs. Horner acting "The Stranger" (with a strolling company from the Standard Theatre) in "Mr. Munns's Schoolroom." The stage was a little wider than your table here, and its surface was composed of loose boards laid on the school forms. Dogs sniffed about it during the performances, and the carpenter's highlows were ostentatiously taken off and displayed in the Proscenium.

They had to leave early to catch a train, but sent the ingredients for a complicated punch to the company with their compliments. "The effect we had previously made upon the Theatrical Company by being held in the first two chairs—there was nearly a pound in the house— was altogether electrical."[92] On the whole, he found in country theaters much the same faults that he decried in London ones. Perhaps he thought the country playhouses still more disordered than those in London: in a speech for the General Theatrical Fund, he said he had been in one recently "where no particular pieces belonged to the immense night of the bill, where generally people walked in and out, where a sailor fought a combat with anyone he chanced to meet and who happened to be in possession of a sword. . . ." But he referred in his conclusion to "the neglected temples of the drama, where it is so hard to get a living . . ."[93] without distinguishing between country and town.

When Dickens traveled abroad, he sent home opinions of the local theaters, which he invariably visited. In Ireland, he did not like the Dublin theater but did find in Limerick "a charming theatre. The best I ever saw, to see and hear in."[94] He seems indeed to have been a good judge of acoustics, to which as manager he always paid careful attention. Though he was not fond of Italian acting, he found the principal theater in Genoa, says Forster, to be

> excellent. Instead of a ticket for the private box he had taken on the first tier, he received the usual key for admission which let him in as if he lived there. . . . In the summer there was a good comic company, and he saw the *Scaramuccia* and the *Barber of Seville* brightly and pleasantly done. There was also a day theatre, beginning at half-past four in the afternoon; but beyond the novelty of looking at the covered stage as he sat in the fresh pleasant air, he did not find much amusement in the Goldoni comedy put before him.

In *Pictures from Italy* Dickens describes the three principal theaters of Genoa: the Carlo Felice, the "most important," where he found the audiences "hard & cruel," hissing the least infelicity of performance; the Teatro Diurno, or Day or Open Theater, with indifferent actors and a French repertoire; and the Theater of Puppets, with a company from Milan, to which he gave far more attention than to the day theater or opera house.[95]

He thought that La Scala in Milan was "fallen from its old estate, dirty, gloomy, dull, and the performance execrable." But in Venice he found "the most brilliant and beautiful theatre conceivable—all silver and blue, and precious little fringes made of glittering prisms of glass." He didn't like the performance of an opera in the San Carlo theater, but he did like a theater there:

for astonishing truth and spirit in seizing and embodying the
real life about it, the shabby little San Carlino theatre—the
rickety house one story high, with a staring picture outside:
down among the drum and trumpets, and the tumblers, and
the lady conjurer—is without a rival anywhere.[96]

In 1847. Dickens was in Paris, and wrote that "The Theatres
are admirable just now." In 1853, vacationing in Boulogne, he went

to the theatre last night, to see the *Midsummer Night's
Dream*—of the Opera Comique. It is a beautiful little theatre
now, with a very good company; and the nonsense of the
piece was done with a sense quite confounding in that connection. Willy Am Shay Kes Peer; Sirzhon Fall Stayffe; Lor
Lattimeer; and that celebrated Maid of Honour to Queen
Elizabeth, Mees Oleeveeir—were the principal characters.[97]

It must have been rather like watching a TV Western dubbed in
Japanese. By 1855, Dickens was less enchanted with Parisian drama,
writing to Georgina that "The theatres are not particularly
good. . . ." Still, in that same year he urged Macready to come to
Paris, and in November he wrote to Regnier:

. . . Thank you a thousand times for the delight we derived
from your representation of your beautiful and admirable
piece. I have hardly ever been so affected and interested in
any theatre. Its construction is in the highest degree excellent, the interest absorbing, and the whole conducted by a
masterly hand to a touching and natural conclusion.

Forster said that Dickens did not like the Français in the Rue
Richelieu, no doubt because it so often housed classical drama: "He
used to talk about it whimsically as a kind of tomb, where you went,
as the Eastern people did in the stories, to think of your unsuccessful
loves and dead relations." He also wrote disparagingly of "the

Theatre of Gaiety; at which . . . a brooding Englishman can, by intensity of interest, get himself made wretched for a fortnight."[98]

In the United States, Dickens commented on theaters in New York and Boston. Like Genoa, New York had "three principal theatres," of which "two . . . are . . . generally deserted. The third, the Olympic, is a tiny show-box for vaudeville and burlesque. It is singularly well conducted. . . ." Then he recalled a fourth, "a small summer theatre, called Niblo's. . . . It is not exempt from the general depression under which Theatrical Property . . . unfortunately labors." "There are two theatres in Boston, of good size and construction, but sadly in want of patronage," he wrote in *American Notes*, but when he returned in 1867 his favorite theater there was, according to George Dolby, the Globe, which Dolby called "one of the handsomest and most elegant theatres in the world," with a "good stock company. . . ."[99]

To Paint Sorrow Over

Dickens' critical pronouncements on actors show him to have been as familiar with most of the dramatic performers of his time as with the theaters and plays. His knowledge was by no means limited to their appearances on the stage: many details indicate personal familiarity—for example, he corrected the maiden name of Mrs. Kelly in an article by Wills in *All the Year Round*. Although he could be severe on them as actors, he always felt deep compassion for their personal difficulties. In "Astley's" he described a poor fellow hanging around the stage door

> who wears a blue surtout, clean collar, and white trousers, for half an hour, and then shrinks into his worn-out scanty clothes; who has to boast night after night of his splendid fortune, with the painful consciousness of a pound a week and his boots to find: to talk of his father's mansion in the

New Cut; and to be envied and flattered as the famous lover
of a rich heiress, remembering all the while that the ex-
charmer at home is in the family way, and out of an engagement.

In another piece he spoke of the actor as one who is obliged "to
paint sorrow over, with burnt cork and rouge. . . ." "I wish,
myself," he said in "Gaslight Fairies," "that we were not so often
pleased to think ill of those who minister to our amusement."[100]
   One instance must suffice to illustrate Dickens' humane concern
for actors.

I went to the Dover theatre on Friday night, which was a
miserable spectacle. The pit is boarded over, and it is a
drinking and smoking place. It was "for the benefit of Mrs.
_____," and the town had been very extensively placarded
with "Don't forget Friday." I made out four and ninepence
(I am serious) in the house, when I went in. We may have
warmed up in the course of the evening to twelve shillings.
A Jew played the grand piano; Mrs. _____ sang no end of
songs (with not a bad voice, poor creature); Mr. _____
sang comic songs fearfully, and danced clog hornpipes capi-
tally; and a miserable woman, shivering in a shawl and
bonnet, sat in the side-boxes all the evening, nursing Master
____, aged seven months. It was a most forlorn business,
and I should have contributed a sovereign to the treasury, if
I had known how.[101]

Dickens seems always to have known, or known of, actors. We
have noted his childhood love of the clown Grimaldi, and his pattern-
ing of his own attempt to become an actor on Charles Mathews. He
mentioned almost every other actor of note, and offered critical commentary on most of them. Not everyone found his opinions flawless:
the distinguised theatrical manager John Hollingshead, while approving
of Dickens' own acting, added that in preferring John Owens to Joe

Jefferson, "as in some other things, his judgment was faulty." But Hollingshead probably would have approved of Dickens' admiration of Robert and Mrs. Keeley (nee Miss Goward); Dickens exempted only them "from the general badness" of the Lincoln's Inn Fields dramatization of his Christmas Book, *The Battle of Life.* "I hope," he said after watching a rehearsal, "they will be very good. I have never seen anything of its kind, better, than the manner in which they played the little supper scene, between Clemency and Britain, yesterday. It was quite perfect, even to me." Like two or three of his illustrators, the Keeleys apparently managed to convey what Dickens meant by his characters; perhaps it was here, in 1846, that Dickens began to think of the stage as a medium for realizing his fiction. Mrs. Keeley had played roles in several earlier productions of Dickens' stories, the first probably being in Buckstone's adaptation of "The Bloomsbury Christening" which, as *The Christening,* was acted at the Adelphi in October of 1834. In what William J. Carlton identifies as his first professional review, Dickens called the performance (in the *Morning Chronicle*) "a new trifle" which "met with complete success." He thought the acting of Mrs. Keeley "extremely good," and also praised Buckstone and another actor.[102]

Roles undertaken by Mrs. Keeley in Dickens' later works included Smike in *Nicholas Nickleby,* Mrs. Peerybingle in *The Cricket on the Hearth,* and Clemency Newsome in *The Battle of Life.* In his early reviews and in the later private opinions of his letters, Dickens is uniformly laudatory. He approved of her husband, too: near the end of his life he praised him in a letter to Herman Merrivale, accepting a paper on the Keeleys for *All the Year Round;* he admired the "unusual subtlety and skill" of his portrayal of Verges in a scene with Dogberry, and said that in a play called "the Sargeant's Wife . . . his chronic terror, as servant in a murderous house, was wonderfully fine. [In another play] he *had seen a ghost before the curtain went up.* It was marked in his face and manner in an extraordinary way."[103]

If these brief comments do not convey as much as Dickens'

lengthy and considered statements on such actors as Macready and
Fechter, they nevertheless reveal some of his standards, some facets of
his taste.   Among other actors whom Dickens liked were Mrs.
Nisbett, an actress whose "impersonation of the heroine" in *The Maid
of Castile* "possesses an excellence which quite suffices to render the
piece a favourite one,"[104] a Mr. Wilkinson, whose "dry Humour"
helped save a performance, and a favorite, James Wallach, who in
Mark Lemon's *The Loving Woman* was "beyond all praise. . . .   He
really bore the whole play on his shoulders, and did gallant
service."[105] Surprisingly, there is little mention of the popular actor
Tyrone Power.   In 1840, in a review of *The Lady of Lyons* for the
Examiner, Dickens wrote that the actor, "as rattling and vivacious as
ever, has sent merry audiences laughing to their beds," but he seems
to have been impressed no more by Power's performance than by the
play: he invited a friend to see it, but added, "it's only the Lady of
Lyons and Power."   He recommended Helen (later Helena) Faucit
(still later Lady Martin), who was trained by Macready, as having
"great abilities . . ."; he wrote of her that "Maddle Faucit est de
mes amis," adding a comparison of French and English actresses:
"Les   bonnes   actrices   sont   tres   rares   a   Londres—plus   qu'a
Paris. . . ."[106]

    In general, Dickens liked French acting, but there were excep-
tions, such as the famous Rachel.   "We have been to the Français
where the acting was odious (including Rachel's, who was very like
Celeste). . . ."   "Rachel," he wote to Wills, ". . . has not so much
in her as some of our friends suppose."   T. E. Pemberton blames
such judgments on Dickens' dislike of "classical drama."   Though he
spoke once disparagingly of the troupe of Madame Celeste, when she
managed a theater in England, and compared her to Rachel, he seems
to have liked her as an actress: she and Mrs. Keeley were among the
professionals invited to the trial performances of "Sikes and Nancy" at
St. James Hall in 1868: "such good judges of dramatic effect . . . ,"
his son Charlie called them.   Four years after his use of her to disparage Rachel, he wrote Mark Lemon, "You know what a high

opinion I always have of her good sense and thorough knowledge of her art."[107]

Dickens liked the French actress Rose Cezos, who played the title role in a French adaptation of *Clarissa Harlow*: "A most charming, intelligent, modest, affecting piece of acting it is: with a Death, superior to anything I ever saw on the stage, or can imagine, except Macready's in Lear." He called her a "great sensation" in Scribe's *Irene*. And he thought another famous actress, Mme. Viardot, "most splendid" in "Orphee"; years before, he had sent the first number of *Little Dorrit* to her: "I have such delight in your great genius, and have so high an interest in it and admiration of it, that I am proud of the honour of giving you a moment's intellectual pleasure." Among other French actors Dickens liked Mme. Plessy, of whom he wrote that "If I could see an English actress with but one hundredth part of the nature and art of Madame Plessy, I should believe our English theatre to be in a fair way towards its regeneration," and he liked Regnier: he doubted, he said, that he would ever "see upon an English stage an accomplished artist, able to write and to embody what he writes, like you." Of another French actor, Pierre Cheri La Font, he wrote to Mrs. Pollack that "Your description of La Font's acting is the complete truth in one short sentence. Nature's triumph over art; reversing the copy-book maxim!"[108]

He greatly admired the performance of Frederick Lemaitre as the gambler in a play with the English title *Thirty Years of a Gambler's Life*, which he called "Incomparably the finest acting I ever saw. . . . Never did I see anything, in art, so exaltedly horrible and awful. . . . In the last two [acts], when he had grown old and miserable, he did the finest things, I really believe, that are within the power of acting. Two or three times a great cry of horror went all round the house." When the character first meets the man he is to murder,

> and first saw his money, the manner in which the crime
> came into his head—and eyes—was as truthful as it was ter-

rific. This traveller, being a good fellow, gives him wine.
You should see the dim remembrance of his better days that
comes over him as he takes the glass, and in a strange
dazed way makes as if he were going to touch the other
man's, or do some airy thing with it; and then stops and
flings the contents down his hot throat, as if he were
pouring it into a lime-kiln. But this was nothing to what
follows after he had done the murder, and comes home, with
a basket of provisions, a ragged pocket full of money, and a
badly-washed bloody right hand which his little girl finds
out. After the child asked him if he had hurt his hand,
his going aside, turning himself round, and looking over all his
clothes for spots, was so inexpressibly dreadful that it really
scared one. . . . He fell into a sort of bloody mist, and
went on to the end groping about, with no mind for anything, except making his fortune by staking this money, and
a faint dull kind of love for the child. It is quite impossible
to satisfy one's-self by saying enough of this magnificent performance. I have never seen him come near its finest points
in anything else. He said two things in a way that alone
would put him far apart from all other actors. One to his
wife, when he has exultingly shown her the money, and she
has asked him how he got it—"I found it"—and the other to
his old companion and tempter, when he was charged by
him with having killed that traveller, and suddenly went
headlong mad and took him by the throat and howled out,
"It wasn't I who murdered him—it was Misery!" And such
a dress; such a face; and, above all, such an extraordinary
guilty wicked thing as he made from the moment when the
idea of the murder came into his head! I could write pages
about him. It is an impression quite ineffaceable.[109]

Among other English actors, he said of a Miss Cushnie, whom
he saw in Frederic Neale's *Butcher, Butcher, Kill the Ox, or Harlequin*

and the Magic Money Box (winner of the length-and-rhyme-in-titles contest), "I . . . never saw a performance of that sort so light-hearted, graceful, pleasant, and agreeable," though he did not know the name of the actress at the time. Sarah Jane Woolgar, later Mrs. Alfred Mellon, was another favorite, as were John Daly and Fanny Kemble (later Mrs. Butler), "one for whose genius I have so great and sincere an esteem. . . ." We have seen some slight disparagement of J. B. Buckstone as manager, but in 1855 Dickens exchanged compliments with him at a function of the Royal General Theatrical Fund, saying that "He could answer for it from his recollections as a boy, twenty-five years ago, how much the acting of that gentleman had enchanted him, as no doubt it then did many others, and how he went home to dream of his comicalities."[110] He mentioned in a speech that he enjoyed "the acting of Miss [Charlotte] Cushman," an American actress, and spoke favorably of Fanny Stirling, who "has so gracefully and captivatingly, with such an exquisite mixture of art and fancy and fidelity, represented her own sex. . . ." Pemberton says that Dutton Cook "recounts the great impression made upon him by Miss Marie Wilton's (Mrs. Bancroft's) early impersonations at the Strand"; Dickens wrote to Mrs. Bancroft, calling himself "one of the most earnest and delighted of your many artistic admirers."[111]

Pemberton also quotes Dickens as saying of a Mr. Emery's performance as Mr. Potter in *Still Water Runs Deep*, a comedy by Tom Taylor, "I don't think I ever saw anything meant to be funny that struck me as so extraordinarily droll; I couldn't get over it at all." (The qualification is interesting; like many of us, Dickens seems to have found unintentional humor to be the funniest of all.) He apparently enjoyed T. P. Cooke, whom he later helped to get a pension; he wrote to him of his performance as William in Jerrold's *Black-eyed Susan*, "It was so fresh and vigorous, so manly and gallant, that I felt as if it splashed against my theatre-heated face, along with the spray of the breezy sea." And he applauded an actor named Charles Dillon in Marston's *A Hard Struggle*, saying, "Real good acting, in imitation of nobody, and honestly made out by himself. . . ." And again,

"His representation of Reuben Holt was exactly what acting should be—nature itself.   I can't call to mind any living actor who could have played it so well."[112] But apparently Dickens had not thought well of Carlotta Leclercq until he saw her as Lucy in *The Master of Ravenswood*. Writing of the success of the play, he added,

> But the astonishing circumstance of all is, that Miss Leclercq
> (never thought of for Lucy till all other Lucies had failed),
> is marvellously good, highly pathetic, and almost unrecongiz-
> able in person!   What note it touches in her, always dumb
> until now, I do not pretend to say, but there is no one on
> the stage who could play the contrast scene better, or more
> simply and naturally, and I find it impossible to see it
> without crying! [113]

Kate Terry in *The Duke's Motto* was, according to a letter of 1863, "perfectly charming"; after watching her in a rehearsal of *The Courier of Lyons*, he told Fechter: "That is the very best piece of womanly tenderness I have ever seen on the stage, and you'll find that no audience can miss it."[114] He liked Frederick Robson (Thomas Robson Brownbill), a well-known actor and comic singer, who appeared in a burlesque of *Medea*, admiring "the extraordinary power of his performance (which is of a very remarkable kind indeed). . . . He wrote to Mrs. Yates of "the uncountable hours of happiness you gave me when you were a mysterious angel to me. . . ." And he liked an actress named Mrs. Mowatt, who played in the English version of *Virginie*:

> . . . The character was rendered in a touching, truthful, and
> womanly manner, that might have furnished a good lesson to
> some actresses of high pretensions we could name.   There is
> great merit in all this lady does.   She very rarely oversteps
> the modesty of nature.   She is not a conventional performer.
> She has a true feeling for nature and for her art; and we
> question whether any one now upon the stage could have

acted this part better, or have acted it so well.[115]

He thought that Anne Romer (cousin of Mark Lemon) had "a fresh-ness about her" that was "mighty pretty to see." He told William Creswick that he thought his part in his play, *Ambition*, was "admirably played"—though, since the letter also asks for a box to be reserved for him, the remark may have been a compliment, not a judgment. In an early review he had commented favorably on an actor named Vining, who "had the most to do" in Buckstone's *The Dream at Sea*, "and did it well; many of his scenes exhibited great feeling and power, and would have done infinite credit to many actors of far greater pretensions. . . ."[116]

The letters contain several references to Charles Kean, son of the great Edmund, including an amusing incident in which they almost shared a watercloset in a country inn, but there is only one written comment, "Kean be blowed," which may owe as much to Dickens' friendship for Macready, whom Kean rivaled in Shakespearian roles, as to impartial evaluation. When Macready saw a woman seeking Kean's autograph he wrote, "I fear it is quantity, not quality for her!" And he wrote in his diary that he was driven almost to suicide to be "*mentioned* . . . in the same breath as Mr. C. Kean!" Certainly Dickens was willing to attend plays in which Kean appeared, as at least one letter shows. And in a speech delivered in Kean's presence, Dickens spoke graciously of him, mentioning the many parts "in which Mr. Kean had distinguished himself," attributing to him the "large spirit of an artist, the feeling of a man, and the grace of a gentleman," and calling him a "prosperous ornament" of his profession.[117]

But he did not care for an actor named Williams, who "so con-founded an enlightened British audience . . . on the subject of *Antony and Cleopatra* that I clearly saw them wondering towards the end of the Fourth Act, when the play was going to begin." He disliked sniping at performers—in a speech before the Royal General Theatrical Fund he criticized those who took "comfort and satisfaction . . .

from slightly disparaging those who entertain them"—but his opinion of acting in his time does not appear to have been high. Speaking of amateur actors he saw in a pantomime, he said, "Not a man in it who wasn't quite as good as the Humbugs who pass their lives in doing nothing else." The first critical comment I have found in his letters is negative: he wrote to Cruikshank that he was "glad that you thought the piece [*The Strange Gentleman*] was badly acted (that being very like my own impression). . . ." In addition to comments we have already seen, he thought Adelaide Kemble "desperately unpleasant—almost repulsive." In Paris, he spoke disparagingly of Marguerite-Josephine Weyman George, who looked as though she had the dropsy: "I never in my life beheld such a sight. Every stage conventionality she ever picked up (and she has them all) has got the dropsy too, and is swollen and bloated hideously." Miss Isabel Glyn (later Mrs. Dallas), the English actress, was also not a favorite. One letter contains laughing references to an apparently delightfully bad actor named Conway Lingham, who seems to have been a common joke in the Dickens circle:

> I am happy to say that I have discovered old Lingham (Conway's father) at the Margate Theatre. The son's style, and massive manner, ripened and matured in the father by excessive age, presents a spectacle of the most astonishing and perplexing nature to a contemplative mind.[118]

Dickens saw some hope for a Miss Robertson, but some problems too: "I think Miss Robertson wants power, and has merit, but she has (to my sight and hearing) the grand vice of forming her enunciation on Miss Sedgwick. It has not a natural air in the original, far less so in the copy."[119] It would seem that his strong dislike of anything imitative was owing in part to its being at a remove from nature.

It is interesting to see which famous actors of his time Dickens did or did not like, but his comments on unknown performers also tell us much about his idea of good acting. He liked, especially in actresses, the light, the graceful, the agreeable, the captivating. In men, he approved of gallant and manly (by which he seems to have meant mature) acting. He liked intelligent acting, liked those who thought their roles through and made them consistent and intelligible to the audience. And of course he liked those who avoided formal, conventional, and bombastic delivery in favor of the natural, the true, the simply affecting. He disliked imitation, and praised those who had developed their own style. And he was sensitive to the capacity of a role to bring forth the latent talent of a hitherto unimpressive performer.

The actor whom Dickens most admired was Charles Macready. In 1840 he wrote Macready, after seeing him in Talfourd's *Glencoe*: "I have seen you play ever since I was *that* high, but I never saw you make such a gallant stand as you did last night, or carry anything through so triumphantly and manfully by the force of your own great gifts." And when he saw him as Werner (title role of a tragedy by Byron), often considered his best part, he wrote, "There is nothing I know, or can imagine, so exquisitely beautiful, so manly, noble, dignified. true, and brave, as that most exquisite and touching performance. It's Nature refined to the very highest pitch of refinement—its [*sic*] everything it ought to be, or can be. . . ."[120]

In 1843, Dickens published a review of Macready's performance as Benedick in *Much Ado About Nothing*, defending the tragic actor's decision to undertake a comic role. Among the "many reasons why a tragic actor incurs considerable risk of failing to enlist the sympathies of his audience when he appears in comedy," Dickens noted that "some people are rather disposed to take it ill that he should make them laugh who has so often made them cry" and that the actor "has not only to make the impression which he seeks to produce in that particular character, but has to render it, at once, so obvious and distinct, as to cast into oblivion for the time all the host of grave associations with which he is identified." Finally, the tragic actor has to contend with the feeling "that the path which a man has trodden for many years—even though it should be the primrose path to the everlasting bonfire—must be of necessity his allotted one, and that it is, as a matter of course, the only one in which he is qualified to walk. . . .   Despite these handicaps, "Macready managed to make [the character] fresh, distinct, vigorous, and enjoyable. . . .   If it be beyond the province of what we call genteel comedy—a term which Shakespeare would have had some difficulty in understanding, perhaps,—to make people laugh, [then Macready is no genteel comedian, for he made the audience laugh] both loud and long. . . ." Dickens singled out for special praise "Mr. Macready's performance of the scene in the orchard after emerging from the arbour," judging it by comparison "with anything we know in nature, literature, art; by any test we can apply to it, from within us or without, we can imagine no purer or higher piece of genuine comedy. . . ."   He compared the scene to a painting by Leslie, and argued that

> Those who consider it broad, or farcical, or overstrained, cannot surely have considered all the train and course of circumstances leading up to that place.   If they take them into reasonable account, and try to imagine for a moment how any master of fiction would have described *Benedick's* behavior at that crisis—supposing it had been impossible to contemplate the appearance of a living man in the part, and therefore necessary to describe it at all—can they arrive at any other conclusion than that such ideas as are here presented by Mr. Macready would have been written down? Refer to any passage in any play of Shakespeare's, where it has been necessary to describe, as occurring beyond the scene, the behavior of a man in a situation of ludicrous perplexity; and by that standard alone (to say nothing of any mistaken notion of natural behavior that may have suggested itself at any time to Goldsmith, Swift, Fielding, Smollett, Sterne, Scott, or other such unenlightened journeymen) criticize, if you please, this portion of Mr.   Macready's ad-

mirable performance.

The nice distinction between such an aspect of the character as this, and the after love scenes with *Beatrice*, the challenge of Claudio, or the gay endurance and return of the *Prince's* jests at last, was such as none but a master could have expressed, though the veriest tyro in the house might feel its truth when presented to him. It occurred to us that Mr. Macready's avoidance of *Beatrice* in the second act was a little too earnest and real; but it is hard dealing to find so slight a blemish in such a finished and exquisite performance. For such, in calm reflection, and not in the excitement of having recently witnessed it, we unaffectedly and impartially believe it to be.[121]

There is much worth noting in this passage, particularly the sense of the ability of the stage to show what the novelist can only describe. Of special interest too are Dickens' ability to see dramatic scenes as pictures—an ability we will see again in his comments on Fechter—and his advice to those who found Macready in one scene to be "broad, or farcical, or overstrained" to check their impressions against those made by great writers. This last could be read as advice by Dickens to critics of his own work, advice few scholars were capable of giving until Santayana gave it and made it stick.

When Macready prepared to tour part of the United States, Dickens wrote his American friend Felton:

I would give a great deal that you and I should sit beside each other to see him play Virginius, Lear, or Werner— which I take to be, every one, the greatest piece of exquisite perfection that his lofty art is capable of attaining. His Macbeth, especially the last act, is a tremendous reality; but so indeed is almost everything he does.

Later letters continued to praise Macready's power, passion, and realism. Of his performance in Henry Taylor's *Philip Van Artevalde*

Dickens wrote,

> I feel all words insufficient to tell you what I think of you
> after a night like last night. The multitudes of new tokens
> by which I know you for a great man, the swelling within
> me of my love for you, the pride I have in you, the majes-
> tic reflection I see in you of the passions and affections that
> make up our mystery, throw me into a strange kind of
> transport. . . .

And at the second annual dinner of the General Theatrical Fund, in
his toast to Macready, Dickens alluded to his belief in the drama's
power for uniting mankind through emotion: "Oh! if one touch of
nature makes the whole world kin, think, gentlemen, for how much of
the kindred feeling that is amongst us tonight, or at any time, we are
indebted to such an art, and such a man!"[122]
The day after Macready's farewell performance as Macbeth,
Dickens wrote to him of his lifelong admiration of him, and of his
regret that his career was at an end. Dickens was a member of the
organizing committee for a banquet in Macready's honor following his
farewell performance, and at the dinner called his friend "the great
vision which had been a delight and a lesson, and . . . a support
and a comfort, and which . . . has improved and charmed us, and to
which we look back in elevated relief from the labours of our
lives. . . ."[123] It may be appropriate to end with the recollection that
Nicholas Nickleby, with its immortal company of actors, was dedicated
to Charles Macready.
Some years after Macready left the stage, Charles Albert
Fechter, a French actor, dramatist, and manager, of German descent,
took his place as Dickens' favorite. Dickens never thought Fechter
the equal of his older friend, but he did admire him both as actor
and as theater manager. He said of Fechter's Hamlet that

> It was a performance of extraordinary merit; by far the most
> coherent, consistent, and intelligible Hamlet I ever saw.

Some of the delicacies with which he rendered his conception clear were extremely subtle; and in particular he avoided that brutality towards Ophelia which, with a greater or less amount of coarseness, I have seen in all other Hamlets. As a mere *tour de force*, it would have been very remarkable in its disclosure of a perfectly wonderful knowledge of the force of the English language; but its merit was far beyond and above this. Foreign accent, of course, but not at all a disagreeable one. And he was so obviously safe and at ease, that you were never in pain for him as a foreigner. Add to this a perfectly picturesque and romantic "make up," and a remorseless destruction of all conventionalities, and you have the leading virtues of the impersonation. In Othello he did not succeed. In Iago he is very good. He is an admirable artist, and far beyond anyone on our stage.[124]

When a friend doubted that Hamlet could be done by a French actor, Dickens wrote,

I don't wonder at your finding it difficult to reconcile your mind to a French Hamlet, but I assure you that Fechter's is a very remarkable performance, perfectly consistent with itself (whether it be my particular Hamlet, or your particular Hamlet, or no), a coherent and intelligent whole, and done by a true artist. I have never seen, I think, an intelligent and clear view of the whole character so well sustained throughout; and there is a very captivating air of romance and picturesqueness added, which is quite new.[125]

The two major qualities of Fechter's Hamlet seem for Dickens to have been a unified conception, and romantic presentation. It was this second quality that he stressed in his characterization of Fechter's acting: after explaining that he had admired Fechter before he knew him, so that "my appreciation is not the result of personal regard, but personal regard has sprung out of my appreciation" (had someone twitted Dickens on praising in print actors who were friends?), he said that

> The first quality observable in Mr. Fechter's acting is, that it is in the highest degree romantic. However elaborated in minute details, there is always a peculiar dash and vigour in it, like the fresh atmosphere of the story whereof it is a part. When he is on the stage, it seems to me as though the story were transpiring before me for the first and last time. Thus there is a fervour in his love-making—a suffusion of his whole being with the rapture of his passion—that sheds a glory on its object, and raises her, before the eyes of the audience, into the light in which he sees her.

It was this power, Dickens said, that had made Fechter so successful in the *Dame aux Camelias*, in which his passion for the tarnished heroine elevated her in the eyes of the audience. Dickens also called attention to Fechter's "picturesqueness of manner":

> Note so trivial a thing as the turn of his hand in beckoning from a window, in *Ruy Blas*, to a personage down in an outer courtyard to come up; or his assumption of the Duke's livery in the same scene; or his writing a letter from dictation. In the last scene of Victor Hugo's noble drama [*Ruy Blas*], his bearing becomes positively inspired; and his sudden assumption of the attitude of the headsman, in his denunciation of the Duke and threat to his executioner, is, so far as I know, one of the most ferociously picturesque things conceivable on the stage.

Dickens found "his delivery of Shakespeare's blank verse" to be "remarkably facile, musical, and intelligent. . . ." And he praised his Iago:

> . . . That quality of picturesqueness, on which I have

already laid stress, is strikingly developed in his Iago, and
yet it is so judiciously governed that his Iago is not in the
least picturesque according to the conventional ways. . . .
Mr. Fechter's Iago is no more in the conventional
psychological mode that in the conventional hussar pantaloons
and boots; and you shall see the picturesqueness of his
wearing borne out in his bearing all through the tragedy
down to the moment when he becomes invincibly and consis-
tently dumb.

Saying that "Perhaps no innovation in Art was ever accepted with so
much favour by so many intellectual persons pre-committed to, and
preoccupied by, another system, as Mr. Fechter's Hamlet," Dickens
attributed the success to

its perfect consistency with itself. As the animal-painter said
of his favourite rabbits that there was more nature about
those rabbits than you usually found in rabbits, so it may be
said of Mr. Fechter's Hamlet, that there was more consistency about that Hamlet than you usually found in Hamlets.
Its great and satisfying originality was in its possessing the
merit of a distinctly conceived and executed idea. From the
first appearance of the broken glass of fashion and mould of
form, pale and worn with weeping for his father's death, and
remotely suspicious of its cause, to his final struggle with
Horatio for the fatal cup, there were cohesion and coherence
in Mr. Fechter's view of the character.

Dickens mentioned that some years earlier the German actor Devrient
had "fluttered the theatrical doves considerably" by making such minor
changes as "being seated when instructing the players," but "he had
worn, in the main, the old nondescript dress, and had held forth, in
the main, in the old way, hovering between sanity and madness. I
do not remember whether he wore his hair crisply curled short, as if
he were going to an everlasting dancing-master's party at the Danish

court; but I do remember that most other Hamlets since the great
Kemble had been bound to do so." But Fechter's Hamlet,

> a pale, woe-begone Norseman with long flaxen hair, wearing
> a strange garb never associated with the part upon the
> English stage (if ever seen there at all) and making a pirati-
> cal swoop upon the whole fleet of little theatrical prescrip-
> tions with meaning, or, like Dr. Johnson's celebrated friend,
> with only one idea in them, and that a wrong one, never
> could have achieved its extraordinary success but for its
> animation by one pervading purpose, to which all changes
> were made intelligently subservient. The bearing of his
> purpose on the treatment of Ophelia, on the death of
> Polonius, and on the old student fellowship between Hamlet
> and Horatio, was exceedingly striking; and the difference
> between picturesqueness of stage arrangement for mere stage
> effect, and for the elucidation of a meaning, was well dis-
> played in there having been a gallery of musicians at the
> Play, and in one of them passing on his way out, with his
> instrument in his hand, when Halmet, seeing it, took it from
> him to point his talk with Rosencrantz and Guildenstern.[126]

This commentary shows once again Dickens' concern for unity
in art, for a subservience of each part, however clever and entertaining it might be if left to its own devices, to the needs of the whole.
It shows once again his love of emotion, but also—more than we have
seen before—how aware he was that emotion must serve an artistic
purpose: Fechter's capacity for conveying passion, properly used, can
make a vehicle of *Dame aux Camelias* that less intelligently exerted
emotion could not achieve. It shows his awareness of how one
character in a play can affect the reception of another by the
audience, and it shows a care for stage effects that goes well beyond a
Hank Morgan-like love of mere flair. It shows that delight in fresh-
ness we have seen before—the sense, in contrast to the tired and stale

conventions of art, that the thing is happening for "the first and last time," and it illustrates how this freshness helps a scene. It shows again the Dickensian eye for detail—the turn of a hand, the writing of a letter. It lays bare the lack of subtlety in the representation of Iago by earlier actors. It recognizes the rigors of speaking Shakespeare's poetry, and it notes the difficulty with which an actor challenges stock interpretations of great characters, and the advantage of the successful challenge. This is a review, not part of a book on acting, but it indicates that Dickens could have written such a book.

Of Fechter's role as Claude Melnotte, in Bulwer's *The Lady of Lyons*, Dickens said (note the contrast to his faint praise of Power in the same play):

> Fechter has played nothing so well as Claude since he played in Paris in the 'Dame aux Camelias,' or in London as Ruy Blas. He played the fourth act as finely as Macready, and the first act much better. The dress and bearing in the fifth act are quite new and excellent. . . . I cannot say too much of the brightness, intelligence, picturesqueness, and care of Fechter's impersonation throughout. There was a remarkable delicacy in his gradually drooping down on his way home with his bride, until he fell upon the table a crushed heap of shame and remorse. . . . His gradual recovery of himself as he formed better resolutions was equally well expressed; and his rising at last upright again . . . brought the house down.[127]

And again Dickens is struck by Fechter's ability to make parts contribute to the whole: the "scenic appliances are subdued to the Piece instead of the Piece being sacrificed to them. . . . Every group and situation has been considered, not only with a reference to each by itself, but to the whole story." The very last critical mention of an actor that I have found in his letters was of Fechter's farewell peformance before touring the United States: he "acted very finely. I

thought the first three acts of his Hamlet very much better than I had
ever thought them before—and I always thought very highly of
them."[128]

The Shattered Glass

The drama of his time was like a child to Dickens: he loved it
with all its faults, but he always wished it could be better, and
mourned and complained of its weaknesses.   Probably all ages have
lamented the death or coma or at least malaise of the drama (and of
most other things) in their time, but much of the nineteenth century
had good reason to feel itself in a dramatic death-watch; as Emlyn
Williams put it, "The first three-quarters of the nineteenth century
constituted the feeblest era of the British theatre; so feeble, indeed, as
to be moribund."   Dickens sent out call after call for a doctor.
Serious drama was on the decline; most theaters, as he said, were offering   "romantic   dramas   of   intense   interest   and   with   terrific
denouements, where the mischief-working character is a being so terrible that he cannot be named. . . ."   He commented sarcastically on
the patent required for any theater purporting to produce legitimate
drama, questioning "the wisdom of the patent which gives a monopoly
in doing that which it never does."   In "The Amusements of the
People, II," he said ". . . We would make that office of Dramatic
Licenser, which, like many other Offices, has become a mere piece of
Court favour and dandy conventionality, a real, responsible, educational
trust."   And in the first part of the same article: "Heavily taxed,
wholly unassisted by the State, deserted by the gentry, and quite un-
recognized as a means of public instruction, the higher English Drama
has declined."   He held the upper class, indeed, to be responsible for
much of the harm: "The nobility and gentry . . . seldom enter a
theatre unless it be a foreign one; . . . when they do repair to an
English temple of the drama, [they] would seem to be attracted thither
solely by an amiable desire to purify, by their presence, a scene of

vice and decorum; and . . . select their place of entertainment accordingly." Private theaters were characterized by "unsavory squalor, and a sense of degradation to Shakespeare and the drama. . . . He castigated the managers of reputable theaters for placing their own interests ahead of good performances: in 1843 he was angry at Charles Mathews and his Haymarket Theater for not releasing his best actors to join with Drury Lane to offer what he considered an "excellent bill" which would have included *The Rivals*.[129]

The prologue Dickens wrote for Fletcher's *The Elder Brother* is not memorable poetry (he said "It has the two merits of being short and modest"), but it is worth quoting in part because of its admiration of an earlier, healthier, dramatic age:

> A Play by Fletcher; Written in that age
> When the deep-hearted and strong-worded Stage
> Had life in England, and could yet rehearse
> Ford's, Heywood's, Webster's, Marlowe's,
>   Shakespeare's, verse.

A later line refers to "this shatter'd glass," which Dickens defined as "*The Theatre generally.*"[130]

He wrote to Effingham Wilson, warmly supporting his proposal (in a pamphlet: *A House for Shakespeare*) not only for turning Shakespeare's home into a national monument, but also for establishing a national theater where his works could be performed, but doubting that this latter could be accomplished "within fifty years." At the second annual dinner of the General Theatrical Fund, he spoke for the cause: "May we yet behold the English drama . . . in some theatre of his own, rising proudly . . . into new and vigorous existence." When Samuel Phelps undertook revivals of Shakespeare at the Sadler's Wells, Dickens "took keen interest in them,"[131] says Pemberton.

He bridled, as always when similar things happened in other

arts, at any condescension shown the drama; he wished neither to elevate it above the people nor to allow the upper class to look down on it. When at a later meeting of the General Theatrical Fund Charles Kean, who chaired the meeting, made too much of the recent command performances at Windsor Castle (in which he had taken part), as though they lent an unusual honor to drama, Dickens made his own comment on "the regeneration of the Drama":

> I think it next to impossible but that it must come to pass, because the Drama is founded on an external principle in human nature. . . . I do not think it within the power of any potentate on earth . . . to raise the Drama up, or pull the Drama down. In this room, in Windsor Castle, in an African hut, in a North American wigwam, there is the same inborn delight and interest in a living representation of the actions, passions, joys, and sorrows of mankind. In England, of all countries on the earth, this interest is purified and exalted by the loftiest masterpieces of human fancy, and the proudest monuments of human wit. Such an art . . . I hold to be imperishable. . . .

Imperishable no doubt, but certainly not impervious: again and again Dickens sounded the alarm for "the neglected temples of the drama. . . ." In 1858 he wrote R. H. Horne that he could not help him get a tragedy he had sent him put on the stage: he went over several theaters and managers—Buckstone, the English Opera House, Drury Lane, Kean, and Phelps—and demonstrated the uselessness of trying to put on tragedy at or by each—by Phelps, for example, because he had tried valiantly before, and had ended badly. Only melodrama, it seems, would succeed: it was about that same time that Dickens wrote to Webster, advising him to "dash at the town with a thorough good melodrama." Dickens' sister-in-law and daughter, as editors of his letters, said that he took great interest in Westland Marston's play, *The Patrician's Daughter* (and wrote a prologue for it) because "It was, to a certain extent, an experiment of the effect of a tragedy of modern times and in modern dress; and the prologue . . . was intended to show that there need be no incongruity between plain clothes of the century and high tragedy." "On the whole," he wrote in 1867,

> the theatres, except in the articles of scenery and pictorial effect, are poor enough. But in some of the smaller houses there are actors who, if there were any dramatic head- quarters as a school, might become very good. The most hopeless feature is, that they have the smallest possible idea of an effective and harmonious whole, each 'going in' for himself or herself. The music-halls attract an immense public, and don't refine the general taste.

Dickens saw few signs of hope for serious drama, in England or America: from Baltimore he reported that "All manner of theatricals are at the lowest possible ebb here."[132]

The problem, as Dickens saw it, was not a lack of interest; all people loved the play. But despite his faith in the ability of even the lowest levels of society to respond to imagination, Dickens knew that not all could respond at the same level to art; part of the difficulty, he believed, was that the legitimate theater faced overwhelming com- petition from so many other forms of entertainment—drawn, as he said, from "various countries, English, Swedish, French, Italian . . . all kinds of strange animals, lions, tigers, Ethiopians and Nightingales," these last referring, apparently, to wild-beast shows, Ethiopian singers, and Jenny Lind. But again and again he iterated his faith that the inherent attraction of people to true drama would save it:

> He had always taken the highest interest in the prosperity of the Drama, because he believed that a noble Drama tended to purify the human heart, and was a most important agent in the work of education and civilization.

He would not dismiss the hope that the British Drama would ultimately "look up", after a pretty low contemplation of its feet; because he could not believe that any art which so appealed to the various passions and affections of human nature could become extinct. A love of the Drama in some shape was implanted in the hearts of all people.[133]

Charles Dickens wore the theater at his heart's core. He loved it for the same reason he loved other forms of art: it had the capacity to present and evoke the passions of humanity. But for him it did both better—with more immediacy and sense of reality, with the fairy-like magic incarnation of the pulsing present moment—than any other art form could accomplish, and so, though his own talent was not shaped to its requirements, he liked it best, and got as close to it as he could in any way that he could—by reading it, reading about it, or seeing it, but probably most of all by being in it, as manager, actor, and dramatic reader. His reputation as dramatic critic is deserved, but in the main it rests upon a specific, limited kind of criticism. Though what he wrote on plays as plays was good indeed, he did not write enough of it to earn all the praise he has been given: certainly his forte is as reviewer of plays presented, not as critic of plays themselves. Still, he demonstrates considerable knowledge of classical English drama and of the history of the English stage; no doubt he read widely in drama, and perhaps in unrecorded conversations he talked at length about what he read; but what he wrote about was what he witnessed: the living moments of the stage. About that subject, he certainly knew as much as any man or woman of his time. He thought those living moments could do more for humanity than anything else that art or science could devise. Those moments could entertain, could bring men and women together through deeply-shared feeling, could take us through all the joy and agony of life without exacting life's terrible payments. As he himself created some of those moments in his brilliant readings, he even thought they could convey to his audience the reality of his own supreme imagination.

4

The Dramatic Readings: the Fairy Immortality

Among the many satisfactions Dickens derived from managing and acting, the most valuable may have been the use to which he found he could put them as a means of conveying his imaginative world beyond the confines of his own art. To understand, in addition to what we have seen, his idea of drama and how he could employ it for his own purposes, it is helpful to turn to a piece he wrote in 1850. In "A Christmas Tree," a record of his earliest childhood memories as recorded in an imaginary trip down a Christmas tree composed of his first awareness of things, Dickens tells us of the impressions made upon him by the stage:

> And now, I see a wonderful row of little lights rise smoothly out of the ground, before a vast green curtain. Now, a bell rings—a magic bell, which still sounds in my ears unlike all other bells—and music plays, amidst a buzz of voices, and a fragrant smell of orange-peel and oil. Anon, the magic bell commands the music to cease, and the great green curtain rolls itself up majestically, and The Play begins! The devoted dog of Montargis avenges the death of his master, foully murdered in the Forest of Bondy; and a humourous Peasant with a red nose and a very little hat, whom I take from this hour forth to my bosom as a friend

(I think he was a Waiter or an Hostler at a village Inn, but many years have passed since he and I have met), remarks that the sassagassity of that dog is indeed surprising; and evermore this jocular conceit will live in my remembrance fresh and unfading, overtopping all possible jokes, unto the end of time. Or now, I learn with bitter tears how poor Jane Shore, dressed all in white, and with her brown hair hanging down, went starving through the streets; or how George Barnwell killed the worthiest uncle that ever man had, and was afterwards so sorry for it that he ought to have been let off. Comes swift to comfort me, the Pantomime— stupendous Phenomenon!—when clowns are shot from loaded mortars into the great chandelier, bright constellation that it is; when Harlequins, covered all over with scales of pure gold, twist and sparkle, like amazing fish; when Pantaloon (whom I deem it no irreverence to compare in my own mind to my grandfather) puts red-hot pokers in his pocket, and cries "Here's somebody coming!" or taxes the Clown with petty larceny, by saying, "Now, I sawed you do it!" when Everything is capable, with the greatest ease, of being changed into Anything; and "Nothing is, but thinking makes it so." Now, too, I perceive my first experience of the dreary sensation— often to return in after-life—of being unable, next day, to get back to the dull settled world; of wanting to live for ever in the bright atmosphere I have quitted; of doting on the little Fairy, with the wand like a celestial Barber's Pole, and pining for a Fairy immortality with her. Ah, she comes back, in many shapes, as my eye wanders down the branches of my Christmas Tree, and goes as often, and has never yet stayed by me![1]

The passage tells us almost all we need to know about Dickens and drama, from the exclamation marks and the word-selection— *wonderful, vast, magic, great, majestic* —to the descriptions, to the final comment. The descriptions support the sense of a magic world, one superior to the dull sublunary where inanimate things require human exertion: here, the lights rise and the bell rings apparently of their own volition, and the curtain rolls itself up. The bell is like no other bell on earth, just as the dog and humorous peasant are like no dog or man Dickens has known elsewhere, and the latter's conceit surpasses all other jokes for eternity. But though this is a special place, it is not a mere imaginary place; it is not at all "unreal." It is better than life, but not otherwise different from it. One uses the physical senses to respond to it—all five senses, if the peel comes from an orange which has been touched and tasted. Dickens feels a personal relationship with the peasant; he remembers him as he would remember any man he had met elsewhere, and is as unsure of his occupation as he might be of that of anyone after many years had passed; Pantaloon is virtually a relative. The dog's wisdom is surprising, and the man's joke is the epitome of humor, but dog, man, and joke are still of this world, just as the avenging of the master, and the starving of Jane Shore, and the murder by George Barnwell are, though somehow more telling than vengeance, starvation, and murder can be in the real world, still just as real. The wonder and magic of that which is both real and somehow better than real, which one can enjoy whether it produces unmatchable laughter or provokes to bitter tears, is explained near the end: all that is here has been created by human thought, which means that the harsh inflexible rules of reality have been lifted. But the magic lies both in this fact, and in the fact that all appearance of human agency has been removed: just as a bell rings and music plays and the curtain lifts without benefit of human exertion—or seems to—so the characters and their actions seem undirected by human hand. The stage is a magic world because 1) unlike the dull settled world, it is made by man to appeal to man; 2) still, all evidence of human effort has been hidden, and things seem, as in the real world, to occur by themselves, even though we are aware that the same magic that lifted the curtain has brought them before us.

The only defect of this magical world—a world of "fanciful
reality"[2] as Dickens' friend John Forster called it for him—is that,
though the peasant's conceit may prevail to the end of time, the performance does not; one must at last return to the "dull settled world"
created without human thought—that is, without imagination. The last
sad sentence expresses the lifelong attempt of Dickens to consort with
this immortal fairy in various forms (which must include, one
assumes, writing his novels), and his lament, like Keats's knight on
the cold hillside, that she insists on leaving him.

It would be too much to say that this mythic reality was the
sole cause of Dickens' fascination with the stage. He was attracted to
much that had precious little reality of any sort in it—to bad plays as
well as good ones, wretched performances as well as convincing ones;
he loved the circus, magicians, animal acts, anything that could be
called entertainment. Certainly the play was often for him, as much
as for anyone, an escape from life. And he loved to entertain others,
not only on the boards but in the intimacy of his circle of friends.
"An incident related by him often became upon the instant a little
acted drama. His mimetic powers were in many respects
marvellous. . . . He seemed to be a Proteus." George Dolby said
that, though quiet and reserved among strangers, Dickens was often
"on" with his close friends, entertaining them like a performer. It
was "a phase in Mr. Dickens's nature, which was apparent only to a
limited circle of friends with whom he felt himself quite at his ease,
and to entertain whom, in that genial way of which he seemed to be
sole possessor, he would take any amount of pains and trouble."[3]
Forster said that

> He seemed to be always the more himself for being some-
> body else. . . . "Assumption has charms for me so
> delightful—I hardly know for how many wild reasons—that I
> feel a loss of Oh I can't say what exquisite foolery, when I
> lose a chance of being someone not in the remotest degree
> like myself."

The motivation for such escape was not merely, as it would have been in most others, dislike of self, or need to disguise self from self; as Sir Arthur Helps penetratingly commented, Dickens "never dramatized himself to himself. . . ."[4] Perhaps it was not even dislike of the misery that self sometimes encountered.   As it was for Dostoevsky's Undergrounder, it was rather the intolerable sense that the self must always be what it is, always in the world in which it finds itself, unable to be anything else in any other reality, bound by the inflexible laws of existence in Blake's fallen world, in which Nothing is capable of changing itself into Anything else, and thinking can make nothing so.   As the trip down the Christmas tree so clearly shows, the theater freed Dickens from the immutable.

So, no doubt, did the novel, poetry, music, all art.   But Dickens believed that the stage offered more than any other art form; it was, he said, "at once the most obvious, the least troublesome, and the most real, of all escapes out of the literal world."   The highest form of drama, tragedy—"the noblest flight of human genius"—was the most real: "the Art that of all others strikes to the Soul like Reality. . . ."   At times he spoke of the play as pretense, or of the actor as "a friend who has beguiled us of a moment of care, who has taught us to sympathize with virtuous grief cheating us to tears for sorrows not our own," but far more often it was the conviction of reality which drama conveyed of which he spoke, and of that reality as an improvement upon the world's, or at the least as a representative of the world at its best.   In the actor's art, he said, "we always find some reflection, humorous or pathetic, sombre or grotesque, of all the best things that we feel and know."[5]

Upon occasion, apparently, Dickens found in the real world this kind of power to touch what we feel and know; when he did, he said he preferred it even to drama.   When his father was imprisoned in the Marshalsea for debt, and Dorrit-like had held a meeting in which he got up a petition for bounty with which to drink the King's health on his birthday, young Charles sat in the corner, watching: "I would rather have seen it than the best play ever played. . . ."   But such an instance was rare; far more often it was the theater which "placed us for a time in a wider and less selfish world in lieu of that which is so much with us early and late."[6]

In "A Curious Dance Round a Curious Tree," Dickens wrote what Harry Stone has called "a theory of dramatic catharsis"; it clearly defines the attraction of play as escape from the unhappy consequences of harsh reality, while preserving all the excitement of life. While visiting St. Luke's Asylum, he says he might instead

> have betaken myself to that jocund world of Pantomime, where there is no affliction or calamity that leaves the least impression; where a man may tumble into the broken ice, or dive into the kitchen fire, and only be the droller for the accident; where babies may be knocked about and sat upon, or choked with gravy spoons, in the process of feeding, and yet no Coroner be wanted, nor anybody made uncomfortable; where workmen may fall from the top of a house to the bottom, or even from the bottom of a house to the top, and sustain no injury to the brain, need no hospital, leave no young children; where everyone, in short, is as superior to all the accidents of life, though encountering them at every turn, that I suspect this to be the secret (though many persons may not present it to themselves) of the general enjoyment which an audience of vulnerable spectators, liable to pain and sorrow, find in this class of entertainment.[7]

The move from madhouse to playhouse is significant. Like the demented, the pantomime distorts reality, but does so by thought, and creates a world which, instead of incapacitating him, proves beneficial. But it is not quite accurate to call this "dramatic catharsis," because, unlike the pantomimist, the dramatist does not distort reality, at least not to the extent of making his characters "superior to the accidents of life": poor Jane Shore starves in the play, and George Barnwell's uncle is murdered. No art can be really real, but for Dickens a strong part of the magnetism of the play lay in its combination of verisimilitude and improvement upon—rather than abandonment of— reality.   Neither of these achievements was of great value without the other: anything (outside of the necessary magic) that hinted at the un- reality of the dog of Montargis was a fault; anything that exposed the peasant as incapable of uttering the superlative conceit was a mistake. Although Dickens could enjoy almost anything upon the stage, however bad, again and again he criticized actors, producers, and playwrights who erred in either offending against reality or failing to improve upon it.   Over-acting was one of the great sins, fatal in a good theater and successful only in cheap private theaters where amateurs sought a quick and easy reputation; Dickens gave advice on how to do the Duke of Gloucester there:

> "Orf with his ed" (very quick and loud;—then slow and
> sneeringly)—"So much for Bu-u-uuckingham!" Lay the em-
> phasis on the "uck"; get yourself gradually into a corner,
> and work with your right hand, while you're saying it, as if
> you were feeling your way, and it is sure to do

—sure, that is, to do in any sense of the actuality of Gloucester. Even a poor actor was tolerable if he avoided such unbelievable excess; Dickens said of the performance of one such that it was "a great comfort to have that kind of meat underdone."   But good acting eschewed over- or underacting, and strove for verisimilitude.   He praised a performance by the son of Charles Mathews, and commented on his doing an Italian dance:

> It was not the cold artificial dance of an actor going through
> a figure, because it was his part, or the burlesque posturing
> of a low comedian, determined to raise a laugh at all
> hazards: it was the sunny, sparkling joyousness of an Italian
> peasant, revelling in the beauty of everything around him,
> and dancing for very lightness of heart and gaiety.   Anything

more elegant and delightful we never saw. . . .[8]

   Mechanical and thoughtless acting also damaged veri- similitude. Dickens spoke of actors in one play who "never looked at one another, but delivered all their dialogue to the pit, in a manner so egregiously unnatural and preposterous that I couldn't make up my mind whether to take it as a joke or an outrage." Forster said that the French actor Plessy "enchanted" Dickens; perhaps he did at one time, but near the end of his life Dickens wrote, "the Lord deliver us from Plessy's mechanical ingenuousness!"[9] *Unnatural* was one of his favorite pejoratives; its opposite, along with such words as *truthful* and *lifelike*, was a favorite compliment. He found in an Italian theater "the most extraordinary acting I ever beheld. As an exact copy of the life out of doors; set before one without much art—not heightened here, and kept out of view there, but presented broadly and plainly as the real thing itself is—it's quite wonderful." An actress was praised because "She very rarely oversteps the modesty of nature. She is not a conventional performer. She has a true feeling for nature and for her art. . . ." Another actor's performance "was exactly what acting should be—nature itself."[10] One of the things he most admired in the acting of his friend Macready was its "tremendous reality." He liked that performance which aimed not so much at the audience but at realizing itself, conveying the sense that the actor did what he did—like the peasant dance of Young Mathews— because it was in him to do it, not because he wished to create an effect. James Wallach was "a highly meritorious Edgar," he said, because "His manner of delivering the description of Dover cliff—watching his blind father the while, and not looking up as if he saw the scene he describes, as it is the manner of most Edgars to do—was particularly sensible and good." And Charles Fechter's Iago was great because in the role he avoided

   the conventional ways of frowning, sneering, diabolically grinning, and elaborately doing everything else that would induce Othello to run him through the body very early in the play. Mr. Fechter's is the Iago who could, and did, make friends; who could dissect his master's soul, without flourishing his scalpel as if it were a sign-of-the-Saracen's-Head grimness; who could be a boon companion without *ipso-facto* warning all beholders off by the portentous phenomenon; who could sing a song or clink a can naturally enough, and stab men really in the dark,—not in a transparent notification of himself as going about seeking whom to stab.[11]

Dickens was sensitive to anything on the stage that struck a false note; he often applied the word *dangerous* to that which might, by appearing ludicrous or incongruous, damage a scene. He commented on a play with which he was helping Charles Fechter:

When I went over the play this day week, he was at least 20 minutes, *in a boat, in the last scene,* discussing with another gentleman (also in the boat) whether he should kill him or not; after which the gentleman dived overboard and swam for it. Also, in the most important and dangerous parts of the play, there was a young person of the name of Pickles who was constantly being mentioned by name, in conjunction with the powers of light or darkness; as, "Great Heaven! Pickles?"—"By Hell, 'tis Pickles!"—"Pickles! a thousand Devils!"— "Distraction! Pickles?"

When, in another drama, an actor twenty years too old to play Caesar walked on the stage and said, "'He calls me Boy'—a howl of derision arose from the audience. . . ." Dickens objected to the custom of having "the Senate of ancient Rome represented by five-shillings' worth of supernumery assistance huddled together at a rickety table, with togas above the cloth and corduroys below. . . ." Props were useful, but could be dangerous: in *Nicholas Nickleby* Dickens laughed at dramatists who built plays around them (in the novel, they consist of a pump and two washing tubs), and he did his own readings on a stage without background of any sort to show "how much a single performer could do without the aid and stimulus of any of the ordinary adjuncts of the stage; how many effects of a genuinely startling character could be produced without the help of scenery, costume, limelight, or mechanical contrivance." Some props did more harm than good: because Greek dress (and names) had become associated in the public mind with stage farce, Dickens feared their effect on an audience in a serious play, and advised his friend Bulwer to change the locale of his play from Greece to Russia. He urged Macready to remove a picture from a scene:

> It haunts me with a sense of danger. Even a titter at that
> critical time, with the whole of that act before you, would be
> a fatal thing. The picture is bad in itself, bad in its effect
> upon the beautiful room, bad in all its associations with the
> house.[12]

Properly used, of course, a costume or prop could add to the reality of a scene, not only by conveying the appearance of the world, but by giving an actor a concrete thing to which he could react. Dickens admired the manner in which the French actor William Lemaitre, playing a guilty murderer, covertly examined his clothes for bloodstains, started when he saw the color of wine brought to him, and used the murder weapon to reveal his mental state:

> He got half-boastful of that walking-staff to himself, and half-
> afraid of it; and didn't know whether to be grimly pleased
> that it had the jagged end, or to hate it and be horrified at
> it. He sat at a little table in the inn-yard, drinking with the
> traveller; and this horrible stick got between them like the
> Devil, while he counted on his fingers the uses he could put
> the money to.

On the whole, Dickens seems to have felt that the theater of his time did much better with scenery—with "pictorial effect"[13]—than with other parts of performance; he did not say why, but it is no bad guess that he found props, like Lemaitre's walking staff, often more capable of conveying reality, and of evoking emotion, than the actors and plots could do.

But the worst offender against the mythic reality of drama was convention. "When I go to the Play," Dickens lamented, "why must I find everything conventionally done—reference to nature discharged, and reference to stage-usage the polar star of the dramatic art?" On seeing a rehearsal of Bulwer's *Not So Bad as We Seem* at the Haymarket, Dickens wrote a friend,

> If you had seen the dense conventionality of some of them at the Rehearsal! Mr. Stuart, who does the Duke, actually steamed with conventionality. I saw it passing off from the pores of his skin. Nor could I by any means persuade them that when the Duke was saying to Wilmot what would infallibly cost him his ducal head if it were overheard, he would not be likely to keep two servants with their ears at the keyhole. As Mr. F. Wilster, the Prompter, convincingly remarked to me, "We never have two servants appear at a door in a flat when there is an entrance, without reappearing when there is an exit." So the Duke endangered his head according to theatrical precedent, and spoke his speech before the servant. . . ."

The dramatist might be able to keep the Duke from losing his head, but he would not be able to make his audience believe in and respond to his play when convention deprived it of probability. Dickens thought the convention of poetic inversion, at least when poorly done, also harmful: he spoke of one play which was "made up of expressions so curiously inverted that it is difficult on first reading them to understand their meaning. . . ." As for conventional characters, one of the main causes of the inferiority of nineteenth-century drama, Dickens was famous not only for railing against them but for opposing his own fictional creations to them. An article of the time said that managers often failed to adapt Dickens' novels to the stage with any success because of this fault.[14]

Dickens called attention to the same kind of fault in the work would-be playwrights submitted to him: "The father is such a dolt, and the villain such a villain, the girl so especially credulous and the means used to deceive them so very slight and transparent, that the reader *cannot* sympathize with their distress." And he supplied his own list of conventional roles, complete with conventional plot:

> There is a rightful heir, who loves a young lady, and is beloved by her; and a wrongful heir, who loves her too, and isn't beloved by her; and the wrongful heir gets hold of the rightful heir, and throws him into a dungeon, just to kill him off when convenient, for which purpose he hires a couple of assassins—a good one and a bad one—who, the moment they are left alone, get up a little murder on their own account, the good one killing the bad one, and the bad one wounding the good one. Then the rightful heir is discovered in prison, carefully holding a long chain in his hands, and seated despondingly in a large arm-chair; and the young lady comes in to two bars of soft music, and embraces the rightful heir; and then the wrongful heir comes in to two bars of quick music (technically called a 'hurry'), and goes on in the most shocking manner, throwing the young lady about as if she was nobody, and calling the rightful heir 'Ar-recreant—ar-wretch!' in a very loud voice, which answers the double purpose of displaying his passion, and preventing the sound being deadened by the sawdust. The interest becomes intense; the wrongful heir draws his sword, and rushes on the rightful heir; a blue smoke is seen, a gong is heard, and a tall white figure (who has been all this time, behind the arm-chair, covered with a table-cloth), slowly rises to the tune of 'Oft in the stilly night.'

This is no other than the ghost of the rightful heir's father, at sight of which the wrongful heir becomes apoplectic, and is literally 'struck all of a heap,' the stage not being large enough to admit of his falling down at length.   Then the good assassin staggers in, and says he was hired in conjunction with the bad assassin, by the wrongful heir, to kill the rightful heir; and he's very sorry for it, and won't do so any more—a promise which he immediately redeems, by dying off-hand without any nonsense about it.   Then the rightful heir throws down his chain; and then two men, a sailor, and a young woman (the tenantry of the rightful heir) come in, and the ghost makes dumb motions to them, which they, by supernatural inference understand—for no one else can; and the ghost (who can't do anything without blue fire) blesses the rightful heir and the young lady, by half suffocating them with smoke: and then a muffin-bell rings, and the curtain drops.

Clearly, the muffin-bell and the blue smoke have only the most distant kinship with the magic bell and green curtain of the "Christmas Tree" world of drama.   In "The Theatrical Young Gentleman," Dickens laughed at the theater-goer who could appreciate only conventional acting, and was "very acute in judging of natural expressions of the passions, and knows precisely the frown, wink, nod, or leer, which stands for any of them, or the means by which it may be converted into any other; as jealousy, with a good stamp of the right foot, becomes anger, or wildness, with the hands clasped before the throat, instead of tearing the wig, is passionate love."   His great dislike of French classical drama is probably owing to the conventions of the form—conventions so venerable and therefore unalterable that they both attracted a staid Thackeray character in *The Newcomes* and put him to sleep.   "One tires of seeing a man," Dickens said, "through any number of acts, remembering everything by patting his forehead with the flat of his hand, jerking out sentences by shaking himself, and piling them up in pyramids over his head with his right forefinger."[15]

As some of the above quotations show, for Dickens the value of verisimilitude lay in its contribution to the creation of feeling. Accompanying such key words of praise as *truthful*, *natural*, and *real* are the equally important *fresh*, *vigorous*, *tender*, *gallant*, *passionate*, and *affecting*. The sense of reality was essential to drama because an audience would not feel unless it believed; for Dickens the strength of all art lay primarily in its enabling us to respond to the world in a way in which, in our own daily contact with it, we are unable to do. Drama, with its unique blend of verisimilitude and capacity for evoking emotional response, was (when well performed) the most nearly-perfect evocation of which art was capable. Again and again Dickens' admiration of a dramatic performance couples reality and feeling. Writing to a friend, he described himself as being, in a dream, "as real, animated, and full of passion as Macready . . . in the last scene of *Macbeth*."[16]

Acting which was true to life, so that it could be believed and could speak to the audience about its world—not about some ideal or artificial place where feeling could not be believed, but its own world—must be united to acting which at the same time moved the spectator. Dickens admired an actress who rendered her character "in a touching, truthful, and womanly manner. . . ." Charles Fechter, in Hugo's *Ruy Blas*, combined "French suddenness and impressibility" with the Englishman's slower and more deliberate rise to fury to produce "a powerful concentration of human passion and emotion, [which belongs] to human nature." The power of the emotion he conveyed lay in its immediacy: "When he is on the stage, it seems to me as though the story were transpiring for the first and last time"—as opposed to those dreary scenes in which conventional acting reminded Dickens of sitting though fifty like performances. Often he praised originality: Charles Dillon, in *A Hard Struggle*, offered "very good acting, in imitation of nobody, and honestly made out by himself." Good acting, even when it expressed a proper state of

mind, was not good if it omitted emotion: Dickens urged Mark
Lemon to get an actress in a play of his to "shew more feeling.   She
lost it in the endeavor to look frank.   It is quite right that she should
be frank, but it is altogether out of nature not to be more touched
and touching."   Here nature and feeling are, indeed, one.   Of reality
and emotion, emotion is for Dickens the more important: the first is
necssary because it makes possible the second.   He could even tolerate
and find enjoyable unrealistic acting which enabled one to feel: in the
Queen's Theater he said he saw "the prettiest piece of acting I have
seen for a long time.   It is burlesque acting (I am sorry to add) but
quite original and singularly graceful and pleasant."[17] Even if the
acting were exaggerated it might, if it avoided the deadly drag of conventionality, looked attractive, and elicited response, do its job.

Several of our quotations have added still another quality to
Dickens' ideal stage presentation: the visual.   The magic coupling of
verisimilitude and feeling could not achieve its goal of uniting men
through emotion—"one touch of nature makes the whole world kin"—
unless it exerted a powerful aesthetic ocular effect upon the viewer.
The viewer of a play should see a picture which, as much as any
painting, both pleased and made sense to him.   One of the great
virtues of Fechter was his ability to create stage pictures:

Picturesquesness is a quality above all others pervading
Fechter's assumptions.   Himself a skilled painter and
sculptor, learned in the history of costume, and informing
those accomplishments and that knowledge with a similar in-
fusion of romance (for romance is inseparable from the
man), he is always a picture,—always a picture in its right
place in the group, always in true composition with the background of the scene.

He commented on the dress of actors: Mrs. Nisbett's "attire was picturesque in the extreme, composed of bright colours and glittering or-
naments after the gypsy fashion, but full of barbaric grace, and cal-

culated to set off to advantage the fine form and features of the wearer." He noticed stage lighting: the thing he commented on at most length about a performance of *Faust* was "Stage management remarkable for some admirable, and really poetical effects of light."[18]

But a striking picture must also be readable, understandable. Dickens is not famous for his use of the word *rational*, but he frequently applied it to good drama. The play was "the most intellectual and rational of all our amusements," and the public owed Macready's acting company at Covent Garden "a debt of gratitude for the intellectual and rational enjoyment which they had afforded. . . ." As always, he refused to limit art to the cognosceti: the play was "a powerful and useful means toward the education of the people." Some of his best comments are on the cognitive capacity of performances: Fechter's Hamlet was great because it was "the most coherent, consistent, and intelligible Hamlet I ever saw",[19] and Macready's King Lear, already remarkable "for a masterly completeness of conception," was made still more so by his reintroduction of the Fool, whom Dickens shows linked to and illuminating Lear and his daughters, as well as balancing the sublimity and grandeur of the scenes in which he appears by his "quiet pathos" and homely nature. Much as Dickens loved stage devices—"tags," as he called them—that could startle and evoke feeling, he disapproved of mere show which displaces sense; after a performance of *The Black Crook* in New York he decided that, despite the attractive showiness of the thing, "The people who act in it have not the slightest idea of what it is about," and so he could not understand why it had been "playing every night for sixteen months(!) . . ."[20]

For Dickens, then, the play at its best was imaginative but realistic, picturesque, rational, and productive of feeling. So it may be for many lovers of the stage, but for Dickens this combination produced a mythic reality in which he believed as firmly as he did in the lesser, harsher, barer reality which most of us accept as the only truth. Dickens could not live without alternative to the dull settled world, with no fairy immortality, no wand to wave, nothing to become anything else, two and two, as Dostoyevsky's Undergrounder lamented, always adding up to four, and the planets, as Blake complained, always as confined to their chartered rounds as the Thames to its banks.   The Undergrounder was defeated by reality; Blake predicted its unmasking only in the Millennium; Dickens devoted his life to loosening its icy grip upon his time.   The world of imagination—of fiction, art, and especially of drama—was not for him a mere pretense which afforded temporary escape, but a separate and equal reality. He spoke often to Forster about the overpowering reality of his own stories and people, and he most valued that praise, Forster said, which recognized them "as bits of actual life, with the meaning and purpose on their part, and the responsibility on his, of realities rather than creatures of fancy."   He thought of his characters as real: the deaths of Little Nell and Paul Dombey affected him as strongly as the loss of his own baby, Dora.   When he finished the death scene in *Dombey and Son* he wrote, ". . . Paul is dead.   He died on Friday night about 10 o'clock; and as I had no hope of getting to sleep afterwards, I went out, and walked about Paris until breakfast-time next morning." Writing of *The Chimes* he said, "Since I conceived, at the beginning of the second part, what must happen in the third, I have undergone as much sorrow and agitation as if the thing were real; and have wakened up with it at night."[21] Gladys Storey said that "There is no doubt that the children of his imagination came before his children of the flesh, which may have accounted for Mrs. Perugini saying: 'The only fault I found with my father was that he had too many children.'"   Sometimes he was tempted to feel that his "fanciful reality" was the only reality: he was fascinated by a remark made by a Spanish monk who showed to Sir David Wilkie Titian's painting of the Last Supper, and said that he often thought that the figures in it were "in truth the Substance, we the Shadows."   Having left off writing *Dombey and Son* for some time, Dickens said that at last he "began to doubt whether I ever had anything to do with a book called Dombey, or ever sat over it, day after day, until I half began, like the Monk in poor Wilkie's story, to believe it the only reality in life

and to mistake all the realities for short-lived shadows."[22] Living
among the shadows, he peered into the picture of imagination and saw
the real reality there: ". . .When . . . I sit down to my book, some
beneficent power shows it to me, and tempts me to be interested, and
I don't invent it—really do not—but *see* it, and write it down." Such
was the power of his seeing, Forster said, that it never permitted
Dickens to complete a story as he had first planned it.[23]

Writing In Company

But as real as Dickens' fictional world was to him, and as great
as he was at conveying it to others, he seems never to have felt that
he had made it sufficiently real or clear.[24] We have seen him enlist-
ing the assistance of illustration, but though this provided help, it was
at best a flawed instrument. Its inadequacies were three: it could not
move, it could not speak, and it had to be done by somebody else.
He continued to use the illustration as long as he published books,
but at the same time he discovered another visual art which offered
him, in his pursuit of a means of totally realizing his fictional reality,
the great assets of motion, sound, and best of all, self-production.
He discovered the stage.

We have already seen that Dickens loved the theater from
infancy: before he was through he was to write for it, act upon it,
direct, devise a portable stage—do almost anything that could be done
in connection with it. He was a poor playwright, an ingenious
deviser, a very good to excellent actor, and (in amateur productions,
as in all these activities but the first) a supreme director. But his
greatest triumph in connection with the stage came in the last years of
his life when, as a professional, he trod the boards to read from his
own works. He had always been aware of the kinship between the
novel and the play, and was always interested in what could be done
for a novel by dramatic representation. Speaking at a meeting of the
Royal General Theatrical Fund, he said it was appropriate for him to

chair the meeting because

> Every good actor plays direct to every good author, and
> every good writer of fiction, though he may not adopt the
> dramatic form, writes in effect for the stage. He may write
> novels always, and plays never, but the truth and wisdom
> that are in him must permeate the art of which truth and
> passion are the life, and must be more or less reflected in
> that great mirror which he holds up to nature.

Forster said that Dickens' "higher calling" included the lower one of
acting; he also quoted Ruskin as saying that in his novels Dickens
"chooses to speak in a circle of stage fire. . . ."[25]

In 1844 Dickens informed Robert Keeley, manager of the
Lyceum, that he objected "to the *principle* of adapting novels for the
stage," but in all probability he had in mind only the unauthorized
adapting of his own novels—without recompense, without power to
approve, even without the opportunity, usually, to help them be better
than horrible. In conferring his blessing on Frederick Yates's
production of *Nicholas Nickleby* at the Adelphi, he wrote that his

> general objection to the adaptation of any unfinished work of
> mine simply is, that being badly done and worse acted it
> tends to vulgarize the characters, to destroy or weaken in the
> minds of those who see them the impressions I have en-
> deavored to create, and consequently to lessen the after-
> interest in their progress.[26]

Long before this Dickens had adapted a piece of his own short fiction
for the stage, and he was active in helping others to do the same; he
had no objection to making a novel into a play, as long as the poor
novelist had something to say about it. As editor, he seems to have
been alert to the advantages of either genre as he considered work
submitted to him. As early as 1838, he wrote to Theodore Martin,
of a piece submitted for *Bentley's Miscellany*, that it was "not, I think,

quite the thing for us, but why don't you turn it into a two-act comedy? It would make an excellent little piece for the stage and looks so like one even now, that when I read it I could scarcely help thinking you had originally written it in that form." In 1859 he wrote to Regnier in France to inquire whether *A Tale of Two Cities* might be dramatized for the French stage (it was not).[27]

Dickens was most often involved in the translation of novel into play by his assistance to some of the unrelenting hordes of theater managers who found great profit in subjecting his works to the process. Sometimes plays based on his serialized works would be on the stage before he had finished the novel, with the flattest and tritest working out of his plot to an improbable ending. Forster says that the plays made from Dickens' books were "the subject of complaint with him incessantly." Upon occasion, that he might see his work represented by something less than the abominable (just as he could hardly bear to see his scenes and characters misrepresented in illustrations) he would, when given the chance, oversee and improve the production. "I really am bothered to death by this confounded dramatization of the Xmas Book," he wrote in 1846 about *The Battle of Life*. "Unless I had come to London I do not think there would have been much hope of the version being more than just tolerated— even that, doubtful." He could not allow the creatures of his imagination to be just tolerated, and so somehow he found time to help. He felt his hard work on *The Battle of Life* paid off, to some extent:

> The scenery and dresses are very good indeed. . . . The great change from the ball-room to the snowy night is most effective, and both the departure and the return will tell, I think, strongly on an audience. I have made them very quick and excited in the passionate scenes, and so have infused some appearance of life into those parts of the play. But I can't make a Marion, and Miss May is awfully bad. She is a mere nothing all through.

Drama, as means of conveying his creatures of imagination, obviously had its defects, when Dickens was not the performer. But he kept trying: when he wrote to Robert Keeley that he could not supply a prologue to his (and Mrs. Keeley's) rendering of *Martin Chuzzlewit*, he added, "I will glady come down at any time you may appoint . . . and go through it with you all."[28]

One or two of Dickens' letters convey a sense of pleasure in such work, but Forster says that on the whole these "efforts to assist special representations were mere attempts to render more tolerable what he had no power to prevent. . . ." Unable to halt a production of *A Tale of Two Cities*, he "devoted myself for a fortnight to the trying to infuse into the conventionalities of the Theatre, something not usual there in the way of Life and Truth." When Benjamin Webster, whom he admired, brought out a version of *The Haunted Man*, Dickens begged him not to perform it, saying he was "quite persuaded and convinced that if you bring the piece out tomorrow night, it will not succeed" because of its "slovenly and imperfect state. . . ." The play was a success, but only because, as Dickens wrote Angela Coutts, "I discovered yesterday that barbarous murder was being done upon me at the Adelphi, and was fain to go down there and pass the day in bettering their interpretation of my haunted friend."[29]

T. E. Pemberton gives us an idea of the kind of thing that must have driven wild the author who could not bear to have the reality of his imagination mangled: in one performance of *The Chimes*, he said, "the actress who was to play the blind girl, Bertha, was suddenly taken ill, and unable to appear; but the stage-manager was equal to the occasion, and sent on another young lady to *read her part*!!!" Little wonder that Dickens described himself as being "direfully slaughtered" by such productions, called the cast of one performance "black despair and moody madness," and, at a performance of *Nicholas Nickleby* at the Surrey, "in the middle of the first scene . . . laid himself down upon the floor in a corner of the box and never rose from it until the drop-scene fell. . . ." Watching the rehearsal of another version of the same novel, he objected to "sundry choice sentiments and rubbish regarding the little robins in the fields which have been put in the little boy's mouth by Mr. Sterling the adapter." Dickens quotes some of the sentiments: "I've heard that good people that live away from this place feed the pretty harmless robins when the cold days and dark night are on—perhaps they would feed me too, for I am harmless—very. I'll run to them at once, and ask them." Mrs. Keeley, who played Smike, is supposed to have said, "I shall never forget Dickens' face when he heard me repeating these lines. Turning to the prompter he said, 'Damn the robins; cut them out.'"[30]

But if Dickens would gladly have cut out all the adaptations of his novels that disgraced the stage in his time, clearly it was because of their poor quality, not their dramatic representation of his fiction. He himself was largely responsible for the dramatization of one of the novels of his master, Scott; it was his desire, he said, "to put Scott, for once, upon the stage in his own gallant manner." The performance was "an enormous success," in good part because "there is scarcely a movement throughout, or a look, that is not indicated by Scott. So you get a life romance with beautiful illustrations, and I do not expect ever again to see a book take up its bed and walk in like manner."[31] Dickens did not make allusions to his Lord lightly; there was for him a true sense of the miraculous in the realization of the novel upon the stage. (The quotation suggests, too, something of the imperfection of the novel, which needs to complete itself by this miraculous transformation.) Frustrated by the failure of others to come close to doing for him what he helped to do for Scott, he at last decided to do it for himself: he would adapt and produce and act in his own stories.

It has been assumed that Dickens gave the series of readings in the last years of his life because 1) he wanted to make money; 2) he loved contact with an audience, and delighted in their applause; 3) his marital life was in such disarray that he sought escape in any kind of activity, and may even in the exhausting schedule he set for himself, while in increasingly poor health, have sought death. All correct, certainly, though the second should not be used, as it has been, to denigrate Dickens; he liked applause, but not in any cheap or slavish sense. He simply liked personal contact with his audience, believing it to be good for public men; in a brief speech before his reading from *The Cricket on the Hearth*, he said, "I have long held the opinion, and have long acted on the opinion, that in these times whatever brings a public man and his public face to face, on terms of mutual confidence and respect, is a good thing," and added that he proposed to read from his book "quite as composedly as I might proceed to write it, or to publish it in any other way." Thus one more reason must be added: Dickens believed passionately in his mythic reality, sought all his life for means by which to render it ever more completely and intelligibly to his audience, and found in his readings another kind of "publishing," one which enhanced his ability to realize it, even beyond the combined powers of his prose and his artists' illustrations. He held, he said, "the hope that I could drop into some hearts, some new expression of the meaning of my books, that would touch them in a new way."[32]

Few men or women are perfectly happy in their work; nearly all know moments of ennui, frustration, erosion, and despair. Dickens loved his desk and pen as much as any writer, but on a surprising number of occasions he declared his dissatisfaction with several aspects of his occupation. Writing was imprisoning anguish: "Men have been chained to hideous prison walls and other strange anchors 'ere now, but few have known such suffering and bitterness at one time or another, as those who have been bound to Pens." Facing the task was particularly trying: beginning his favorite novel, *David Copperfield*, he wrote that "deepest despondency, as usual, in commencing, besets me." Writing put him in a bad mood: starting on *The Cricket on the Hearth*, he said, "I am in the preliminary seclusion and ill-temper of the Xmas book." He described his condition while beginning a work: "sitting, frowning horribly at a quire of paper, and falling into a state of inaccessibility and irascibility which utterly confounds and scares the House." Planning *Hard Times*, he said he was "in a dreary state . . ."; working on *Little Dorrit*, he found himself in "a hideous state of mind in which I walk down stairs once in every five minutes, look out of window once in every two, and do nothing else."[33] He spoke constantly of the restlessness he felt when he tried to write: "I go wandering about at night into the strangest places, according to my usual propensity at such a time—seeking rest, and finding none." As he was first thinking of *Bleak House* he said that, "I sit down between whiles to think of a new story, and, as it begins to grow, such a torment of a desire to be anywhere but where I am; and to be going I don't know where, I don't know why; takes hold of me, that it is like being *driven away*." To another friend at the same time he wrote of beginning to write as a kind of illness: "Violent restlessness, and vague ideas of going I don't know where, I don't know why, are the present symptoms of the disorder."[34] Movement did not help: in 1856 he went to Paris to write, but described the same old symptoms:

> Prowling about the rooms, sitting down, getting up, stirring
> the fire, looking out of window, tearing my hair, sitting
> down to write, writing nothing, writing something and tearing
> it up, going out, coming in, a Monster to my family, a
> dread Phaenomenon to myself, etc etc etc.

He wrote of the "restlessness which is the penalty of an imaginative life and constitution. . . . The vague unhappiness which tracks a life of constant aim and ever impels to some new aim in which it may be lost, is . . . curious to consider. . . ." He seemed impelled like the Ancient Mariner to describe this anguished state, especially endured as he began a novel:

> At such a time I am as infirm of purpose at Macbeth, as
> errant as Mad Tom, and as ragged as Timon. I sit down to
> work, do nothing get up [*sic*] and walk a dozen miles, come
> back and sit down again next day, again do nothing and get
> up, go down a railroad, find a place where I resolve to stay
> for a month, come home next morning, go strolling about
> for hours and hours, reject all engagements to have time to

myself, get tired of myself yet can't come out of myself to be pleasant to anybody else, and go on turning upon the same wheel round and round and over and over again until it may begin to roll me toward my end.[35]

He often spoke, too, of the difficulties he had in the actual writing. Trying to write in Paris, he told Forster that he "Couldn't begin, in the strange place; took a violent dislike to my study, and came down into the drawing-room; couldn't find a corner that would answer my purpose; fell into black contemplation of the waning month; sat six hours at a stretch, and wrote as many lines. . . ." Sometimes he blamed his state on his location: staying in a friend's house near Kensington, he said, ". . . This odious little house seems to have stifled and darkened my invention."[36] He spoke of "my final wrestle with Copperfield," and when he began B*leak House* said that "It is dreadfully difficult to work at the new book on these dull days" of January. "Hard at work" on the novel at last, he declined an invitation: "If I let myself out of my room under such circumstances, I have lost my power over myself for the day."[37]

Apparently it was not always easy to "see" what he wished to write down. Sometimes the muse would not come: "I have been, and am, trying to work this morning; but I can't make anything of it, and am going out to think." (Thinking, we remember, was the force behind the fairy wand.) Working on *Bleak House*, he lamented his inability to "grind sparks out of this dull blade." And while trying to see something for *Hard Times* he experienced "a great pressure of Wooden-Headedness on gifted author." When he succeeded in seeing and writing down, the effect was debilitating: "There are some things in the next 'Copperfield' that I think better than any that have gone before. After I have been believing such things with all my heart and soul, two results always ensue: first, I can't write plainly to the eye; secondly, I can't write sensibly to the mind." So much so that his postscript declared him "not equal to the flourish" under his signature. "What a dream it is," he wrote to Macready, "this work and strife, and how little we do in the dream after all. Only last night in my sleep, I was bent upon getting over a perspective of barriers, with my hands and feet bound. Pretty much what we are all about, waking, I think?"[38] Pretty much what he experienced when trying to see and write down, certainly.

More and more, in the last years, he expressed dissatisfaction with his work. "I have grown hard to satisfy, and write very slowly, and I have so much bad fiction, that *will* be thought of when I don't want to think of it, that I am forced to take more care than I ever took." Possibly, at the end, he even came to dislike his task. While he was working on *The Mystery of Edwin Drood,* George Dolby asked him "how he liked returning to the writing of a serial story, and he replied at once that he 'missed the pressure' of former days; which I took to mean that as his circumstances were comfortable now, the work was irksome." Was the pressure that of making money? Some years earlier, Dickens associated the pains of writing with a greater need: getting ready to start *Bleak House,* he told Mary Boyle, "This is one of what I call my wandering days before I fall to work. I seem to be always looking at such times for something I have not found in life. . . ."[39]

Is all this, after all, no more than most writers feel as they wrestle with the agony of creating? Perhaps, but not many writers have been so driven to express so often and so darkly the pangs of giving birth. Probably not all writers find the sense of suffering, of inadequacy, increasing through their careers, certainly not when the last work they complete is as great as *Our Mutual Friend.* But an examination of the dates of the above quotations indicates an increasing dissatisfaction: before the 1840's, Dickens had hardly a word of complaint; after it, he speaks ever more frequently of his restlessness, his pain, his ill moods, the onus of writing, the need for inspiration, the greater difficulty in pleasing himself, and the yearning for something. One thing is certain: during these years, despite his statement to Forster that he "had never thought of the stage but as a means of getting" money, he told many people that he not only thought often of a career in the theater, but sometimes said that he would have preferred it to that which he chose. "I have often thought," he wrote Forster in 1844, "that I should certainly have been as successful on the boards as I have been between them." He told Grace Greenwood that "he believed he had more talent for the drama than for literature, as he certainly had more delight in acting than in any other work whatever. . . ." In 1842 he wrote "that nature intended me for the lessee of a National Theatre—and that pen ink and paper have spoiled a Manager."[40]

When he finished a long and exhausting job of producing, directing, and acting in an amateur performance, instead of sighing with relief, he was unhappy.

> I have no energy whatever—I am very miserable.   I loathe domestic hearths.   I yearn to be a Vagabond.
>
> Why can't I marry Mary!   Why have I seven children—not engaged at sixpence a night apiece, and dismissible for ever, if they tumble down, but taken on for an indefinite time at a vast expence, and never—no, never, never—wearing lighted candles round their heads!
>
> I am deeply miserable.
>
> A real house like this, is insupportable after that canvass [*sic*] farm wherein I was so happy.   What is a humdrum dinner at half past five, with nobody (but John) to see me eat it, compared with *that* soup, and the hundreds of pairs of eyes that watched its disappearance!

The call to another amateur production, he said, "stirs my blood like a trumpet. . . ."[41]

Months before he died, he expressed his desire once more; Charles Kent tells the famous story:

> Going round by way of Lambeth one afternoon, in the early summer of 1870, we had skirted the Thames along the

Surrey bank, had crossed the river higher up, and on our way back, were returning at our leisure through Westminster, when, just as we were approaching the shadow of the old Abbey at Poet's Corner, under the roof-beams of which he was so soon to be laid in his grave, with a rain of tears and flowers, he abruptly asked, "What do you think would be the realization of one of my most cherished day-dreams?" adding instantly, without waiting for my answer, "To settle down for the remainder of my life within easy distance of a great theatre, in the direction of which I should hold supreme authority."[42]

Everyone dreams of finding a thing to do that is less wearisome and more rewarding, but when such dreams are the idle wishes of the moment, the dreamer usually does not know much about the other something (which is why it seems better). Dickens knew all there was to know about drama. On more than one occasion he spoke of the exhausting labor it required, and of the frustration and disappointment it could create. Yet he was drawn always to the stage, and as years passed he seemed more and more attracted, for all the irritation he expressed to Forster, to the idea of having his own fiction represented upon it. Gradually, he worked his way toward the idea—overriding the objections of such friends as Forster and Angela Burdett Coutts—of eliminating the objections to such representation (the poor adaptation and poor performances) by taking on the task himself.

He had always enjoyed reading from his works. As we have seen, he read to his illustrators; he also read to Forster to get his critical reaction; and he read to groups of friends for mutual pleasure, the most famous occasion probably being that sketched by Maclise in 1844, when he read from *The Chimes*. To convey meaning in this way to his reader, to perceive that he comprehended—that was what Dickens wanted. "It was as if," said Edmund Wilson, "he had actually to embody, to act out in his own person, the life of his imagination." If Dickens was challengeable as actor in the plays of others but supreme in his own readings, this is surely the reason. (For some, it should be noted, Dickens' acting was also characterized by the ability to reach his audience, to make them feel. A review of his performance as Richard Wardour in *The Frozen Deep* said that

> Mr. Dickens has all the technical knowledge and resources of a professional Actor; but these, the dry bones of acting, are kindled by that soul of vitality which can only be put into them by the man of Genius, and the interpreter of the affections. . . . Altogether, the audience return home from Tavistock House rather indisposed for some time to come to be content with the time-honoured conventionalities of the public stage. . . .)[43]

It is not coincidental that several perceptive members of Dickens' reading audience employed analogies to art to describe the effects he achieved. We have seen how Dickens attempted to use illustrations to realize his characters beyond the limits of fiction; now some of those who heard his readings seemed to feel that he was picturing his imagined world in another but similar way. *The Cheltenham Examiner* spoke of a scene in *Nicholas Nickleby* that "was 'painted'" by his reading "with a vividness and pathos which told with thrilling effect. . . ." *The Scotsman* said of his readings that "His works could have no more perfect illustrator." Kent saw the readings as going beyond illustration: Dickens' descriptions of scenes "were not simply word-painting," he said, "but realization." And later commentators, attempting to convey the effect of his readings, also have referred to art. Philip Collins concluded from his extensive study of commentary on the readings that "To hear [Dickens] read, instead of reading the book oneself, was like meeting someone instead of getting a letter from him—or like seeing a stereoscopic instead of a two-dimensional photograph, or a great painting instead of an engraving of it. . . ."[44]

Like illustration in the books, the reading platform became for

Dickens a medium for conveying what his daughter Kate called the "excessive realism of his mental vision," which made whatever he read about so real for him that he sometimes disliked illustrations of books he had previously read because "the picture in his mind was often so vivid as to preclude the possiblity of its being conceived in any other way." That which he "really did not" imagine but "saw," and then tried to realize by writing down and by using drawings, he now attempted to realize by acting. By most accounts, he realized superbly. Kent said that "he realized everything in his own mind so intensely, that listening to him we realized what he spoke of by sympathy." Turgenev said that "there were several first-class actors in his face alone who made you laugh and cry," and Charles Kent said that he brought conviction and reality even

> to the very least among the minor characters. . . . A great fat man with a monstrous chin, for example, was introduced just momentarily in the briefest street-dialogue, towards the close of [A Christmas Carol], who had only to open his lips once or twice for an instant, yet whose individuality was in that instant or two so thoroughly realized, that he lives ever since then in the hearer's remembrance. When, in reply to some one's inquiry, as to what was the cause of Scrooge's (presumed) death?—this great fat man with the monstrous chin answered, with a yawn, in two words, "God knows!"— he was before us there, as real as life, as selfish, and as substantial.[45]

Dickens had done for the fat man what the actor described in his Christmas tree article had done for the peasant: made him real to the viewer.

George Dolby said that Dickens took "scarcely less pleasure and delight in his public readings than in the pursuit of his legitimate calling . . ."; I wonder if he did not take at least as much—I almost dare say more. Once, to Edmund Yates, he himself said that he did.

He would like, he told Yates, to have been a great actor. But you are a great novelist, Yates protested. "That's all very well," Dickens replied, "but I would rather have been a great actor, and had the public at my feet." The final image is misleading: Dickens always hated the lionizing process, and surely did not mean at his feet to worship, but, as with children before a story-teller, to hear. The readings gave him, in any case, what the novels could not. Writing to Forster, who had always opposed the public readings, he said, "I must do *something*, or I shall wear my heart away. I can see no better thing to do that is half so hopeful in itself, or half so well suited to my restless state." To Wilkie Collins he wrote that he wanted to "escape from myself. For, when I do start up and stare myself seedily in the face, as happens to be my case at present, my blankness is inconceivable—indescribable—my misery amazing." Forster and all his followers have attributed this "restless state" solely to the marital troubles of the time, and no doubt the readings were a relief from that unhappiness: Philip Collins points out that Dickens' first private reading from his work in 1847 and his return to the idea of public readings in 1857-58 both coincided with troubles in his private life. But great as those troubles were, they may not have been the sole cause of his unhappiness. Forster himself says that in the mid-1850's Dickens' "books had lost for the time the importance they formerly had over every other consideration in his life."[46] Probably there were several reasons for this; I suspect that one was the frustration he felt with the limitations of his art, the desire to find some impossible medium which could establish immediate contact with his audience, and could convey more powerfully than his novels his own imaginative reality. If so, how well we may now understand the irresistible attraction readings had for him—so irresistible, many believe, that he died rather than give them up. Here was his desire, realized; here were his characters, "before us there, as real as life . . . and as substantial." Dickens had finally found the way, even beyond the art of illustration, to show his readers what he meant. The New York *Tribune* saw his readings as "only the natural outgrowth of what he has been doing all the days of his life. To have heard these readings is to have witnessed the spontaneous expression of a great nature in the maturity of its genius." In *David Copperfield,* Agnes tells David how his "old friends . . . read my books as if they heard me speaking its contents." When he wrote his books, as we learn from several anecdotes, Dickens often wrote out loud; G. H. Lewes said that "Dickens once declared to me that every word said by his characters was distinctly *heard* by him. . . ."[47]

Dickens would seem to have been an even better actor in his own roles than in those written by others. Admiration began with "the cunningly contrived and admirably lighted platform, which was the outcome of his keen eye for theatrical effect," and ended with the entire performance—"a whole tragic comic heroic *theatre* visible, performing under one *hat,*" as Carlyle put it. Charles Kent said he had the power of the Ancient Mariner to mesmerize his audience. Edgar Johnson goes into more detail:

> In the public readings of Dickens's last dozen years he attained to the very peak of his career as a dramatist and actor. The dramas and the comedies he himself enacted, alone on his own stage, were indeed dealt with according to his own pleasure and his own judgment, for he molded them out of his own writings, and the players, "a skilled and noble company," every member of which was his own protean self, were absolutely under his command. In essence, he had achieved his "cherished day-dream" of holding supreme authority over a great theater.[48]

Several reviewers join Kent in refuting—at least for the readings—Forster's contention that Dickens' ability was limited to the comic: the *Scotsman* said that in his readings "he was as clever a comedian" as Charles Mathews, but with "a power of pathos to which even that most versatile of players has not the slightest pretension. Hence his reading is not only as good as a play, but far better than most plays, for it is all in the best style of acting." Professor Adolphus Ward also thought him as good in "pathetic" roles as in humorous, but argued that "he isolated his parts too sharply . . . ," which I take to mean that he tried too hard to make his characters distinct from each other—no doubt because he took pride in his ability to do so, but also because he wanted so much to make clear to all what he meant by each. Several reviewers commented on this ability: Dickens "to an extraordinary extent assumes the personality of each," and "All the characters seem to live." His face, said Leigh Hunt, had "the life and soul of fifty human beings."[49]

Professional actors apparently approved as much of Dickens' theater in a hat as did laymen. Early in 1870, among twelve scheduled readings, he gave three in the morning so that actors could attend. Dolby said that "He succeeded, to perfection, in the presence even of so thoroughly critical an audience." The great William Macready—who was, as Philip Collins notes, a severe judge of actors—said that Dickens "reads as well as an experienced actor would," and was heard "undisguisedly sobbing and crying" at the private reading of *The Chimes*. After hearing readings from *David Copperfield* Macready was rendered speechless, Dickens says, and finally managed:

> No—er—Dickens! I swear to Heaven that, as a piece of passion and playfulness—er—indescribably mixed up together, it does—er—no, really, Dickens!—amaze me as profoundly as it moves me. But as a piece of art—and you know—er—that I—no, Dickens! By----! have seen the best art in a great time—it is incomparable to me. How is it got at—er—how is it done—er—how one man can—well? It lays me on my—er--back, and it is of no use talking about it!

He wrote that it was "altogether a truly artistic performance." And when he heard the Sikes-Nancy scene, he could say no more than "in my—er—best times—er—you remember them, my dear boy—er—gone, gone!—no, it comes to this—er—**two Macbeths!**"[50]

As in all things, one of the keys to Dickens' success as reader was hard work. Dolby said that "seldom . . . do we find a man gifted with such extraordinary powers, and, at the same time, possessed of such a love of method, such will, such energy, and such a capacity for taking pains." In preparation for his reading at St. James's Hall in 1866, Dolby said, Dickens rehearsed "considerably over two-hundred times" in less than three months. Of the first fifty readings he got up for public performance he wrote to Forster that he had "*learnt them all*, so as to have no mechanical drawback in looking after the words. I have tested all the serious passion in them by everything I know; made the humorous points much more humorous; corrected my utterance of certain words; cultivated a self-possession not to be disturbed; and made myself master of the situation." When did he not? Only once did he find himself "out" of a part, and this he caught well in advance of the performance. "Imagine my being so entirely out of 'Dombey,'" he wrote Wills from Paris, "that I have been obliged to go down this morning and rehearse it in the room!"[51]

But another factor in his success was the ability to give his audiences deep emotional perception. It was a delight to him that he could do so, and he reveled in their responses to him both as creator and performer. It was, after all, the ability many of his readers admired in his novels. "What a power he has," Macready exclaimed, "of penetrating his reader with his idea." The same was said of his speeches: they "seemed to come from the very heart of the speaker and to go straight to the heart of the listener." To Maclise, who had expressed his appreciation of Dickens' acting of Richard Wardour in *The Frozen Deep*, he said, "the interest of such a character to me is that it enables me, as it were to write a book in company instead of in my own solitary room, and to feel its effect coming freshly back upon me from the reader."[52] To convey meaning in this way to his reader, to perceive that he comprehended—that was what Dickens wanted.

Critical response to the readings supports the assertion that they improved his audience's understanding of his work. It was said that his performance of *The Chimes* "added much to his admirers' awareness of the qualities to be found in this story." (Philip Collins, from whom I take this quotation, expresses surprise that, in view of the comparatively limited success of *The Chimes* as a reading, Dickens spent so much time revising it; perhaps the reason lies in his conviction that the reading revealed qualities not previously found.) Kent said that when he read he disappeared, and his characters stood before them; the minor characters, whom "no one had ever realized" before hearing him read, came "with the surprise of a revelation." Kate Field attested to Dickens' ability to bring his characters to life; after attending his reading from *Dombey and Son* she wrote,

> You may have loved him since childhood, . . . but until you have made Toots' acquaintance through the medium of Dickens, you have no idea how he looks or how he talks. When Toots puts his thumb in his mouth, looks sheepish, and roars forth "How are you?" I feel as the man in the play must feel when, for the first time, he recognizes his long-lost brother. . . .[53]

One critic said that in Dickens' reading of "Sikes and Nancy" Fagin "seems actually before us"; another wrote of Dickens' performance of Nancy that "Here the acting of Mr. Dickens is much beyond his writing. . . ." Still another asserted that the readings lent greater reality to certain scenes which were deficient in that quality in the novels; in "Bardell and Pickwick," Dickens had "succeeded in giving the scene an air of probability which in the original version it does not wear." Collins notes that in this reading Dickens' "conception of the characters differed significantly from the usual interpretations"; it is as if Dickens were saying, "No, *this* is how what I have written should be understood." Good scenes became great ones: "What has struck you heretofore as a diamond no better than its fellows is magically transformed into a **Kohinoor**. And when I say 'magically

transformed,' I mean it in all soberness." Lesser things were improved: a reviewer said that hearing Dickens reading "Barbox
Brothers" made it "very much more agreeable and interesting than a
private perusal."[54]

Though Turgenev admired Dickens' reading, he contrasted it to
that of Gogol, who "did not seem to care whether there were any listeners or what they were thinking of." Several viewers thought that
Dickens tended to the theatrical, which they considered as evidence of
his desire for easy effect. But if he strove for effect, perhaps the
term *theatrical* in its pejorative sense is not entirely appropriate: the
difference between Dickens and Gogol is not that one loved his work
and lost himself in its reading to the exclusion of his audience while
the other sought merely to impress, but that Gogol was content with
making his reading perfect unto itself and for himself, while Dickens
believed that no performance—written or spoken—could approach perfection unless it reached its audience, unless it produced a reaction that
was both emotional and cognitive. Members of his reading audience
testify again and again how penetratingly he had done this. "I was
dreaming dreams," the novelist Dick Donovan (J. E. Preston
Murdock) said. "Charles Dickens had carved his name on my
heart. . . . He seemed to . . . stir within me feelings and desires
of which up to then I had only had a vague consciousness." Robert
Lytton (the poet Owen Meredith) wrote Dickens: "You play with the
heart . . . as tho' it were a creature of your own
construction. . . ."[55]

None of this is to say that Dickens was not also drawn to the
reading stage by the opportunity to experience an admiring audience.
He wrote of the tremendous appeal audience response had for him.
When Douglas Jerrold facetiously supposed that Dickens had given up
Martin Chuzzlewit in order to write a comedy, he replied,

> I have my comedy to fly to. My only comfort! I walk up
> and down the street at the back of the Theatre every night,
> and peep in at the Green Room Window—thinking of the

time when "Dick—ins" will be called for, by excited
hundreds, and won't come, 'till Mr. Webster . . . shall
enter from his dressing room, and quelling the tempest with
a smile, beseech that Wizard if he be in the house (here he
looks up at my box) to accept the congratulations of the
audience. . . . Then I shall come forward and bow—once—
twice—thrice—Roars of approbation—Brayvo—Brarvo—Hooray—
Hoorar—Hooroar-- one cheer more. . . .[56]

It is facetious, but it does not mask nor does it intend to mask the
real pleasure Dickens would take were such a thing to occur.   It
hardly occurred as he imagined it, ever, for him as dramatist, but it
did for him as actor, and did as much as could ever have been
dreamed for him as reader of his own works.   But the pleasure lay
not merely in the applause; it came also from the comprehension.

Even on the reading platform, however, Dickens had some difficulties in showing what he meant.   Even in this joining of the
powers of fiction and stage, he did not create the perfect medium with
which to reach his audience.   He experienced two major difficulties.
First, as some criticisms we have already seen have indicated, in his
desire to realize his imagination he pressed too hard.   Some readers
have felt the same way about his novels, and have attributed the
pressing to a similar motive.   If in his works "the desire for effect
[was] too obstructive," said G. H. Lewes, it was owing to his effort
to use his "power effectively" to reach and improve "the lot of the
miserable Many. . . ."   In his readings, said Francesco Berger, "he
allowed himself certain mannerisms of voice and gesture which in the
theatre, he would not have resorted to."   A reviewer argued that in
the pathetic passages of the readings Dickens was "too effective—too
stagey, in fact."   In his reading of "The Poor Traveler," said *The
Saturday Review*, he used "a series of little turns or tricks adopted by
which an idea is continually brought round and round, and forced
upon the attention. . . .   Mr. Dickens . . . threw out the whole
strength of his power of reading to make them tell. . . .   He has

. . . thrown away the genuine success he might have achieved, by
having recourse to the paltry artifices of stage effect." There was,
R. H. Hutton said, "something a little ignoble in this extravagant
relish of a man of genius for the evidence of the popularity of his
writings. Dickens must have known that theatrical effects are by no
means the best gauge of the highest literary fame." So important a
contemporary scholar as Philip Collins agrees with Hutton: "It is a
judgment . . . which must carry some weight."[57] Perhaps, but the
load is lessened, surely, by what we have seen. Before an audience
that could understand him, Dickens eschewed mere theatrical effects in
his readings, and sought apperception at least as much as he sought
approbation. Mr. Collins himself attests to this: "many accounts," he
says, ". . . show that he gave his audiences that enriched sense of
the power and subtlety of a text which a critical commentary attempts
to convey by analysis and argument." Disliking exegesis as he did,
Dickens provided it for his novels only by acting them. In his
criticism of Dickens for striving for effect, R. H. Hutton also uninten-
tionally explained why he did: Dickens, he said, "had too much eye
to the effect to be produced by all he did. . . . He makes you feel
that it is not the intrinsic insight that delights him half so much as
the power it gives him of moving the world. The visible word of
command must go forth from himself in connection with all his
creations."[58] In popular plays, Dickens certainly did appreciate stage
effects, but he never confused them with good art, and if at times he
used them in his readings, it was not poor judgment or the desire for
a cheaply-bought reaction that made him do so. Hutton's last sentence provides the key: for Dickens the play was not in itself the
thing, but only the thing by which he might catch the imagination of
his audience. To put it more accurately, it was not a Mousetrap; it
was a portal to his mythic reality, and he used whatever he felt he
needed to draw his listeners through it.

Dickens' second problem in his readings was that in his effort
to go beyond his own novels he encountered a difficulty similar to
that which he had so well defined years earlier, when his friend

Macready had, after establishing himself as a tragic actor, taken on the comic role of Benedick. Among several problems, Dickens suggested that

> First impressions, too, even with persons of a cultivated understanding, have an immense effect in settling their notions of a character; and it is no heresy to say that many people unconsciously form their opinion of such a creation as *Benedick,* not so much from the exercise of their own judgment in reading the play, as from what they have seen bodily presented to them on the stage. Thus, when they call to mind that in such a place Mr. A. or Mr. B. used to stick his arms akimbo and shake his head knowingly; or that in such another place he gave the pit to understand, by certain confidential nods and winks, that in good time they should see what they should see; or in such another place, swaggered; or in such another place, with one hand clasping each of his sides, heaved his shoulders with laughter; they recall his image, not as the Mr. A. or B. aforesaid, but as Shakespeare's *Benedick*—the real *Benedick* of the book, not the conventional *Benedick* of the boards—and missing any familiar action, miss, as it were, something of right belonging to the part.[59]

Reviewers and students of Dickens' readings have noted a similar problem. When he undertook such favorites as Mrs. Gamp or Sam Weller, Collins says, "audiences were easily disappointed by the outcome . . . if it clashed with their own cherished notions of how the character must be played." The imaginations of the readers of Dickens' novels created the same difficulty for him as earlier actors had made for Macready: they created pictures with which he was forced to compete. Doubtless this was the trouble one Bostonian had with Dickens' presentation of Sam. In the first reading of 1867 in that city, George Dolby observed a man leaving the theater early, and

thinking that he might be ill, asked what was wrong.   The man
responded,

> "Say, who's that man on the platform reading?"
> "Mr. Charles Dickens," I replied.
> "But that ain't the real Charles Dickens, the man as
> wrote all them books I've been reading all these years."
> "The same."
> After a moment's pause, as if for thought, he replied,
> "Wall, all I've got to say about it then is, that he knows no
> more about Sam Weller 'n a cow does of pleatin' a shirt, at
> all events that ain't *my* idea of Sam Weller, anyhow."[60]

John Hollingshead said that if Dickens' acting of Mrs. Gamp "fails to
produce an impression upon the audience commensurate with its artistic merits, it is because the character . . . is so broadly and deeply
impressed upon the printed page, that nearly every reader is able to
build up for himself a clear idea of this great friend. . . ."   Many
viewers agreed: their ideas of Sam and Sairy had grown so in their
own imaginations that not even Dickens could modify the imagined
reality.   As Adolphus Ward put it, Sam had "become to all of us a
mythical personage incapable of realization in this imperfect world."[61]
        In short, Dickens found himself, in his effort to go beyond his
own novels, running into a catch-22: his very success as a writer in
stirring the imaginations of his readers now blocked his further attempts to convey, through the greater immediacy of the stage, his own
fanciful reality.   Not even Charles Dickens, seeking to bring to bear
the combined forces of fiction, illustration, and drama, could make
imagination real.   But the praises poured on his performances indicate
that he came perhaps as close as human power can to freeing himself
and others from the tyranny of the dull settled world.   Intelligent
critics like Kate Field commended his effort to combine fiction and
theater.   "Dickens," she said, "was as much born to read *Mr. Bob
Sawyer's Party* as he was to create it."   For her, at least, Dickens

managed to escape his own realty: in acting Justice Stareleigh, she said, "Dickens steps out of his own skin."[62]

Certainly Dickens was ever-alert to the reactions of his audiences, always sensitive to what they liked. After a reading from *Nicholas Nickleby* he said, "I am inclined to suspect that the impression of protection and hope derived from Nickleby's going away protecting Smike is exactly the impression—this is discovered by chance—that an Audience most likes to be left with." But if he always tried to reach his listeners, he also seems to have expected them to hear intelligently, perceptively. It is significant that in the readings success appears often to have been defined by the ability of Dickens' audience to get what he meant. One viewer was struck by this. "He depended, as I remember," said David Christie Murray, "in a most extraordinary degree upon the temper of his audience. I have heard him read downright flatly and badly to an unresponsive house, and I have seen him vivified and quickened to the most extraordinary display of genius by an audience of the opposite kind." This does not sound like the performance of a man who read merely to acquire evidence of his popularity. Dickens' own comments upon his readings repeatedly concentrate upon whether or not his audiences got what he meant, on whether they found reality in his readings, as well as entertainment. "Among my English audiences," he said,

> I have had more clergymen than I ever saw in my life before. It is very curious to see how many people in black come to Little Dombey. And when it is over they almost uniformly go away as if the child were really Dead—with a hush upon them. They certainly laugh more at the Boots's story of the Little Elopement than at anything else; and I notice that they sit with their heads on one side, and an expression of playful pity on their faces—as if they saw the tiny boy and girl, which is tender and pleasant, I think?[63]

"As if the child were really dead"; "as if they saw"; is it not as if what Dickens had, as he said to Forster, not imagined but really seen and written down—a reality which he felt compelled, indeed like the Ancient Mariner, to convey to others—had finally had its complete transmission to the mental vision of his audience?

Always the emphasis is upon getting a reaction from the spectators, especially an unusual reaction—not merely enjoyment, certainly not just applause to swell his ego, but a special, understanding response.   Edward Dowden said that Dickens' eye "kept roving throughout his audience from face to face, as if seeking for some expression of the effect he was creating."   Dowden's intent is to disparage, but perhaps it was not merely for response to mere stage effect that Dickens was looking; some of his viewers said that he strove not for effect but for truth: "Where an ordinary artist would look for 'points' of effect he looked for 'points' of truth,"[64] one such reviewer remarked of his acting.   "I have made one reading from DC," Dickens wrote.   ". . . It seems to have a strong interest, and an expression of a young spirit in it that addresses people of sensitive perception curiously."   After he read it at Norwich, he wrote to Collins that "I don't think a word—not to say an idea—was lost."   After performing it and *A Christmas Carol* in Paris, he wrote to Wills that

> You have no idea what they made of me. I got things out
> of the old "Carol"—effects I mean—so entirely new and so
> very strong, that I quite amazed myself and wondered where
> I was going next. I really listened to Mr. Peggotty's nar-
> rative in 'Copperfield' with admiration. When Little Emily's
> letter was read, a low murmur of irrepressible emotion went
> about like a sort of sea.[65]

Clearly *effects* as Dickens uses it here is not what Dowden meaant by the word.   Charles Kent said that during the same Paris performances, when Dickens portrayed Steerforth sincerely shaking the hand of Peggoty, then condescendingly shaking the hand of Ham, he heard a Frenchman in the front row whisper "Ah-h!"   "The sound of that one inarticulate monosyllable," said Kent, "as he observed when relating the circumstances, gave the Reader, as an artist, a far livelier sense of satisfaction than any . . . imparted by mere acclamations. . . ."   James T. Fields said that Dickens liked his Paris audience best because "it was the quickest to catch his meaning."   In his reading at Sunderland, Dickens said, he did "a vast number of new things" because of the effect of "a rapturous audience . . . and the stage together: which I never can resist. . . ."   "I can most seriously say," he wrote to Bulwer, "that all the sights of the earth turn pale in my eyes, before the sight of three thousand people with one heart among them, and no capacity in them, in spite of all their efforts, of sufficiently testifying to you how they believe you to be right. . . ."[66]

5

Music: Such Sweet Sounds

After the deep immersion in drama which we have witnessed, Dickens' involvement in music will seem slight. He possessed little musical talent, knew fewer musicians than theater people, and was not drawn incessantly into the musical sphere. Still, music was an important part of his environment, and figured in his novels. He demonstrated a respectable knowledge of many of the musicians and musical instruments, and of much of the music—both popular and classical—of his time. As in other arts, content (especially the melancholic) seems at times to have been more important than quality, but on the whole evidence of good taste and judgment is plentiful.

"In the realm of music," says Edgar Johnson, Dickens' "background hardly extended beyond romantic songs, comic ditties, and the old English ballad-operas, which he liked better than he did the Italian opera. He makes no mention of either symphonies or chamber music, and there is no indication that he ever heard of Wagner, but he relished 'jolly little Polkas and Quadrilles,' and liked Auber's *Masaniello* and *Fra Diavolo*. . . ." But then—almost as if, having said what one expects to hear about Dickens, he can now say more—Johnson adds, ". . . He enjoyed [Parisian] opera, loved *Il Trovatori* and the *Barber of Seville*, and was deeply moved by Gounod's *Faust* and Gluck's *Orpheus*. . . . He was enchanted by

Joachim's playing on the violin, and . . . was fond of Mendelssohn's *Lieder* and of Mozart and Chopin."[1]

Dickens' background in music was not as slight as Johnson's first statement suggests. As Harry Stone says, "Dickens had long had entree to the musical world. His sister Fanny had been a student at the Royal Academy of Music and later had pursued a musical career. In his teens Dickens was drawn into her circle of friends, heard much musical talk, and came to know many singers and musicians." His father-in-law, George Hogarth, was a "distinguished music critic." Gad's Hill often welcomed "cultivators and professors": there is mention of several such in the letters, as when Dickens wrote that Henry F. Chorley, music critic for the *Athenaeum* and writer of libretti, "was here before starting for Spain" in 1861—obviously not for the first or last time. And in his writing Dickens showed at least a speaking knowledge of many of the musicians of his time; in one article in *Household Words* he and George Sala mention four prominent musical performers. Early in his career he wrote reviews of operas, and made critical comment on music in plays.[2]

Though Dickens possessed little musical talent, he seems to have had a fairly good voice, and he tried his hand at several musical instruments. John W. Bowden said that "he had no aptitude for music," but his daughter Mary objected: her father "had a most excellent ear and a good voice, " and "was intensely fond of music, and would listen to playing or singing by the hour together" (she is the source of Johnson's information that Dickens especially liked Mendelssohn's lieder, as well as Chopin and Mozart). From childhood to maturity he sang, often in accompaniment to his accomplished sister, as Mary Weller reported. At the Mitre in Rochester when his father visited friends, "little Charles used occasionally to sing, in a clear treble voice, some of those old songs which he was always fond of. . . ." On the ship *Cuba*, on the second of his American trips, he wrote Mamie that

I think I have acquired a higher reputation from drawing out the captain, and getting him to take the second in "All's Well," and likewise in "There's not in the wide world" (your parent taking first), than from anything previously known of me on these shores. . . . We also sang (with a Chicago lady, and a strong-minded woman from I don't know where) "Auld Lang Syne," with a tender melancholy, expressive of having all four been united from our cradles. The more dismal we were, the more delighted the company were.

According to Lightwood, Dickens' friends all bore "testimony to his vocal power and his love of songs and singing."[3]

As for instruments, Kitton said that Dickens tried but could not learn to play either the piano or the violin, but he did become fairly accomplished on an accordion which he purchased in 1842; he played "perpetually" on one he borrowed from a steward on his passage home from America: "I regaled the ladies' cabin with my performances." Each night he played for Kate a song from *Clari*, the opera in which he had taken part in 1833; the song was "Home Sweet Home." Back in England, at Broadstairs, one of his first acts was to write to his brother Fred to bring his accordion down to him. Though he did not play the piano, the instrument was part of his household from 1844, even, apparently, when he lodged on the Continent: in Genoa at the "Pink Jail" (the Villa Bagnerello), he wrote that "We expect a Piano up from Genoa today."[4] In 1846 he reported from Lausanne that "We have really a very good German piano," and commented that the daughters of a neighbor played on a Lausanne piano, "which must be heard to be appreciated." The piano would seem to have been a musical instrument to Dickens, not a piece of furniture or a decoration. He did not keep instruments in his house unless they were used: when someone offered him a flute reputedly owned by Byron, he replied, "Mr. Dickens cannot play that instrument himself, and has nobody in his house who can. . . ." In later years he apparently did try the instrument: a visitor to his house reports that he said that after dinner, "I retire to my study, amuse myself with the flute. . . ."[5]

Dickens' fondness for and knowledge of music are reflected in his work. James T. Lightwood said that ". . . There is, perhaps, no great writer who has made a more extensive use of music to illustrate character and create incident than Charles Dickens." The references in his work "reflect to a nicety the general condition of ordinary musical life in England during the middle of the last century. . . . For the story of music in the ordinary English house, for the popular songs of the period, for the average musical attainments of the middle and lower classes . . . we must turn to the pages of Dickens' novels." Percy Scholes records that "nearly forty instruments are mentioned by Dickens and well over a hundred different songs" in his works. Titles considered for the journal that was to become *All the Year Round* also suggest how Dickens occasionally thought of writing in terms of music: *Household Harmony, Home Music, English Bells,* and *Weekly Bells.*[6]

He seems to have had an ear for music. Writing from Florence, where he was traveling with Wilkie Collins and the painter Augustus Egg, Dickens complained that Collins

> is very learned, and sometimes almost drives me into frenzy by humming and whistling whole overtures—with not one movement correctly remembered from the beginning to the end. I was obliged to ask him, the day before yesterday, to leave off whistling the overture to William Tell. "For by Heaven," said I, "there's something the matter with your ear—I think it must be the cotton—which plays the Devil with the commonest tune."

He complained humorously, too, of the singing of his American secretary, George Putnam.[7] But he liked good amateur singing; to Francis Crew, bookseller and stationer but also amateur singer of some repute, he wrote, "You cannot but be aware of how charmed I

always am with your delighful voice, nor less admirable taste. . . ."
And he wrote Forster from Lausanne that the sisters Lady Virginia
and Lady Mary Taylour, granddaughters of the composer Sir John
Andrew Stevenson, "inherit the musical taste, and sing very well."
Twice in later years, he imagined himself back in Lausanne, walking
"outside the Inn at Martigny—the piano sounding inside, and Lady
Mary Taylour singing." Perhaps woman and music formed for him a
combination particularly affecting because of his memory of his first
great love, Maria Beadnell, who played the harp: he wrote to her in
1855 that "I have never seen a girl play the harp, . . . but my attention had been instantly arrested."[8]

Amateur music, though, could be agony as well as pleasure; in
addition to mere badness, Dickens found it often monotonous, pervasive, and full of bathos. In particular, amateur instrumental music
often bothered him, especially when he tried to work at his retreat in
Broadstairs. In 1843 he wrote to Miss Coutts that

> I have been here six years, and have never had a Piano next
> door; but this fortune was too good to last, and now there is
> one close to the little bay window of the room I write in,
> which has six years' agony in every note it utters. I have
> been already obliged to take refuge on the other side of the
> house, but that looks into a street where the "Flis" stand,
> and where there are donkeys and drivers out of number.
> Their Music is almost as bad as the other. . . .[9]

Two weeks later he wrote to say that ". . . The Piano goes away on
Friday. My mind misgives me that some other Instrument will take
the house afterwards. I have seen a man looking at the bill, who has
been heard playing the flute in the Evening under solitary cliffs."
The saga was resumed the next month:

> The Piano is gone, and the flute is out of hearing—at Dover.
> But a barrel organ, a monkey, and punch, a Jim Crow, and

a man who plays twenty instruments at once and doesn't get the right sound out of any one of them, are hovering in the neighborhood.   Also a blind man who was in a Sea Fight in his youth; and after playing the hundredth psalm on a flageolet, recites a description of the engagement.

Four years later, what Forster called "the plague of itinerant music" was even worse: Dickens wrote to him that

> Vagrant music is getting to that height here, and is so impossible to be escaped from, that I fear Broadstairs and I must part company in time to come.   Unless it pours of rain, I cannot write half-an-hour without the most excruciating organs, fiddles, bells, or glee-singers.   There is a violin of the most torturing kind under the window now (time, ten in the morning) and an Italian box of music on the steps—both in full blast.[10]

Music beneath the window followed him into all his summer retreats. In Brighton there were "Life Guards' Bands under the window"; in Boulogne, at a nearby camp there were "soldiers, training to be trumpeters, [who would] come and blow their lives away, in hopeless practice at their instruments, outside our gate."   At his "French Watering-Place," on the bathing beach,

> there is usually a guitar, which seems presumptuously enough to set its tinkling against the deep hoarseness of the sea, and there is always some boy or woman who sings, without any voice, little songs without any tune: the strain we have most frequently heard being a appeal to 'the sportsman' not to bag that choicest of game, the swallow.[11]

In Naples, "itinerant music" was objectionable because of its monotony: Dickens found that "The same men, with the same instruments, were singing the same songs, to the same tunes, all along the

seashore in the morning, as when I was there nine years ago."
Dover, he wrote to Mary Boyle, was "too bandy (I mean musical, no
reference to its legs). . . ."[12]

In 1864 he joined with others in support of a bill by Michael
T. Bass for the control of street music in London.   All there, he
wrote, "are driven nearly mad by street musicians . . . brazen instruments, beaters of drums, grinders of organs, bangers of banjos,
clashers of cymbals, worriers of fiddles, and bellowers of
ballads. . . ."   But he continued to appreciate good street music near
his dwelling: from Parma he wrote his wife that "There has been
music on the landing outside my door to night.   Two violins and a
violincello.   One of the violins played a solo; and the other, struck
in, as an orchestra does now and then—very well."   And in America
he regretted the absence of such music: in New York, he asked, "Are
there no itinerant bands; no wind or stringed instruments? No, not
one."   In Richmond the people "had musical instruments playing to
them 'o nights, which it was a treat to hear again."   On the ship
home, it was another matter: "We had no lack of music, for one
played the accordion, another the violin and another (who usually
began at six o'clock, A.M.)   the key-bugle; the combined effect of
which instruments, when they all played different tunes . . . at the
same time . . . , was sublimely hideous."   In England, too, he could
be tolerant of noisy street music at times: he wrote Mamie from
Gad's Hill of a parade ending its march at Falstaff's Inn across the
way, including "a band with a terrific drum. . . .   I have presented
the band with five shillings, which munificence has been highly
appreciated."[13]

Dickens by no means slighted music in his attendance of public
performances.   A. E. Brooks Cross says that "Dickens had a strong
contempt for opera as a form of dramatic entertainment and ridiculed
it on many occasions," but the letters show that he regularly
patronized the opera; in 1849, for example, between the end of April
and the beginning of September he took in at least four performances,
seeing Catherine Hays in Donizetti's *Lucia di Lammermore*, Jenny Lind

in Bellini's *La Sonnambula,* Weber's *Die Freischutz,* and Donizetti's *Lucrezia Borgia.* References to operas attended continue throughout the letters—for example, in 1852: "Musically, we had a wonderfully fine Italian Opera at Covent Garden. . . ."[14] From Venice in 1853 he wrote that "There was a very fair operra [*sic*] and a capital ballet." From Turin: "There is a large and most beautiful theatre, where we saw the Prophete last night—not well sung (except Viardot's part by Madame Stolz) but admirably put upon the stage." From Paris, he wrote of watching Scribe—"the author of 400 pieces"—getting increasingly nervous at a dinner party as the hour of performance of *Manon Lascaut* approached; Dickens went a week later to see it, and called it "most charming. Delightful music, an excellent story, immense stage tact, capital scenic arrangements, and the most delightful prima donna ever seen or heard, in the person of Marie Cabel. . . . She sings a laughing song in it . . . which is the only real laughing song ever written." And from Rome: "Verdi is still the rage. [We saw] a poor enough opera of his—very well done indeed, at San Carlo. . . ."[15]

Cross to the contrary notwithstanding, Dickens' love of drama also formed a powerful part of his interest in opera: when he saw Bellini's *Il Pirato* in Paris, with three famous singers in leading roles, it was not their music upon which he commented, but their acting:

> . . . The passion and fire between [Grisi], Mario, and Fornassi, was as good and great as it is possible for anything operatic to be. They drew on one another, the two men—not like stage-players, but like Macready himself; and she, rushing in between them; now clinging to this one, now to that, now making a sheath for their naked swords with her arms, now tearing her hair in distraction as they broke away from her and plunged at each other; was prodigious. . . .

But he certainly paid attention to operatic music, too, as his comments

on details or aspects of performances indicate.   At Carraca, Italy, he
said "There was a very fair opera: but it is curious that the chorus
has been always, time out of mind, made up of labourers in the
quarries, who don't know a note of music, and sing entirely by ear."
(The letter also confirms the constant attention musicians paid to
Dickens when he traveled: he spoke of the orchestra for the performance "turning out in a body afterwards and serenading us. . . .")
In Paris in 1863, he wrote Georgy that he went "to hear 'Faust' last
night.   It is a splendid work, in which that noble and sad story is
most nobly and sadly rendered, and perfectly delighted me.   But I
think it requires too much of the audience to do for a London opera
house.   The composer must be a very remarkable man indeed. . . .
I could hardly bear the thing, it affected me so."   (Dickens seems to
have been aware of contemporary English indifference to opera.)   He
also must have known *Saul*: at least he knew the "Dead March," to
which two characters refer in his novels.[16]

The opera formed a part of his cultural memory: speaking from
the chair of the Royal General Theatrical Fund, he said that he well
remembered "when the opera of *Gustavus* was first produced at Covent
Garden. . . ."   He prided himself on his knowledge of operatic performances: in 1862 he wrote Wills that "Dick bets Stanny that
'Masaniello' was produced, as an opera, at Drury Lane Theatre thirty
years ago. . . ."   And in 1858 he wrote to de Cerjat that "There is
an Italian Opera at Drury Lane, price eighteen-pence to the pit, where
Viardot, by far the greatest artist of them all, sings, and which is full
when the dear [expensive] opera can't let a box. . . ."[17]

Certainly he loved good professional singing.   Lightwood said
that "His knowledge of song and ballad literature was extraordinary";
he found 164 songs and pieces of music in his works, and said that
"Moore's Irish Melodies had also a special attraction for him."   In
England, Dickens wrote to the soprano Jane Shireff of "the pleasure
which you have so often afforded me, in common with all playgoers
and admirers of beautiful music."   He wrote to Isaac Adams, who
had serenaded him and his wife at Hartford, thanking him "for your

most beautiful serenade," and saying "how much delight it afforded us"; it was a "charming performance," with "such sweet sounds" and with an "innate power of expression and perfect appreciation of the Poet's meaning. . . ." Again, at times he seems to have judged vocal music rather by the emotional appeal of its content than by its intrinsic quality: he wrote of Adams and "a German friend" that "*They* were most beautiful singers: and when they began, in the dead of night, in a long, musical, echoing passage outside our chamber door; singing, in low voices to guitars, about home and absent friends and other topics that they knew would interest us; we were more moved than I can tell you." Of the Yale chorus, on the other hand, he was not so fond because "It hadn't the heart of the other."[18] "Heart" presumably refers to the quality rather than the subject matter of the performance. Of an American troupe of four singers, called the Hutchinsons, who visited England in 1846, he wrote a friend, "They must never go back to their own country, without your having heard them sing Hood's Bridge of Sighs. My God how sorrowful and pitiful it is!" Despite the regret he expressed that Jenny Lind and similar performers drew audiences away from plays, he called her "almost the greatest genius, to my thinking, that the world has ever produced." He seems to have heard most of the important singers of his time, and much of its vocal music. Rarely did he decline a chance to hear singers, as he was obliged to do in 1848 when Miss Coutts got up a party to hear the *Messiah* at Exeter Hall.[19]

It would appear that Dickens read critical reviews of musical performances, at least those concerning musicians in whom he was interested. Writing to the father of Christiana Weller, a young pianist with whom he became infatuated for a time, he advised him not to advertise her coming performance in London by repeating critical notices she had received in the country:

> In reference to the Press (where I think you are a little mistaken) take my word that the quieter you keep in London on that score the better. The provincial criticisms of

> Miss Weller are not so remarkable for their good-taste that
> that they are likely to do any good here.   Indeed I am sure
> their injudicious obtrusion would do her serious dis-service,
> and prejudice her very much.

Whatever his opinion of the provincial criticism, he certainly approved
at that time of the pianist: he wrote to Benjamin Lumley, manager of
Her Majesty's Theatre, that she was "a brilliant and extraordinary
Piano Forte player," and when she played (at the Hanover Square
Rooms, instead), he wrote to her applauding "your brilliant achievement last night.   You rose with the occasion, nobly.   Nothing could
have been more successful, graceful, charming—triumphant, in every
particular."   And in a postscript he added that her sister Anna, who
also played, was "great."   Ten years later, his opinion of Christiana's
talents—influenced, probably, by an altered idea of her character—had
dwindled, and when he made a slighting reference to her talent, which
her father perhaps justly resented, Dickens could only defend his
revised judgment by arguing that "there is a wide gulf of difference
. . . between the graces and talents that justly captivate in private,
and their power of competition in public performances with the picked
artists of Europe"—which was disingenuous, since his praise of
Christiana ten years before had been of a public performance.
Dickens ended his letter with a disclaimer: "I have not the least
knowledge of music I only love it,"[20] the lapse in punctuation perhaps
signalling his state of embarrassment, but he was not so much caught
in poor musical judgment here as, perhaps, in his usual hyperbole
when responding to a performance, and his tendency to swing in the
opposite direction when enthusiasm had, for whatever reason, cooled.
    There is much other evidence of Dickens' knowledge of music.
He was apparently familiar with musical terms, at least enough so that
he could transmit to Frank Stone George Hogarth's advice that, for a
picture, "the proposed title *Adagio con moto* would be 'quite ridiculous
and preposterous, and would involve a most extravagant musical
mistake', but that *Andante con moto* would be perfectly correct."   He

knew that the little fiddle carried by dancing masters was called a "kit," and seems to have been aware that in the first half of the nineteenth century the piano was not thought a proper instrument for men.[21] He knew that the flute unscrews into three pieces, and was aware that there are two methods for providing wind for an organ (a "blower," and foot pedals). Answering a query about a reference in one of his novels, he wrote, "I know a bassoon by sight pretty well, and have some reason to, having had a part of my childhood haunted by musical instruments of every description." He knew at least enough of church bells to speak, in *Barnaby Rudge*, of a "triple bob major." He was confident enough of his own judgment—and apparently of its reputation among others—to assure J. G. Lockhart, when seeking his permission to have Henry Austin set his *Spanish Ballads* to music, that he could "answer for his music being appropriate to the words, and full of melody. . . ."[22]

He selected (of course) the music to be performed at the several plays which he directed: at the benefit performances for Hunt and Poole at Manchester he decided, "I should like to have the Overture to Fra Diavolo, before the Comedy; the Overture to La Gazza Ladra, before the interlude; and the Overture to Massaniello before the Farce. The Music between the Acts, as cheerful as possible." For the plays given in 1848, he permitted a little more selection by others, only indicating the kind of music he wanted: "before the Merry Wives, it must be something Shakespearean. Before Animal Magnetism, something very telling and light—like Fra Diavolo. Wednesday night's music 'in a concatenation accordingly', and jolly little Polkas and Quadrilles between the pieces. . . . If any additional strength should really be required in the Orchestra, so be it." Lightwood says that he was "frequently his own bandmaster and director of the music." The theater in Tavistock House had a "small but efficient orchestra."[23]

Dickens clearly believed in the power of music to improve the human spirit. Its best influence lay, naturally, in its support of the imagination: it was a part of that Christmas tree which symbolized his

earliest imaginative life, and he spoke of it in connection with imagination as part of his first awareness: "I feel in a half kind of
fancy, remembering the wonderful things which music has of course
suggested to me from my earliest childhood. . . . As long as
mankind lived, and loved, and hoped, so long music, which draws
them upward in all their varying and erring moods, could never cease
out of the world."   Music, he said, "is suggestive of all fancies.
You know it can give back the dead; it can place at your side the
congenial creature dear to you who never lived.   You know that the
blind see in it; the bedridden have hope in it, the dead hear it."   It
is no surprise that he liked music as a part of worship: he expressed
his pleasure at finding in the Reverend Edward Taylor's Seamen's
Bethel in Boston "a little choir of male and female singers, a violincello, and a violin," and noted that "the service commenced with a
hymn."   Observing one of the Ragged Schools, he heard the class
end with

> a hymn, sung in a subdued tone, and in very good time and
> tune. . . .   Separated from [the students'] miserable bodies,
> the effect of their voices, united in this strain, was infinitely
> solemn.   It was as if their souls were singing—as if the
> outward differences that parted us had fallen away, and the
> time was come when all the perverted good that was in
> them, or that ever might have been in them, arose implor-
> ingly to heaven.[24]

It is no surprise, either, that Dickens was affected by music in such
humble surroundings, as well as in great cathedrals.   And it certainly
is no surprise that he used music in a simile to describe how he felt
when a good audience responded to one of his readings: "like the
touch of a beautiful instrument."   He took especial pleasure, one
remembers, when an audience of simple people "got" the message of
his readings, believing that all men and women are capable of
responding to art; the same was true of music: the common man in

Italy, he wrote, "has a decided natural liking for it.   The Italian Opera being rather dear . . . , [his] taste is not highly cultivated; still, music pleases and softens him, and he takes such recreation in the way of hearing it as his small means can buy."   The connection between taste and money, rather than class, is instructive.   One of Dickens' pieces contains a scene in which poor people are found enjoying a musical performance, apparently much more than are people at the opera.[25]

If music could not soothe the savage beast, it could soften the female breast, and Dickens urged Miss Coutts that in their work at Urania Cottage for wayward women they should include

> Music, as a means towards our end. . . .   I think it extremely important that the assistant should at least be able to play simple Tunes on the Piano; and I am looking about, high and low, for a cheap second-hand one. . . .   The fondness for music among these people generally, is most remarkable; and I can imagine nothing more likely to impress or soften a new comer, than finding them with this art among them. . . ."

He soon followed up the idea with a request to John Hullah, who taught choral singing, for a teacher of music at Urania: "I am very anxious for the instruction beginning without delay, as I attach immense importance to its refining influences."   Two months later he was pressing Miss Coutts to approve of lessons twice a week: Hullah "is so very earnest about the twice a week, and in his representations of trials once a week having always failed, that I trust you will . . . let the thing be tried. . . .   Two hours in the week is not much— each lesson is only an hour long—and there is nothing necessary to be prepared between lesson and lesson."   Later letters continued to urge the benefits,[26] but in September he was obliged to inform Hullah— carefully refraining from any comment—that Miss Coutts had decided to terminate the "scientific kind of instruction" given by "Mr.

Bannister" in favor of "some female teacher of lower qualifications" more suitable to the girls' need of "devotion and relaxation, rather than . . . abstract study or accomplishment." Perhaps Dickens kept after Miss Coutts: in the following year, it was arranged that a "single weekly lesson" should be given by Hullah, which sounds like a compromise. Finally, not even that worked out: in December of 1849 Dickens wrote Miss Coutts that teaching under Hullah at Urania Cottage "is at an end." But Dickens continued to favor music in the lives of humble people; in Lowell, Massachusetts, he imagined that it would startle many Englishmen to find that in that working town "there is a joint-stock piano in a great many of the boarding houses." And, in the midst of his indignation at American slavery, he was glad to find that in places Negroes were allowed to sing while working: he listened while "some twenty sang a hymn in parts, and sang it by no means ill. . . ."[27]

He was not infrequently responsible for the inclusion of music on public occasions: in addition to selecting music for the plays he directed, he proposed to John Hullah that he "form a chorus of your people" (i.e., his students) to sing "God Save the Queen" at the command benefit for Macready, about to leave for the United States, and the performance was given. And when he planned a dinner for R. H. Horne when that friend left for Australia, he noted that "Coote is coming as a guest—and a piano." He wrote the Duke of Devonshire that he hoped to form a band of students from the Royal Academy of Music to play the overture for *Not So Bad as We Seem*. And music was an important part of his private life. "When at home," says Lightwood, "he was fond of having music in the evening." Among noted musicians who played there were Joseph Joachim, Clara Novello, Charles Halle, William S. Bennett, and Pauline Viardot; among musical friends were Thomas Moore, Mendelssohn, Meyerbeer, Jenny Lind, Francesco Berger, and Arthur Sullivan.[28] To the last of these, regarding his music for the *Tempest*, Dickens wrote, "I don't pretend to know much about music, but I do know that I have been listening to a very great work." At times while his family and guests were singing and playing he would read, but also listen attentively: his daughter told of an incident in which he jumped up from his book to correct a singing error. Courtesy obliged him to endure bad music by guests in his own house, but at times he managed to strike back:

> One night a gentleman visitor insisted on singing "By the sad sea waves," which he did vilely, and he wound up his performance by a most unexpected embellishment, or "turn." Dickens found the whole ordeal very trying, but managed to preserve a decorous silence till this sound fell on his ear, when his neighbor said to him, "Whatever did he mean by that extraneous effort of melody?" "Oh," said Dickens, "that's quite in accordance with rule. When things are at their worst they always take a *turn.*

Music continued to be a part of his home life to the end of his days: in the last summers at Gad's Hill Mamie "played and sang all his favorite tunes and songs" for her father."[29]

Fewer musicians applied to Dickens for help than did artists, playwrights, and novelists. In 1848 he wrote to John L. Hatton, pianist, conductor, singer, and composer of songs, to say that he knew no musical persons in the United States to whom he could give Hatton an introduction for his anticipated tour, but that he was glad to testify to his merits as musician and composer. And inasmuch as he was not a gifted amateur in music, as he was in drama, Dickens' participation in organizations devoted to music was much more limited. But he gave of his time when called on, chairing for example the annual meeting of the Royal Society of Musicians in 1860,[30] and demonstrated his interest in the welfare of musicians in several comments in his letters and articles. If music was not for Dickens the powerful force that drama was, if it did not take up as much of his aesthetic life as art did, it was nevertheless a continuing interest and activity. Like them, its primary appeal seems to have been the human story, replete with human feeling, that it could convey, with ballad and lieder (and to a lesser extent opera) offering the greatest appeal. Though he appreciated and probably could judge other kinds of music more fully than has been thought, his love of things human held sway here as it did everywhere.

6

Poetry: Earnest Admiration

Dickens' interest in poetry is not often mentioned, no doubt because his own efforts in that genre were negligible. But if his verse deserves little attention, his experience of poetry rewards study, for it extends our awareness of his wide reading and adds to our understanding of his knowledge of literature and of his aesthetic. Dickens was active in the field of poetry: he read a good deal, wrote occasional verse, and as editor struggled to maintain poetic standards in his journals. Some of his comments on poetry, as in music, seem more concerned with content than with quality: his judgment may have been at times affected by congenial ideas, attitudes, and feelings. Nevertheless, he seems to have understood the elements of poetry—he comments upon meter, rhythm, and such devices as inversion—and he had definite ideas about how figures of speech should be employed (he shares Ogden Nash's suspicion of extensive use of metaphor, for example). He spoke too of such things as how a poet should see, as well as present, his concept. He loved poetry which elicited emotional response, of course, but he had a healthy dislike of the false, the fey, the artificial—of "twaddle"; he abominated the poetic pose. He preferred in poetry that which was novel, picturesque, graceful, and natural. He was sensitive to such an infelicity as the derivative, and knew enough poetry to recognize it. As editor, he picked out and en-

couraged young talent, though he was not infallible in his judgment;
beyond his work as editor, he gave unstintingly of his time to any
hack who sought his opinion.　On all such he urged the delight of
writing verse for one's own enjoyment, and the potential agony of
trying to write it for a living.

Much of Dickens' experience of poetry came from his work as
editor.　Arthur Adrian says that a study of the poems in Dickens'
journals reveals "some interesting aspects of his editorial policy: the
contributors to whom he catered, the types of offering he considered
suitable for a popular periodical, and the critical criteria he applied in
his selection."　Among important poets, George Meredith was the
most frequently published in *Household Words*; others were Landor,
Hunt, Coventry Patmore, Thomas Hood the younger, and Richard
Blackmore.　Several of Dickens' friends were represented—Bulwer,
Horne, Edmund Yates, Charles Kent, Chauncey Hare Townshend, to
name a few—but friendship was not in itself an admission ticket:
poems by Locker-Lampson and Laman Blanchard were rejected, "the
latter," Adrian says, "in one of the most memorable notes in editorial
history.　Having submitted some verses entitled 'Orient Pearls at
Random Strung,' [Blanchard] got them back again with the comment,
'Dear Blanchard, too much string—Yours, C. D.'" Dickens insisted
that poetry be part of his journals:　among other ideas for things to
be included in *Household Words* was that it should be "always having,
if possible, a little good poetry . . ."; he told Forster that he wanted
to have "poetry in every number if possible. . . ." It did not always
turn out to be possible: letters to his subeditor Wills mention poem
after poem that had "absolutely nothing whatever in it. . . ." Typical
comments are "The game is really not worth the candle,"[1] and "a
thousand times worse than nothing and won't do."　"We are better
without a Poem than with a Poem without an idea.　Don't put in
'The Best.'"　By 1858, he was begging: "Pray, pray, *pray*, don't
have Poems unless they are good.　We are immeasurably better
without them.　'Beyond' is really Beyond anything I ever saw, in
utter badness."　And by 1862 he gave strict orders: "On no con-

sideration put in any Poem that I have not seen. When I come upon
a strange Poem in print and publication, my distress is abject."[2]

He found so little good verse that he was obliged to make com-
promises: "Taboo (for the present, certainly) the Poem. I think it
very bad." Again, "The Poem is so very poor, that it had better
come out bodily until we have a very strong number. The metre is
so wretchedly made out." He included many a poem because there
was nothing better: of a group submitted by R. H. Horne in 1852 he
judged "one of his poems very indifferent,"[3] but put them all in.
When he could, he tried to improve salvagable ones: a poem by one
Hobson, "so poor a thing," had "awful haltings . . . but I have
made the best of it." And of another:

> I have bothered and worried at the Poem (which is neither
> English, nor verse) hoping to make something of it, but have
> not succeeded after all. Strike it out. If I can fuse into it
> an idea I have of its natural end, you shall have it in the
> next parcel. If you hear no more of it, give it up as un-
> mendable.

Frequently he tried to get the poet to improve his work: he asked
Wills to return to W. C. Bennett his "The Deeds of Wellington,"
asking him, "if he should observe a halting line anywhere, [to] make
it bolder if he can." Of something submitted for the Christmas
Number of 1855 he said, "The Poem must really be polished before
it can appear: it is so painfully defective and broken. . . ."[4]

Apparently he did not publish poetry in a foreign language; he
wrote to Wills, "Howitt, all right. But take his German poetry out
altogether, or make him render it in English also."[5] The practise is
consistent with Dickens' idea of the audience for his journals: largely
middle class, the lower levels of which would not bilingual.

There is constant effort to improve the quality of poetry in a
number. "I don't see anything in the 'Children in the Wood' except
a power of making nothing out of a most beautiful story. The

enclosed little poem by Townshend is far better (I have two more in hand), and will improve the No. as a substitution for the present." And again:

> You say you have a stronger Poem. If so, and you can get it into this No. instead of the Sonnet, it will be a decided improvement. "Marie's Fever" is so twaddly that I should like to see something stronger in the place of a "literary Lady's Maid." The No. becomes horribly weak in that place.

But the last poem was included in the issue of July 30, causing Dickens to write that "'a Literary Lady's Maid' and 'Corporate Dreams,' coming together, make me thrill and shudder with indescribable anguish." He seems to have been particularly careful of the tone of poetry in the Christmas numbers: "No to the Poem. There is no good in it; it is conceited and morbid; directly counter to the spirit of the Xmas No." Detailed commentary in the letters to Wills demonstrates that he read the poems carefully.[6]

When he found any talent at all he tried to cultivate it; he wrote Wills of one such unidentified writer that "The young poet is not quite to any purpose at present, but I would certainly encourage him." And he did find good material: "The Poem is very good," he said of one printed in the 11/8/62 issue of *All the Year Round.* Of a poem by Robert Lytton: ". . . Decidedly Yes, as being novel and picturesque." And of another group of submitted verse: "Yes to the Poems—too golden-haired, and marble, and all that; but meritorious I think."[7]

Only a few poets are afforded continuing editorial comment by Dickens; the best—Meredith, for example—are hardly mentioned, for the obvious reason that Dickens needed to say little about them to his subeditor, and the worst are named only to be obliviated. William Cox Bennett is mentioned on more than one occasion; he did not always please Dickens (no lesser poet in his stable ever did). Of a long poem, probably by Bennett, entitled "The Deeds of Wellington," Dickens queried Wills, "Do you think it would be worth while to publish the enclosed, with an alteration here and there, in next Wednesday's Number—so as just to catch the funeral? I hate the thing myself, but it might go down with a good many."[8]

He liked Ollier, a regular contributor, but was occasionally critical of his work. In 1850 he wrote a letter to him, saying that *Household Words* would accept "good occasional contributions," but declining to offer "any regular employment to Mr. Ollier." Two years later he called him "an excellent and true young poet, as I think," but only one other reference is positive. His first mention of him to Wills is in regard to a line he used from Byron, which he told Wills to get Ollier to change. And another poem, "Amy's Return," he called "so full of strange conceits and strange metre, that I am very doubtful of it. . . ." But Ollier's "A Vision of Old Babylon," printed in *Household Words* in 1856, drew approval, though with qualification: . . . Very good. But it is a remarkable thing, especially when that contrast is to be presented between the flourishing and the wasted Babylon, that thriving city has not a single living figure in it! It is a very curious example of the incomplete way in which some writers see their pictures." As we have seen, Dickens liked to see people in pictures: without drama, what was there in anything? The final comment on Ollier is negative: a poem submitted by him "is maudlin,"[9] and should be omitted.

The only other poet of interest in the editorial correspondence is Mary Berwick, whom Dickens soon discovered to be Adelaide Anne Procter, daughter of the poet. His first acceptance of her submitted work was tentative: "I have given Miss Berwick's 'Knight Errant,' the benefit of the doubt, and sent it to the Printers. The Spring lines I re-enclose. I would decline them, on the ground that after the Spring Sonnet we have settled Spring for this year." But when he learned her identity, he wrote to her to convey "my congratulations on the delicacy and talent of your writing. . . . You have given me so much pleasure, and have made me shed so many tears, that I can only think of you now in association with the sentiment and grace of your verse." Perhaps in the eight months between the two comments Miss Berwick's verse had improved, but probably Dickens simply thought better of her work when he learned that her talent was inherited. Later he was to say, according to Forster, that "In the spring of the year 1853 I observed a short poem among the proferred contributors, very different, as I thought, from the shoal of verses perpetually setting through the office. . . ." Either Miss Berwick submitted something a year before the first reference I have found, which is in 1854, or Dickens mistook the year as much as he misremembered, or misreprented, his first reaction. James Lightwood said that many of Berwick's "sacred verses have found their way into our hymnals,"[10] but I have discovered none in the Episcopal *Hymnal* of 1940.

It hardly need be added that Dickens' critical advice was sought by many who hoped, not that he would include their work in his journals, but that he would both improve them by his critical comment and help them get published elsewhere. With but few exceptions, Dickens steadfastly refused to attempt the second, but always courteously undertook the first. To a Mrs. Price he wrote that "I regret to say that I am quite powerless to assist you in the publication of your poems," and also tried gently to dissuade her from trying to get them into print: ". . . Your verses . . . are very agreeable and womanly, but I do not discern in the specimens you have sent me, any novelty, either of thought or expression, that is likely to attract attention." A young man named Samuel Newton received similar advice:

> . . . You have a facility of versification, and . . . can can sometimes express your thoughts in a spirited and rapid manner. Whether there is sufficient originality in the thoughts themselves, or in the form of their expression, to constitute you a Poet . . . is a question I will not take upon myself to decide. . . . Think of the vast crowd of young

men who can write verse, and of the handful who can write poetry. . . .[11]

The date of the letter tells us something of the time Dickens gave to aspiring writers, even those without talent: it was written on New Year's Day.

Though he did not involve himself in getting poets into print, Dickens did on occasion try to help them financially; he did not limit his assistance to the talented poet. Writing to Miss Coutts in 1849, he asked for her permission to "put you down as a Suscriber to a certain book of poetry" by Charles Whitehead, not because the book (*The Solitary, and Other Poems*) had any merit, but because Whitehead was the author, "some years ago, of a very clever novel indeed, called Richard Savage," and was now indigent. Dickens wrote similar letters to Carlyle, Milnes, Bulwer, and Macready, calling Whitehead "no utterer of base coin in rhyme"—apparently as much as he could bring himself to say about the poetry. Four years before, he had advised Whitehead that ". . . Poetry is a dangerous pursuit . . . of all other most unlikely ever to lead you to fame, happiness, or profit."[12] Given the opportunity now to say "I told you so," his effort instead to assist the struggling writer is positively Pickwickian.

Poetasters would seem to have pursued Dickens as eagerly as beggars of all descriptions did: in Glasgow on a reading tour, he reported that he was "in close hiding from a local poet who had christened his infant son in my name, and consequently haunts the building." On one of the few occasions on which Dickens did try to help a poet get published, he wrote to Evans, seconding the effort of R. H. Horne to secure his firm as publisher, saying, "He has written some remarkable poems in H. W.—as the Electric Telegraph, the Christmas Carols, the Camera Obscura, and so forth."[13] His frequent protestations that he had little influence with publishers would appear to have been correct: the offer was declined by Bradbury and Evans.

The poet to whom Dickens offered the most advice was his adopted working man, John Overs. In October of 1839, Overs sent him several "Songs," apparently on the months: Dickens thought the one on May "extremely pretty," but suggested that Overs send it to a publisher without the others: "I think you succeed most when you are not comical. . . ." Even this little encouragement may have been kindness rather than objective judgment, a partial compensation for his rejection of a verse play Overs had sent him the previous month: ". . . The verse contains most singular instances of inverted expression (which I may describe more familiarly as putting the cart before the horse) and many words not to be found in the language. . . ." By the end of the year, Dickens was trying to discourage Overs' poetic efforts: ". . . In nine tenths of the distressing cases" of struggling writers who were "made known to me," he said, "there is as much natural ability as in yours . . . although it has seldom developed itself under the same disadvantages." He tried to express to Overs the agony of the writer whose occasional publication of a piece here and there encourages him to dream of making his living by such a means. "If a ballad were printed here or a paper accepted there, do you think you would better your condition or be a happier man? I am bound to tell you—having the miseries of such a condition urged upon me by hundreds every day and hour of my life—that you would not." But Overs persevered, and Dickens continued to help him. In 1840 he wrote that he had "read your Legend of Canterbury with great interest and pleasure. It would have been a most creditable performance to anybody. . . ."[14] Near the end of the year, he commented that of a pair of "Profiles" Overs had sent to *George Cruikshank's Omnibus* "The Postillion is much the better of the two." In 1841 he wrote him that his poem, "The Trysting Tree," published in the *Kentish Coronal*, was "a very good song . . ." and later that year thanked him for sending his "verses, which are very good." Three years later, he was still looking over his humble friend's work, offering criticism and advice on publication: "I have marked here and there such slight observations as occurred to me. I think it very good all things considered, though here and there a little obscured and forced." Dickens suggested procedure for submitting it for publication, but declared himself "not hopeful."[15] In that year Overs died, and the kind exertions of Dickens ended at last.   His efforts to nurture this slight talent may be contrasted with the response of Harrison Ainsworth who, when he took over *Bentley's Miscellany*, immediately advised Overs to confine himself to prose.   No doubt Ainsworth was right, which will make Dickens' efforts seem to some merely foolish, but perhaps to others only the more generous.

Another aspiring poet whom Dickens tried to help was a young clerk named Robert S. Horrell, who sent him verse which he could write, as he said, only in spare moments.   In one of the busiest years of his life, Dickens replied in as long a letter as he ever wrote, finding all the kind things he could possibly say, offering judicious criticism, and trying gently to discourage Horrell, not from writing, but from dreaming of making his living as a poet.

First, as the more grateful task, let me say what I have to say of praise. . . . A love of the good and beautiful, and a desire to illustrate it in one so circumstanced is always a thing to be commended—to be very highly commended.   It should increase your own happiness whether it adds to the happiness and entertainment of mankind or no, and from pursuits so worthy and humanizing, I would not turn you aside by one encouraging word.   The pursuit of excellence in any path which has the light of Truth upon it, is in the abstract, a noble employment, and like the search for the Philosopher's Stone will reward you with a hundred incidental discoveries though you fall short of the one great object of your desire.

Beyond this, I think that you have many good thoughts—occasionally a power of expressing them, very simply and well—a love of nature and all creation—and, of course, (for these are its necessary companions) deep feeling and strong sympathy.

On the other hand, you have much to learn.

Dickens told Horrell his verse was "harsh and irregular," his "conceits strained and unnatural," and his imagery "fraught with more sound than sense." He cited examples:

> To spell a tiger from all thoughts of harm—to clasp blood springs with tendril fingers (which appears difficult, to say the least)—to make the sun unfurl his bannered robe—to engrave words with fire—to describe the birds as couching with gasping pants of bliss—to tear a man to pieces with links—to fold love's banner o'er a lady's brow—are so near absurdities that I hardly know what else to call them. You may find, I know, startling and monstrous conceits in the writings of our greatest Poets; but you must remember that *they* were great, not because of these blots, but in despite of them, having for every one a crowd of beautiful and grand thoughts which bore down all before them. Never imitate the eccentricities of genius, but toil after it in its truer flights. They are not easy to follow, but they lead to higher regions.
>
> You have too much about faery land, and faery things—by far too much mention of nerves and heart strings— more agonies of despondency than suit my taste—mysterious promptings too in your own heart which are much better there, than anywhere else. It is not the province of a Poet to harp upon his own discontents, or to teach other people that they ought to be discontented. Leave Lord Byron to his gloomy greatness, and do you
>
> Find tongues in trees, books in the running brooks,
> Sermons in stone, and good in everything.

The remarks on startling conceits may explain why Dickens does not mention the metaphysical poets; possibly the distaste for "mysterious promptings" helps to explain why he, according to Forster, disliked Wordsworth. Dickens went on to praise a poem apparently called "The Young Painter's Last Dream," which "pleased me very much in its opening; the change of time and coming on of morning are very beautifully described, and the aspect of his room and the familiar things about it I really think *highly* of." But he objected strongly to the sad end of the poem, suggesting that Horrell had "quite perverted its proper object and intention."

> To make that face his comfort and trust—to fill him with the assurance of meeting it one day in Heaven—to make him, dying, attended, as it were, by an angel of his own creation—to inspire him with gentle visions of the reality sitting by his bedside and shedding a light even on the dark path of Death—and so to let him gently pass away, whispering of it and seeking the hand to clasp in his—would be to complete a very affecting and moving picture. But, to have him struggling with Death in all its horrors, yelling about foul fiends and bats' wings, with starting eyes and rattles in his throat, is a ghastly, sickening, hideous end, with no beauty, no moral, nothing in it but a repulsive and most painful idea. If he had been the hero of an epic in seventy books, and had out-Lucifered Lucifer in every line of them, you could scarcely have punished him at last in a more revolting manner. . . .

Dickens never understood ugliness for its own sake in art; if Horrell's character was to die a terrible death, he ought to deserve it. Dickens commented upon a few more poems, finding one too much like "a song of Mr. Lover's," another "very good," and closing with very slight encouragement, and practical advice.

> . . . I don't think you would ever find a publisher for a
> volume of such compositions. . . . There are a great many
> people who write as well—many who write better. . . . At
> the same time, I see no objection to your sending some
> piece of moderate length . . . to such a Magazine as
> Blackwood's; and no improbability—no unusual improbability
> I mean—in the way of its acceptance and insertion. If you
> do this, give yourself the advantage of plain penmanship and
> a sheet of paper large enough to hold the lines, or it will
> never be read. And don't write to the Editor to tell him
> who you are or what you are, for he will care very little
> about that, and the public will care less.

And he finished with advice about writing similar to that which he
had given to Overs:

> You wish to know whether you do right in sacrificing
> so much time to what may fail at last. If you do so at the
> cost of any bitterness of heart, or any disgust with the
> employment in which you are engaged, you certainly do
> *wrong.* If you have the strength of mind to do your duty
> cheerfully, and to make these toils a relaxation and solace of
> which nobody can deprive you, you do *right.*

He advised Horrell to send something he had written "carefully and to
please yourself" to several magazines, and, if "each failure bring with
it vexation and disappointment, lock up your papers, burn your pen,
and thank Heaven you are not obliged to live by it."[16] Good advice,
no doubt, though if every writer heeded it probably few would ever be
published. But what impresses one most about this letter is its
length: the amount of time that Dickens was willing to expend upon
fellow writers of virtually no talent is astonishing.

Horrell apparently answered the long letter with a flurry of
excuses for his faults; Dickens was again kind enough to answer him
at length, but far too committed to conscientious writing to tolerate the

alibis; he sternly lectured his young pupil for excusing faults instead of eradicating them.[17] Not even this, though, could make Dickens give up on Horrell: in April of the year he offered encouragement, and further detailed criticism:

> . . . I suggest to you that in lieu of the "shriek" at page 5, a groan or a sigh or murmur would be more in consonance with the spirit of the piece. At page 7 marred is awkward I think. Sullied would be better. And going back to page 5 again, I would rather see "good creature" or something to that effect than "Ha! woman" when he is apostrophizing the nurse.

The following year, he violated one of his rules and tried to help Horrell get into print. "He . . . has decided ability," he wrote Harrison Ainsworth, now editor of *Bentley's Miscellany*, and sent him a Horrell poem: "I think it very pretty, and I have no doubt you will also. But it is Poetry, and may be too long." Dickens' last letter to Horrell, not long before Horrell died, shows him still trying to help the modest talent by sending pieces to Ainsworth, now for possible inclusion in *Ainsworth's Magazine*.[18]

It hardly need be added that Dickens rarely volunteered opinion on published work sent him, and never forced his opinion, of poetry or anything else, upon anybody. A favorite device of his to avoid offering judgment of things sent him—probably when such opinion, if honest, would have been unfavorable—was to thank the sender before, Dickens would say, he had time to read it, though he was looking forward to doing so.[19]

It is difficult to draw conclusions from Dickens' comments upon the efforts of aspiring poets when their efforts are not available to us. He seems to have had a good grasp of mechanics, at least so much as enabled him to discern elementary faults in meter and imagery, though he did identify one poem as blank verse that was actually in fourteeners. His letter to Horrell shows his dislike of bombast, rantings. and posturings; as in all art, he liked the natural, and reacted against anything he considered strained or artificial. Also, he rejected negative content which struck him as unnecessary: pessimism often seemed to him to be either pointless or a pose, and he particularly disliked violently sorrowful endings that in his judgment damaged the potential positive thrust of the work. Many of his comments are directed to content, not to form; some of these support the judgment that he often assessed art more by what it said than how it said it. "By Rail to Parnassus" (again, this is probably by Henry Morley, but bears at least the approval, and perhaps something of the hand, of Dickens) certainly is so inclined: after quoting verse by Hunt in prose form. the speaker in the piece says that "those words stand in the book [*Stories in Verse*] line under line because they are poetry; but they speak quite as well to the heart written like prose, straight on together—also because they are poetry." (If I understand this correctly, Dickens' point is that line division is not essential.) The narrator also comments that Hunt's stories "are only told in verse in order that the music may give force and beauty to the sense . . ." which sounds uncomfortably close to the eighteenth-century idea that form is but an external decoration laid upon content. Not infrequently Dickens' comments on a poet are confined to his content: thus he tells Samuel Rogers that he is "a Poet whose writings (as all the World knows) are replete with generous and earnest feeling. . . ."[20]

Whether such comments are prompted by inattention to form or are a means of avoiding comment on form when such comment would be derogatory, however, is a question not easily to be decided; all one can do is advise once more against the conclusion that, because Dickens did not do something, he could not do it. Certainly there are instances in which it would be easy to decide that Dickens liked a poem solely for its content, but which offer evidence that he could also have been attracted by quality of composition. He wrote, for example, to David M. Moir, physician and author, encouraging him to publish his *Domestic Verses*. It is tempting to judge that Dickens liked these poems because they were on a favorite theme of his: the

death of children (four of Moir's)—even when handled by an amateur
poet; Dickens' letter speaks of the "tenderness and pathos" of the
verse. But Wordsworth, Tennyson, Warren, and Jeffrey also urged
publication of the book, surely not solely because of its content.
Some of Dickens' attention to subject rather than form is valid literary
opinion: Stang points out that in several articles in his journals
"Dickens insisted that the conventional subject matter of poetry was
worn out and that the poet should turn to the products of the in-
dustrial revolution taking place around him, which he was studiously
trying to ignore." "Poets," he said, "should take their material
chiefly from actual life." A letter to Wills about a book of poems by
John Critchley Prince, entitled *Hours with the Muses*, comments both
on the quality of his verse and, constructively, of his content:

> The faults of Prince's poems, besides its [*sic*] intrinsic mean-
> ness as a composition, is, that it goes too glibly with the
> comfortable idea (of which we have had a great deal too
> much in England since the Continental commotions) that a
> man is to sit down and make himself domestic and meek, no
> matter what is done to him.

At the very least, he was obviously aware that even the best subject
could be ruined by poor form, as he showed when he rejected a story
for *Household Words* because it showed only the "power of making
nothing out of a most beautiful story."[21]

A little of what Dickens wrote gives some idea of the extent or
quality of his knowledge of poetry. He recognized the similarity of
one of Horrell's poems to one by Lover, which suggests familiarity
with contemporary poetry. He seems to have been capable of discussing poetry with poets, and to have been familiar with American as
well as British poetry: Poe told James Russell Lowell that he and
Dickens had, as the editors of the Pilgrim Edition *Letters* put it, "two
long interviews in the course of which they discussed American
poetry. . . ."[22] In 1842 he sent Lady Holland a book of American

verse, probably Rufus Griswold's *Poets and Poetry of America* (1842),
with comments upon some of the poets.   His letters and speeches
demonstrate a familiarity with a respectable number of English poets;
assuming that he did not comment upon every poet he read, his
reading of verse may be considered as rather more than average for
an educated English gentleman, always with the exception of those
classical writers forced upon the attention in formal education.

Without a doubt Dickens admired poetry as a genre, but there is
nothing to suggest that he considered it a higher art than prose.   He
disliked assumption of airs in any would-be or real genius,. but he
seems particularly offended by poets who insisted upon being Poets,
perhaps thereby expressing his resentment of those who felt poetry to
be supreme.   When he wrote his Introduction to Adelaide Procter's
Legends and Lyrics, he made this clear:

> No claim can be set up for her, thank God, to the posses-
> sion of any of the conventional poetical qualities.   She never
> by any means held the opinion that she was among the
> greatest of human beings; she never suspected the existence
> of a conspiracy in the part of mankind against her; she
> never recognized in her best friends, her worst enemies; she
> never cultivated the luxury of being misunderstood and un-
> appreciated; she would rather have died without seeing a line
> of her composition in print, than that I should have maun-
> dered about her, here, as "the Poet," or "the Poetess."[23]

Little need be said about Dickens' own verse.   There is far less
of it than any other kind of writing he attempted, but he did try his
hand from time to time, beginning perhaps with jingles he is said to
have written for advertisements of Warren's blacking.   He offered a
weak love poem to Maria Beadnell at age nineteen and another, "The
Bill of Fare," at a private party; later Dickens said he thought the
lines of the first of these worthy of the Devil, "For I'm sure they're
devilish bad," and anticipated that the reader of the second would say

"a bad one it is," a prediction which Angus Wilson among others proved true. Dickens entered an occasional poem in one or the other of the journals with which he was connected; one such is "Song of the North," which he informed Forster he had written for Bentley. He liked to spice up a letter now and then with doggerel or a parody, as in a letter to Mrs. Colden, a parody of Gray's "Elegy" in a letter to Mary Boyle, and a take-off of Moore's "Lesbia hath a bearing eye" to Lemon.[24] Much of his public verse was written to occasion, as was his prologue to Marsdon's *The Patrician's Daughter*, an effort which drew modest praise from the *Examiner*. Dickens had, by "impressing the audience strongly with the scope and purpose of what they had come to see, thoroughly prepared them for welcome and applause." The question no doubt was whether the audience needed such preparation; the *Morning Post* was less gentle, calling it "milk and water," at best "doubtless a very pretty academical exercise." Kitton commented that the poem had "dignified and vigorous lines. . . ." Whatever its merits, Dickens seems to have given the Prologue his usual careful attention: he made a number of changes of words in his second draft, and completely revised the last three lines.[25]

Kitton thought that the Ballad from the sixth chapter of *Pickwick Papers* was "perhaps the most acceptable of all Dickens' poetical efforts." It was set to music by his brother-in-law Henry Burnett, and drew approval from Walter Savage Landor. "Acceptable" is the best that can be said for the ballad: it does have some pleasing sound patterns, but is in monotonously regular lines of alternating iambic tetrameter and trimeter, with all the words in just the right places, and with cliches, no imagery, and one cart before its horse: "scattered been." Another poem, "Romance," from Chapter 43 of *Pickwick Papers*, also elicited some praise: Percy Fitzgerald thought that "Mr. Weller's song . . . is superior to anything of the kind that had appeared since," and Sir Frederick Bridge, organist of Westminster Abbey, set it to music in the late nineteenth century, and reported that "It has had a very great success. . . ." Another poem, "A Word in

Season," published in *The Keepsake* of 1843, was remembered by the *London Review* in 1866 as "a graceful and sweet apologue, reminding one of the manner of Hood." Forster called it "a clever and pointed parable in verse," and Kitton later judged it "a thoughtful little poem," but Dickens later satirized its theme in Chadband of *Bleak House*. Kitton quotes appreciation of two other poems: "The Hymn of the Wiltshire Laborers," in the *Daily News*, which one reviewer said "breathes in every line the teachings of the Sermon on the Mount," and "The Song of the Wreck" in *The Lighthouse*, which A. W. Ward considered "a most successful effort in Cowper's manner." Later critics have not been so kind: Humphrey House strikes the standard tone when he calls Dickens' hymn in *The Wreck of the Golden Mary* "a pale and spiritless affair. . . . Not a syllable falls out of accepted commonplace; there is hardly a trace of interest even." Dickens anticipated all such negative judgment in "Lodgings to Let," in which he scribbled,

> . . . I fear my composing,
> Will be considered very prosing.[26]

For Dickens it was with poetry much as it was with drama: he could not write it, but he loved it. While the first delight of drama for him was in its appearance on the stage, poetry necessarily took him to the printed page, with by no means the total fascination he found in plays, but certainly with considerable appreciation. T. W. Hill said that poetry was well represented in his library, and added, "you may conclude that Dickens liked poetry." Dickens' works "contain more than one hundred and fifty apt quotations from fifty-three poets. . . ."[27] He seems to have liked poetry in all its forms, from ballads to Shakespeare—perhaps preferring ballads to all other forms, as has been suggested, but certainly not, as is implied, limiting his enjoyment to them. One of his favorite poems was *The Loving Ballad of Lord Bateman*, especially in the form given it by George Cruikshank, and he was an enthusiastic reader of seventeenth-century ballads; but, as in music, his enjoyment of poetry extended well into more formal literature. I have found in his correspondence reference to the following: Bryant, Bulwer, Burns, Byron, Campbell, Chaucer, Coleridge (including his translations of Schiller), Barry Cornwall (Bryan Waller Procter), Cowper, Crabbe, Dante, Catherine Fanshawe, Gay, Gray, Hood, Hunt, Juvenal, Lamartine, Landor, Longfellow, Samuel Lover, George Lyttleton, Milnes, Milton, David Moir, Moore, Pope, the Psalms, Samuel Rogers, Scott, Shakespeare, Shelley, Southey, Tennyson, Thackeray, Virgil, and Wordsworth. This does not include all the minor poets of his day, some of whom we have seen him commenting upon, and without a doubt does not include all the poets he read: Dickens was not one to talk or write about his reading, unless occasion arose for doing so. As with music, only his comments on figures of some stature or interest are given here, but many more opinions concerning lesser and unknown versifiers of his time are scattered throughout his letters. To take the poets in alphabetical order, we begin with William Cullen Bryant, to whom Dickens wrote in 1842 that he had "a thumbed book at home, so well worn that it has nothing upon the back but one gilt 'B,' and the remote possible traces of a 'y.' My credentials [for meeting Bryant in his approaching trip to the United States] are in my earnest admiration of its beautiful contents."[28]

When Dickens received poetry from a friend or from a poet he admired, he did not, as was sometimes his practise, avoid the necessity of passing judgment by writing his thanks before he read. In a letter to Bulwer he said,

> I have not written sooner to thank you for King Arthur, because I felt sure you would prefer my reading it before I should do so, and because I wished to have an opportunity of reading it with the sincerity and attention which such a composition demands.
> This I have done. I do not write to express to you the full measure of my gratification and pleasure (for I

should find that very difficult to be accomplished to my own
satisfaction) but simply to say that I have read the Poem,
and dwelt upon it, with the deepest interest, admiration, and
delight; and that I feel proud of it as a very noble instance
of the genius of a great writer of my own time.   I should
feel it a kind of treason to what has been awakened in me
by the book . . . if I were tempted into being diffuse in its
praise.

No doubt Dickens is sincere in his praise, but the lack of specific
comment is disappointing, especially after he assures Bulwer he has
read with close attention.   As always, Dickens is not eager to force
opinion upon anybody, but letters to Bulwer about his plays included
some consideration of details, while this has none.   Appreciation of
another poem by Bulwer is also limited to general praise: "I want to
tell you how deeply I have been impressed by the Boatman.   It
haunts me as only a beautiful and profound thing can.   The lines are
always running in my head, as the river runs with me."   But his last
comment on Bulwer, about his *The Lost Tales of Miletus*, finally says
something specific:

My ear instantly took to the metre.   When it changed, I
changed as easily and sympathetically. . . .   I am not
usually free from a certain inadaptible obstinacy as to
novelties in tacit rhythm, and to this hour am forced to
separate some idea of some friends of ours from the
mechanism with which they are associated—altogether to
separate the one from the other, and to express the thoughts
to my thoughts, in my own manner.
     The extraordinary beauty, picturesqueness, and com-
pleteness, of the Secret Way, . . . fascinated me. . . .
Argiope holds her place in my heart against all her
rivals. . . .   She is peerless against the world of women.
But the narrative itself, the painting in it, the distinctness at-

tained, the glowing force of it, the imagination in it and yet the terseness and closeness of it, these *astonish* me! I declare to you that I have never read any story, whatsoever the manner of its telling, so perfectly amazing to me in these respects quite apart from its winning tenderness and grace. Of Death and Sisyphus at Table—again—I have as clear and vivid a picture as if I had looked in at the window and seen them together: while the last twenty lines of that poem are most magnificent. I suppose the Orlad's Son to have been one of the most difficult of the Tales, to tell, because this legend in one form or another is the most familiar of all by far. But for a perfectly different kind of beauty, my pastoral reading can not match it; and the reed is broken by the Master hand. . . . The sacrifice of the Wife of Miletus, and the picture of the Temple in Cydippe, are the two things next distinctest in the new host.

He concluded by calling the tale, "Secret Way," "that triumph of romance," and calling the whole "this great work" of "amazing variety and wealth. . . ."[29] Here at least is reference to one detail, meter, though Dickens' confession that he separates the thought of some poetry from its form in order to respond to it is unsettling, to say the least. Most of his response to the book is to story, not poetry, and shows his usual command of elements of fiction, but hardly anything of his knowledge of verse.

Dickens did not comment at length on Byron's poetry, but he certainly did not like his life. He seems to have accepted without question the assumption of his time that Byron was a scoundrel, and all his comments on the poet indicate his conviction that Byron's morality tainted his verse. In *Childe Harold* he criticized the expressions "Dazzled and drunk with beauty" and "The heart reels with its fulness" as "less suggestive of Venus than of gin and water. . . ." As early as *Sketches by Boz*, he attacked him for, among other things, "romanticizing murderers." His "gloomy greatness" ought not to be imitated by young poets, though the phrase at least admits Byron to have genius. Still, Dickens must have liked Byron's narrative poems, for on more than one occasion he quoted them from memory: on a walk with a friend he recited six lines of *The Corsair*, and upon another he deleted "and yet it is not night" from a poem submitted to him by Ollier, because it had already been penned "in an older line, preceded by the words 'The moon is up'"; the line was from *Childe Harold*.[30]

Dickens told Thomas Campbell that he placed himself "among the admirers of your genius," but said no more than that. He made no comment on Chaucer, but did quote from "The Pardoner's Prologue." He knew and liked Barry Cornwall (B. W. Procter), spoke appreciatively of his poetry, and on several occasions wrote to thank him for a volume of verse the poet had sent him.[31] His opinion of George Crabbe diminished—"I don't think so highly of Crabbe as I once did (feeling a dreary want of fancy in his poems) . . ."—though he still thought him worthy of the attention Jeffrey had given him in his role as editor of the *Edinburgh Review*. He referred to Dante, showing knowledge of his first circle. Of Thomas Gray he said, "No poet ever came walking down to posterity with so *small* a book under his arm." He liked Thomas Hood, though he called his *Comic Annual* for 1839 "rather poor"; he gave the book a favorable review in the *Examiner* because Hood was ill.[32] He told Frederick Ward, a friend of Hood, that he had "a great regard for Hood; and hold his genius in the highest estimation." James T. Fields said that Dickens "gloried in many of Hood's poems, especially in that biting Ode to Rae Wilson. . . ." He described Hood as "a man of great power—of prodigious force and genius as a poet. . . ."[33] His comment on Leigh Hunt was not so strong, perhaps simply because the occasion of his speaking was not so productive of emotion. In 1842 he told Hunt that he had "much pleasure in seeing" his two-part poem, "The Walk" and "The Dinner," about a walk and dinner they had shared. And he called his *Poetical Works* (1844), "your companionable, and welcome, and valued book." In print, he praised Hunt's *Stories in*

Verse—

> all of them good ones, written in such verse as may be read
> by rich and poor with almost equal pleasure. . . . Read or
> print them how you will, you cannot destroy their music or
> convict them of being by a syllable too wordy; they discharge
> their burden in plain sentences, without even [ever?] going
> out of their way to avoid expressions common in the mouths
> of the people. Every picture in them is poetical in its con-
> ception, and in its expression musical. There is nothing
> far-fetched—there is no mystification; there are just stories in
> verse which may be enjoyed by the entire mass of the
> people.[34]

He lumped Hunt's "Indicator" and "Companion" together with
German novels as "convenient" reading, the sort that could be easily
taken up and as easily laid down again. But in 1855 he thanked
Hunt "for the delightful volume you have sent me. . . . I have
renewed with the utmost pleasure my acquaintance with those old
friends. . . ." And when he wrote the circular advertising dramatic
performances for Hunt's benefit, he described him as "one of the
most genial and graceful writers in the language . . . who . . . has
charmed and improved hundreds and thousands of readers. . . . He
has taught them, better than any other man, what to read, and where
to find it, and how best, by sympathy with ennobling thoughts, to
elevate things around them into sources of delight."[35] That last, of
course, was one of the mainstays of Dickens' aesthetic beliefs.

He read Juvenal: "I have been wondering at Rome that Juvenal
(which I have been always lugging out of a bag, on all occasions)
never used the fire-flies for an illustration." He called Lamartine "a
writer of . . . distinguished and eminent genius" with "beautiful
productions," though the poet's liberal convictions may have attracted
him as much as his talent: Tillotson says he may also have admired
Lamartine's "romantic feeling for nature. . . ." Of course he

admired Landor, after whom he named a son; in 1853 he thanked him for dedicating his "great book" to him.   He called Landor's "Imaginary Conversation" (between Aesop and Rhodope) in *The Book of Beauty* (1845) "among the most charming, profound, and delicate productions I have ever read."   And in reviewing Forster's book on Landor he said that "Landor's fame very surely awaits him,"[36] though he also admitted the point was arguable.

Dickens was an admirer of Longfellow.   ". . . A fine writer," he called him in 1842, and pointed especially to his poems in a book of American verse sent to a friend: "Mr.   Longfellow's pieces are very good."   Commenting on something of his, probably the first two books of *Voices of the Night*, he said, "I really believe them to be nearly all equally good."   In two successive letters the same year he called Longfellow "the best of the American poets. . . ."   Among prospective titles for *Household Words* was "The Forge," taken from Longfellow's poem.   Two months before his death, in a speech at the Newsvendor's Benevolent Institution, he cited "the great name of" Longfellow.[37]

He liked the work of Samuel Lover, but in 1862, despite admiring his "charming lines on the Poet's Home," declined two poems submitted to *All the Year Round* because he had already published two verses on the same subject, and because he did not want to print "translations from the German.   The extent to which poetry of that origin is offered here, is almost incredible."   The same year, however, he accepted some of Lover's "little pieces for insertion this day fortnight."   Dickens liked poems submitted by Lover in 1865, and agreed with their thrust concerning some contemporary problem, but argued that they would aggravate rather than help the situation.   A few months later, though, he again accepted poems: "Glad to retain the verses for insertion."   The following year, he sent Lover proof of one poem for correction, and rejected another as "not strong enough, put side by side with the tremendous realities of the late storms."   Near the end of the same year, he rejected yet another poem: ". . . A thousand thanks but I don't think the brisk little shot is quite in our direction."[38]

Dickens made one comment on the poetry of Richard Monckton Milnes, saying that "the elegance, tenderness, and thoughtful fancy of the Palm Leaves, have greatly charmed me, and have made an impression on me, such as I believe you would yourself desire to produce. . . ." In his Preface to the third volume of *Master Humphrey's Clock* he called Samuel Rogers "a poet whose writings . . . are replete with generous and earnest feeling. . . ." He did not speak of the nondramatic poetry of Shakespeare, but must have read him: he quoted from one of his sonnets in the Preface to *Bleak House*. I find no references to the poetry of Shelley, but Dickens seemed to have made his age's error of lumping him together with Byron as part of, as Wilson puts it, "that antisocial and amoral side of the Romantic rebellion, which was always abhorrent to him." Both poets were mocked in "The Poetical Young Gentleman" in *Sketches by Boz*. In his obituary for Talfourd he said that "in his poems . . . he was widely appreciated," and called him a "charming writer." Dickens liked a short poem by Thackeray: according to George Dolby, his presentation copy of *A Christmas Carol* to Thackeray bore an inscription, "expressive of the pleasure Dickens had derived from a poem of Thackeray's."[39]

Dickens commented upon the poetry of Tennyson more frequently than upon that of any other; Horne said that Dickens was a "great admirer" of Tennyson. The first reference I have found is in 1842, when Dickens began to mention a number of poets; Forster says that in that year the "collected *Poems* of Tennyson had become very favorite reading with him." "I have been reading Tennyson all morning on the seashore," he wrote from one vacation spot, and applied quotations from "The Mermaid," "The Merman," and "A Dream of Fair Women" to the scene before him. "Who else . . . could conjure up such a close to the extraordinary and as Landor would say 'most woonderful' series of pictures in the 'dream of fair women' as

> Squadrons and squares of men in brazen plates,
>   Scaffolds, still sheets of water, divers woes,
> Ranges of glimmering vaults with iron grates,
>   And hushed seraglios!

"I am sorry to see that Sumner . . . speaks slightingly of Tennyson,"
he wrote the same year. "Good God how strange it seems to me that
anyone can do that—though many do." And the following year he
wrote to the man after whom he would name another son that he was
one "whose writings enlist my whole heart and nature in admiration
of their Truth and Beauty. . . ."[40] He sent Christiana Weller, the
young pianist in whose career he had become interested for a time, a
copy of *Poems, 1842*, which Tennyson had given to him. "I have
marked with a pencil in the Index to each, those pieces which I
should like her to read first—as being calculated to give her a good
impression of the Poet's Genius. . . ." In 1844 he wrote to ask
brother Fred to bring him "a copy of Tennyson's poems . . ."; a
copy of the second edition (1843) was in the Gad's Hill Library at
his death, with "numerous pencil marks." "What a great creature he
is!" he exclaimed in 1844. In 1859 he wrote to Forster, "How fine
the 'Idyls' are! Lord! what a blessed thing it is to read a man who
can write! I thought nothing could be grander than the first poem till
I came to the third; but when I had read the last, it seemed to be
absolutely unapproached and unapproachable." Elsewhere he called
the work a "magnificent poem . . . perhaps, the noblest of his
works."[41]

At a speech at the Mechanics Institute of Liverpool he called
Tennyson "a great living poet." But despite his admiration, he
thought that Tennyson's influence on lesser poets was damaging:
rejecting a poem he believed to be by Ollier, "full of strange conceits
and strange metre," he commented, "Tennyson is ruining all these
writers." And he rejected a sonnet by Tennsyon suggested for
reading at Macready's farewell dinner, saying it "would not do. . . .
I have an instinctive assurance that it would fail"[42] in a densely

packed chamber.   One would give much to know what the sonnet was, and why he thought it would not suit a crowded room.

According to Forster, "Dickens had little love for Wordsworth," but love him or not, Dickens certainly knew him.   Paraphrases of Wordsworthian lines occur in several places in Dickens' letters; one such, in 1853, when he was traveling with Collins and Augustus Egg, is "'We are'—not seven, like Wordsworth's children—'three.'"   David Wilkie said that Dickens considered "We Are Seven" "one of the most striking examples of his Genius. . . ."   In the absence of any actual criticism of Wordsworth by Dickens, in consideration of his not infrequent allusions to him, and in view of what strikes me as strong sympathy with Wordsworthian thought—never overtly so identified, but undeniably so—I think Forster's statement may be held in some doubt. Forster himself held Dickens up as "an example of the truth the great poet never tired of enforcing, that Nature has subtle helps for all who are admitted to become free of her wonders and mysteries."[43]

There is one other brief comment, on Scandinavian poetry: Dickens and Miss Coutts found themselves agreeing on the unfortunate effects of the verse of that country on a friend: "Why a man who is for ever fainting away, should be making himself limper with Scandinavian poetry, [I] cannot fathom."[44]

7

The Dickens Aesthetic

Because he did not write the kind of extended commentary on the theory of art that other novelists have undertaken, and because of a persistent bias against his intellect, Dickens has for a century and more been thought of as a man of limited aesthetic understanding, even as a kind of idiot savant. But the absence of formal expression of his principles of art is owing not to inability, but to his reluctance to impose his opinion, his reservations about the value of criticism, his distaste for what he considered critical jargon, and his fear of giving offense. The simple accomplishment of this study has been to gather the numerous instances found in Dickens' correspondence and other writings, as well as from his speeches and from the recollections of those who knew him, that indicate his extensive association with those arts which lay beyond his own genius, as appreciator, helper, patron, participant, and theorist. The aggregate of instances speaks for itself in regard to the extent to which Dickens did these things, but it may be helpful before we conclude to review the Dickensian aesthetic which emerges.

Though Dickens was not in all ways a successful autodidact, his experiences in art, sculpture and architecture, drama, music, and poetry taught him no less about aesthetics than we would expect for a man of intelligence, if perhaps a bit less than we might have wished for a man of genius. In some ways, Dickens did not rise above his origins and his century: without formal education, he never acquired that broad background of history, philosophy, theology, and the classics which we hope gives depth and perspective to everything in our lives, including appreciation of the arts. In painting and drawing, he was often affected more by subject than by artistry, and responded more to dramatic content and uplifting message than to aesthetic achievement. When he did focus upon the artistry of a work, he was inclined through much of his life to judge by such limited standards as a seemingly contradictory fidelity to nature and beautification of subject. He did not comment at length on sculpture, and appears to have been unaware of important contemporary developments in architecture. His knowledge of drama was perhaps not as complete as he has been given credit for: his attention, at least as revealed by what he wrote, was concentrated on living performances of plays far more than upon drama as literature. He was rather more fond of popular and folk music than of classical, and his knowledge of the forms and techniques of poetry are at times questionable.

But like most things, the Dickens aesthetic is a turnable coin, and the other side reveals much that we can respect, even when we may not agree. Dickens was widely acquainted with the art, drama, music, and poetry available in his time. Reluctant though he was to volunteer unsolicited opinion, he said enough to show that he could understand what an artist was after in a painting or drawing, and on the whole his judgment of what he saw was sound. As a viewer of art he grew impressively, breaking out of his early insular attachment to the work of his friends and countrymen to an understanding of the wider, more ambitious and daring efforts of Continental painters: he learned how an artist's reach should exceed his grasp. He was capable of appreciating good sculpture, and responded both to the beauty and the practical needs of architecture. His knowledge of the theater of his time was indeed unsurpassed, and he seems to have understood all that a professional producer, director, stage manager, stage carpenter, actor, and critical audience could know about the theater. He knew Shakespeare almost by heart, and understood him; he was familiar with other Elizabethan dramatists, as well as many playwrights of the Restoration and eighteenth century. He loved music, would seem to have had a good ear, knew something about musical instruments, and apparently listened with pleasure to the highest as well as to more modest compositions. He was a competent editor of poetry, and a constant and informed reader; if he liked some poets such as Tennyson too much for our taste, he shared his judgments with many of the best critical minds of his own time. Finally, he shared such judgments only when his own taste and understanding verified them: in all his appreciation of the arts he strove for independent and honest response, refusing the tame parroting of received opinion, working to comprehend and appreciate beauty without pretense, affectation, or bias, seeking always the immediate and personal communion with art to which the true aesthetic aspires.

The aesthetic he developed was founded upon a set of carefully-reached and firmly-held principles. He began with a love of feeling, of the emotional response to life that art can both render and arouse, confident that the power of the imagination to awaken and invigorate the psyche was the most important sustenance the human spirit could receive. He saw drama as the best means of doing this, and he looked for dramatic qualities in every kind of art. While he appreciated nature and worshipped the Deity, it was humanity that fascinated him, and he placed mankind at the center of the aesthetic experience: how he could read a painting or drawing when it spoke of human nature!

He believed that art should imitate life, and was critical of almost anything that clouded the mirror held up to nature. He did not understand why an artist might play with proportion, might exaggerate or diminish a form—might do anything other than show form his own image. He despised conventional representation, artificiality, the contrived effect—although he was capable of huge enjoyment of such things, and probably developed something of his own literary technique out of his delight: a fondness for the ridiculous formed no insignificant part of his aesthetic. He cared less for the small, the quiet, the contemplative and analytical than for representations of life at high pitch: for him the very best art usually possessed vigor, color, movement, the beating pulse. But despite his own reputation, he was scornful of sentimentality as a means of arousing emotion. He expected the artist to be a careful craftsman, and accepted no excuse for inferior work, for artistic or physical laziness: though he tolerated the indolence of his friend Daniel Maclise, he did not suffer it gladly. His judgment of all artistry was made through meticulous attention to its execution of detail: his best critical opinion combines assessment of each part of a work with an appreciation of how all the parts make the whole. To my mind his response to art is at once wonderfully democratic and aristocratic: all artists appear before his court on an equal footing, regardless of rank, friendship, or reputation, and each must meet the highest standards of achievement if he is to be granted the distinction of true artist.

Probably the final word to be remembered in the Dickens canon of aesthetics is the word *true*: his use of it covers the range of his appreciation of art from simplest to most complex. If in its common application the word meant to him no more than "accurate," "according to nature," at its deeper level I believe it meant the penetration he required of the greatest art: a probing beneath the surface appearance, a deep comprehension, above all an affirmation that passes other human understanding. Our century is not over-fond of positive thinking, to which too many things have, like Churchill's pederast, given a bad name. But if we free ourselves from the limitations of our time, we may admire a man who believed, even when some of the events of his own life spoke to the contrary, that life is, beyond all cynicism on the one hand and Pippa-like optimism on the other, tortuous and trying but essentially good, and that it is the business of art to see so, and to say so.

Most of our study has concentrated upon Dickens' opinion of

arts other than his own, though two chapters, Art and Dramatic Readings, have touched upon prose fiction, and have offered insight into his aesthetic contemplation of his novels. In a separate work, we will examine Dickens' attitude toward literary criticism, his work as editor of fiction and other writing, his opinions about novelists, and his advice to colleagues and neophytes, in an effort to see the Dickens aesthetic at work in literature.

Notes

Key: sources cited frequently are identified by the following abbreviations:

AN—*American Notes for General Circulation.* John S. Whitley and Arnold Goldman, eds. Baltimore: Penguin Books, 1972.

AYR—*All the Year Round.* Edited by Charles Dickens.

BC—*Letters of Charles Dickens to the Baroness Burdett-Coutts.* Charles C. Osborne, ed. London: John Murray, 1931.

BT—Butt, John, and Kathleen Tillotson. *Dickens at Work.* London: Methuen aand Co., 1957.

CA—Carlton, William J. "Charles Dickens: Dramatic Critic," *Dickensian,* 56 (1/60), 11-27.

CJ—Cohen, Jane R. *Charles Dickens and His Original Illustrators.* Columbus: Ohio State University Press, 1980.

CP—*Collected Papers.* Arthur Waugh, Hugh Walpole, Walter Dexter, and Thomas Hatton, eds. 2 vols. Bloomsbury: Nonesuch Press, 1932.

D—*The Dickensian.*

DG—Dolby, George. *Charles Dickens as I Knew Him.* 1885. Repr. London: Everett & Company, 1912.

Diaries—*The Diaries of William Charles Macready,* William Toynbee, ed. 2 vols. New York, London: Benjamin Blom, 1969. 1st pub. 1912.

DS—Pemberton, T. Edgar. *Charles Dickens and the Stage.* London:

George Redway, 1888.

DSA—*Dickens Studies Annual.*

DTR—*The Dickens Theatrical Reader*, eds. Edgar and Eleanor Johnson. Boston: Little, Brown, 1964.

EW—Wilson, Edmund. "Dickens: the Two Scrooges," *The Wound and the Bow.* London: W. H. Allen, 1952. First pub. 1941.

F—Forster, John. *The Life of Charles Dickens.* Intro. by G. K. Chesterton. 2 vols. London: J. M. Dent; New York: E. P. Dutton, 1927. References are to book, chapter, and page, e.g. F VI (book 6), ii (chapter 2), 226 (page 226).

FN—Frye, Northrop. "Dickens and the Comedy of Humors," *Experience in the Novel*, Roy Harvey Pierce, ed. New York and London: Columbia University Press, 1968.

HCD—Johnson, Edgar. *The Heart of Charles Dickens.* Boston: Little, Brown and Company, 1952.

HD—*A Child's History of England* in *Master Humphrey's Clock and a Child's History of England.* Introduction by Derek Hudson. London: Oxford University Press, 1958.

HH—House, Humphrey. *The Dickens World.* London: Oxford University Press, 1941.

HW—*Household Words.* Edited by Charles Dickens.

IR—*Inteviews and Recollections*, ed. Philip Collins. 2 vols. London: Macmillan, 1981.

JE—Johnson, Edgar. *Charles Dickens: His Tragedy and Triumph.* 2 vols. New York: Simon and Schuster, 1952.

JL—Lightwood, James T. *Charles Dickens and Music.* 1912. Repr. New York: Haskell House Publishers Ltd., 1970.

K—Kent, Charles. *Charles Dickens as a Reader.* 1872. Repr. New York: Haskell House Publishers, 1973.

L—Lehmann, R. C. *Charles Dickens as Editor.* New York: Sturgis and Walter, 1912.

LC—*Letters of Charles Dickens.* Georgiana Hogarth and Mary Dickens eds. 2 vols. 1879.

LD—*The Letters of Charles Dickens.* Pilgrim Edition. Oxford:

Clarendon Press. 5 vols. V. I, Madeline House and Graham Storey, eds. 1965. V. II, Madeline House and Graham Storey, eds. 1969. V. III, Madeline House, Graham Storey, and Kathleen Tillotson, eds. 1974. V. IV, Kathleen Tillotson, ed. 1977. V. V, Graham Storey and K. J. Fielding, eds. 1981.

LE—Lehr, Dolores. *Charles Dickens and the Arts.* Unpublished doctoral dissertation. Temple University, 1979. University Microfilm Reprints, Ann Arbor, Mich., 1979.

MR—*Mr. and Mrs. Charles Dickens: His Letters to Her.* Walter Dexter, ed. London: Constable & Co. Ltd., 1935.

NL—*Nonesuch Letters. The Collected Papers of Charles Dickens.* Arthur Waugh, ed. 2 vols. Bloomsbury: the Nonesuch Press, 1937.

OR—Ormond, Leonee. "Dickens and Painting: The Old Masters," D, 79 (1983), 130-151; "Dickens and Painting: Contemporary Art," D, 80 (1984), 2-25.

PA—Paroissien, David H. "Charles Dickens and the Weller Family," DSA, 2 (1972), 1-38.

PC—*Charles Dickens: The Public Readings*, ed. Philip Collins. London: Clarendon Press, 1975.

PD—*The Poems and Verses of Charles Dickens.* F. S. Kitton, ed. New York and London: Harper, 1903.

PE—Pemberton, Thomas Edgar. *Charles Dickens and the Stage.* London: G. Redway, 1885.

PI—*Pictures from Italy. Pictures from Italy* and *American Notes*, in *The Complete Works of Charles Dickens.* V. II. New York: Harper, n.d.

PK—Perugini, Kate. "Charles Dickens as a Lover of Art and Artists," *Magazine of Art*, XXVII (1/1903), 125-30; (2/1903), 164-69.

PP—Compton, Emmaline. *Pen and Pencil.* n.d., n.p. Selections repr. IR.

S—Storey, Gladys. *Dickens and Daughter.* London: Frederick Muller, 1939.

SB—*Sketches by Boz.*   *The Works of Charles Dickens.*   Introduction, Critical Comments, and Notes by Andrew Lang, Charles Dickens the Younger, John Forster, Adolphus Wm.   Ward, and others. New York: P. F. Collier, 1911.

SD—*Speeches of Charles Dickens.*   K. J. Fielding, ed.   Oxford: Clarendon Press, 1960.

SH—Stone, Harry.   *Uncollected Writings from Household Words.* 2 vols. Bloomington: Indiana University Press, 1968.

St—Stone, Harry.   *Dickens and the Invisible World.*   Bloomington and London: Indiana University Press, 1979.

TN—Stang, Richard.   *The Theory of the Novel in England: 1850-1870.* New York: Columbia University Press; London: Routledge and Kegan Paul, 1959.

UT—*The Uncommercial Traveller,* in *The Uncommercial Traveller and Reprinted Pieces, Etc.*   London: Oxford University Press, 1964.

W—Woolcott, Alexander.   *Mr. Dickens Goes to the Play.*   Port Washington, N. Y.: Kennikat Press, 1967; First pub. 1922.

WA—Wilson, Angus.   *The World of Charles Dickens.*   New York: The Viking Press, 1970.

WC—*Letters of Charles Dickens to Wilkie Collins.* Laurence Hutton, ed. N.Y.: Harper, 1892.   Repr. New York: Kraus Reprint Co., 1969.

Unless otherwise indentified, all dates given in the notes are in the nineteenth century.

Introduction

1. Review of *Dickens the Craftsman: Strategies of Presentation*, ed. Robert B. Partlow; *Dickens Studies Newsletter*, 1:3 (12/70), 7.

2. F, I:iii, 45. "Dickens in Relation to Criticism," *Fortnightly Review*, 17 (1872), repr. IR, I:25-26. LD, II:ix; quoted from Lady Pollock, *Macready as I Knew Him* (1884), p. 59. HH, p. 51. *Things I Have Known* (1894), repr. IR, II:204. F, VIII:ii, 195; XI:iii, 376. *The New Spirit of the Age* (1844), repr. IR, I:71, 70. *Life of Charles Dickens* (1870), repr. IR, I:110. "Dickens in Relation to Criticism," *Fortnightly Review*, (2/72); repr. IR, I:26.

3. HH, p. 173. *The Maturity of Dickens* (Cambridge: Harvard University Press, 1959), p. 42. HCD, p. 14. See *The Victorians and After: 1830-1894*, Introduction to *English Literature Series*, 1938; "Charles Dickens," *Dial* (11/1921). *The Victorian Age* (1922), p. 214. "D., Drama and Tradition," *Scrutiny*, 10 (4/42), 358. EM, p. 25. SH, p. 64. "The Unknown Dickens," DSA, 1 (1970), 4. SD, p. xxiv. P, p. 128; p. 135.

4. JE, II:1132. LD, I (12/3/39), 609. K. J. Fielding, "D as J. T. Danson Knew Him," D (1972), 151. "Dickens in Relation to Criticism," *Fortnightly Review*, 17 (1872), repr. IR, I:26. F, II:iv, 96. Jerome Meckier, "Some Household Words: Two New Accounts of Dickens's Conversation," D, 71 (1975), repr. IR, II:289. "Dickens Looks at Homer," D, 60 (1/1964), 52-54.

5. S, p. 44. ST, pp, 54-55. F, I:iii, 45. PP, repr. IR, I:15.

6. *Letters of Mrs. Gaskell* (Manchester, 1966), eds. J. A. V. Chapple and Arthur Pollard, repr. Ir, p. 109. "Dickens in Relation to Criticism," *Fortnightly Review*, (2/72); repr. IR, I:26. "Books that Dickens Read," D, 45 (3/49), 82.

7. LC, II (11/13/62), 353. F, VI:iii, 57.

8. JE, I:270; II:1131-32.

9. LD, III (6/13/43), 512; see also V ((4/22/48), 289. LD, I

(3/6/42), 107; Dickens did not have it quite right: Godwin planned the book backwards from volume 3, but actually wrote it forwards. "Charles Dickens," *Le Gaulois* (6/13/70), repr. IR, II:292.   F, I:vii, 15.

10.   L (11/20/54), 156. LC, II (8/16/65), 275.   "CD: A Memory," *New Liberal Review* (10/1901), repr. IR, II: 348, 345.

11.   "Books that Dickens Read," D, 45 (9/1949) 201.   LC, I (11/1/54), 435-36.   W. T. Harris, Editor's Preface to Hughes, James L., *Dickens as Educator* (New York: D. Appleton, 1901), p. v; p. ix.

12.   Raymond Blathwayt, "Reminiscences of D.: An Interview with Mr. Alfred Tennyson Dickens," *Great Thoughts* (11/12/1910) repr. IR, I:156.   "Forster's Life of Dickens." *Quarterly Review*, 132 (1872), repr. IR. I:114. P, p. 130.

13.   SH, pp. 4, 64.   JE, II:1128; 1130.   WA, p. 222.

14.   Robert Langton, *The Childhood of Charles Dickens* (1912); repr. IR, I:5.   F, I:vii; repr.   IR, I:6.   "Recollections of Charles Dickens," D, 7 (1911), repr. IR, I:8.

15.   HCD (10/8/53), 236; see also F, V:ii, 384.   Constance Cross, "CD: A Memory," *New Liberal Review* (10/1901), repr.   IR, II:345. F, V:vii, 449; VII:v, 166.

16.   LD, III (11/20/44), 226; (2/23 & 25?/45), 73.   F, IV:iv, 314.

17.   NL, II (9/18/53), 488.   LC, II (2/16/55), 451f.   CP, I:338.

18.   LD, IV (11/20/44), 227; V (7/9/48), 369; see note.   F, IV:iv, 320-21; VII:ii, 126—see also HCD (10/25/53), 239.

19.   HCD (11/13/53), 241, 243.   L, p. 313.

20.   EW, p. 39.

21.   "Books that Dickens Read," D, 45 (3/49), 85.

22.   EW, p. 1.

23.   See e.g. DTR and W. Harvey Peter Sucksmith, "Dickens Among the Pre-Raphaelites: Mr. Merdle and Holman Hunt's 'the Light of the World,'" D, No. 380, v. 72, part 3 (9/76), 161.

24.   D, 79 (1983), 131-151; 80 (1984), 2-25. *Charles Dickens and Music* (1912).   "Charles Dickens as Verse Editor," MP, 58

(11/1960), 99-107. "Dickens on Art," MP, 53 (8/1955), 25-38. TN. "The Unknown Dickens," DSA, 1 (1970), 4.

25. LE, p. 1.

26. *Dickens and Ellen Ternan* (Berkeley: University of California Press, 1952), p. 61. S, p. 107.

Chapter 1

Art: For the Sake of the Story

1. See e.g. JE, I:561-2; WA, p. 94; HH, p. 129; F, IV:vi, 348; CJ, p. 7; Tillotson, LD, IV:xi; LE, p. 74.

2. JE, I:561; PK, p. 129.

3. PI, p. 98. Harvey Peter Sucksmith, "Dickens Among the Pre-Raphaelites: Mr. Merdle and Holman Hunt's 'The Light of the World," D, 72 (9/1976), 161.

4. SD (4/30/70), 421.

5. PK, p. 164. OR, pp. 3-6.

6. CJ, p. 38.

7. If we add names mentioned in *Pictures from Italy* and elsewhere, we find a total of nearly seventy artists mentioned, including Titian, Tintoretto, Raphael, Marco-Antonio Rainondi, Rubens, Rembrandt, Van Dyke, Guido, Domenichino, Carlo Dolci, Correggio, Murillo, Paul Veronese, Salvator Rosa, Adriaen Van Ostade, the Carraccis, Spagnoletto, Guilio Romano, William Etty, Sir Charles Eastlake, Francis Danby (or perhaps one of his sons, James or Thomas), Thomas Creswick, William Lee, John Rogers Herbert, William Dyce, Charles West Cope, and the Chalon brothers.

8. F, VII:v, 159. *Things I Have Known* (1894), repr. IR, II:201. OR, p. 3.

9. "New Year's Day," HW (1/1/59), repr. in CP, I:712. See e.g. J. Hillis Miller, "The Fiction of Realism: *Sketches by Boz, Oliver Twist*, and George Cruikshank's Illustrations," *Dickens Centennial Essays*, eds. Ada Nesbet and Blake Nevius (Berkeley: University of California Press, 1971), p. 127. See, e.g., CJ, p. 3: "Dickens's books reveal his exposure and his debt to prints, particularly to those of Hogarth." See for example LD, III (2/25/42) 90-91; LC, I (1/3/50), 248; LD, IV (8/10/45), 351.

10. PK, p. 125. Dickens did, of course, include artists in minor roles in his novels: Henry Gowan in *Little Dorrit* is an artist of sorts, as is Miss La Creevy in *Nicholas Nickleby*, and there are artists in his minor writings, e. g. the sidewalk artist in "His Brown Paper Parcel."

11. LD, V (6/21/49), 556.

12. LD, V (12/16/48), 458.

13. F, VII:iii, 172. "The Shop Side of Art," AYR (12/63), 374-79.

14. *Diaries*, II:336.

15. PK, p. 130. For evidence supporting this, see LD, V (7/23/48), 375; (1/27/49), 480.

16. LC, II (1/19/61), 161-62.

17. OR, p. 6. LD, V (11/19/48), 442; LD, V (12/10/47), 207. Unpublished paper in the Dickens House, repr. IR, II:184. OR, p. 8.

18. LC, II (6/11/59), 111.

19. F, II:xii, 164. The Chalon brothers were popular for their water-colors, which they often exhibited at the Royal Academy; Alfred was also a fashionable painter of ladies' portraits.

20. LD, II (1/31/41), 201.

21. "A Detective Police Party," HW, I:409.

22. PI, p. 25.

23. "Banvard's Geographical Panorama of the Mississippi and

Missouri Rivers," *Examiner* (12/16/48), reprinted in CP, I:182.

24. LD, IV (7/22/44), 159: the French artist was Eugene Deveria. Dickens' use of him to criticize Maclise may indicate that this early he was beginning to find fault with English art.

25. LC, II (3/21/68), 436.

26. LD, II (9/28/41), 395.

27. "Macready as Benedick," *Examiner* (3/4/43), reprinted in CP, I:45.

28. S, p. 116.

29. "Please to Leave Your Umbrella," HW (5/1/58), repr. in CP, I:705-706.

30. "Please to Leave Your Umbrella," HW (5/1/58), repr. in CP, I:704-705.

31. "An Idea of Mine," HW (3/13/58), 699-704, repr. in CP, I:699-700.

32. OR, p. 243. "My Confidences," (1896), repr. IR, I:117. "Some Memories of Charles Dickens," *Atlantic Monthly*, 26 (1870), 243. PI, p. 98.. See note 28, above. BC (11/19/52), 117.

33. PI, p. 19.

34. PI, p. 96.

35. PI, p. 99.

36. *Douglas Jerrold's Shilling Magazine* (8/45), reprinted in CP, I:37.

37. LD, IV (6?/44), 141.

38. LD, III (12/14/43), 608.

39. CJ, p. 143.

40. PI, p. 44.

41. PI, p. 139.

42. LD, IV (11/17-18/44), 220.

43. Ibid.

44. "The Rising Generation," *Examiner* (12/30)48), reprinted in CP, I:190.

45. PI, p. 152.

46. Ibid.

47. HCD (10/30/52), 210.

48. LC, II (7/8/61), 171.

49. LD, III (7/31/42), 299.

50. LD, I (2/22/38), 378.

51. LD, V (1/3/49), 468.

52. AYR (7/24/69), reprinted in CP, II:48.

53. CJ, p. 94.

54. LD, III (8/15-18?/43), 543n.

55. LD, IV (6?/44), 141.

56. LD, II (9/12/41), 378.

57. LD, II (8/19/41), 361; 362.

58. "Insularities," HW (1/19/56), 626.

59. LD, IV (12/12/46), 679.

60. LD, IV, 700.

61. Except perhaps Monroe Engel: see "Dickens on Art," *Modern Philology*, 53 (8/1955), 25-38.

62. CJ, p. 4.

63. *The Complete Letters of Vincent Van Gogh* (Greenwich, Conn.: New York Graphic society, 1958; repr. 1978), 3:374; from letter to Rappard (3/83), p. 5.

64. CJ, p. 5; quoted from Forster, *Life of Dickens*, J. W. T. Ley, ed. (London: Cecil Palmer, 1928), p. 720.

65. LD, IV (7/18/46), 586: Sir A___ E___ has not been identified; Forster says that the man was not used as a model for Dombey, and Kathleen Tillotson suggests that the man was probably only a physical, not a character, study for Dombey.

66. LD, IV (8/2/46), 596.

67. F, VI:ii, 471.

68. LD, IV (11-12/46), 671.

69. LD, II (1/30/41), 199.

70. LD, III (12/20/42), 397.

71. LD, III, 373n4.

72. See e.g. LD, II (3/6 or 7/40), 38.

73. LD, I (11/9/38), 450-51: a letter from Forster to Bentley supporting Dickens' opinion of the offending plate is quoted in part in

the Pilgrim *Letters* (I:451n.).

74. CJ, p. 96.

75. LD, III (6?/44), 140.

76. LD, II ((8/13/40), 115.

77. LD, I (11?/37), 333.

78. LD, I (7/19/38), 450-51: the piece was "Automaton Police Office, and Real Offenders. From the Model Exhibition before Section B. of the Mud Fog Association," *Miscellany*, IV (1838), facing p. 209.

79. LD, I (7/3/39), 559.

80. LD, II (4/29/41), 275.

81. LD, II (5/2/41), 276; III (11/21/43), 601. The editors of the Pilgrim Edition *Letters* speculate that Dickens liked the pieces in the almanac, but not Cruikshank's pictures.

82. LD, V (9/2/47), 156.

83. F, VI:iii, 40.

84. See note 87.

85. Ibid.

86. *Examiner* (7/8/48), reprinted in CP, I:157.

87. *Dickens and the Invisible World* (Bloomington, Indiana, and London: Indiana University Press, 1979, p. 11.

88. LC, I (7/27/53), 359.

89. "Frauds on the Fairies," HW, VIII:97.

90. SD (1/27/52), 136. *Swallowfield and Its Owners* (1901), repr. IR, II:288; 288; PC, p. 154.

91. *Examiner* (12/30/48), reprinted in CP, I:190-93: a part of the review is given by Forster (VI:iii, 43-45), but he alters phrasing in several places.

92. LD, III (12/31/42), 417.

93. LD, III (3/2/43), 453.

94. CJ, p. 159.

95. LD, III (12/22/42), 409.

96. LD, III (9/1/43), 549.

97. PK, p. 129.

98. LD, III (2/27/42), 94; III, 156n.

99. LD, I (6/28/39), 558: "Hamlet" is Maclise's painting.

100. LD, III (7/31/42), 299.

101. LD, III (11/26/42), 383.

102. LD, IV (4/17/46), 535.

103. *Contributions to the Morning Chronicle*, Gordon N. Ray, ed., pp. 145-46; quoted in LD, IV: 535n.

104. LD, I (6/28/39), 558; *George Eliot's Life*, J. W. Cross. ed. (1885), iii, 145; *Frazer's Magazine*, XXII (1840), 113; quoted in LD, I:558n.

105. LD II, (11/25/40), 157.

106. LD, IV (8/7/44), 168-69, and n.

107. *Douglas Jerrold's Shilling Magazine* (8/45), reprinted in CP, I:34-39.

108. LD, III (9/1/43), 550.

109. LD, IV (5/9/45), 304.

110. PK, p.129. OR, p. 10; p. 10.

111. LD, III (1842?), 418; III (12/31/42), 415; III (5/5/43), 483; IV (8/24/44), 184; IV (11/12/44), 217.

112. SD, speech at the Royal Academy Banquet (4/30/53), 164; LC, II (4/18/67), 335. OR, p. 10.

113. "The Late Mr. Stanfield," AYR (6/1/67), 537, reprinted in CP, II:46.

114. F, VII:v, 172.

115. CJ, p. 7.

116. SD (1/6/53), 157.

117. LD, IV (7/3/46), 576.

118. SD (1/2/52), 13-14.

119. "Banvard's Geographical Panorama of the Mississippi and Missouri Rivers," *Examiner* (12/16/48), reprinted in CP, I:182-84.

120. F, VI:iii, 41.

121. F, VI:iii, 41-2: Lamb wrote "On the Genius and Character of Hogarth," *The Complete Works and Letters of Charles Lamb* (New York: Random House, 1935); the passage Dickens refers to is ". .

the very houses, as I heard a friend of mine express it, tumbling all about in various directions, seem drunk. . . ." (p. 312).

122. OR, p. 132; p. 137. LD, IV (3/9/45), 276.

123. OR, p. 138. LD, IV (11/17 & 18/44), 220.

124. NL, I:666.

125. LD, IV (7/22/44), 160.

126. LD, IV (11/12/44), 217; IV (11/17-18/44), 220.

127. F, VII:iii, 142.

128. See LD. V: 277n.: in "To Think or be Thought For," HW, 14 (9/13/56), 193-98, Dickens' authoritative friend Wilkie Collins also engaged in some heretical artistic opinionating, criticizing masterpieces by Raphael and Michaelangelo.

129. LD, IV (3/9/45), 276-77.

130. LD, IV (5/9/45), 305, 307. OR, pp. 139-40.

131. PI, p. 40.

132. PI, p. 95.

133. PI, p. 69.

134. PI, pp. 149, 152.

135. PI, p. 96.

136. PI, p. 141.

137. JE, II:1131.   Harvey Peter Sucksmith, "Dickens Among the Pre-Raphelites: Mr. Merdle and Holman Hunt's 'The Light of the World,'" D, 72 (9/1976), 160-61.

138. LD, IV (11/17 & 18/44), 220; (3/18/45), 284; (5/9/45), 304, 307: the reference to Sterne, slightly distorted, is to *Tristram Shandy*, Book III, Chapter 12.

139. F, VII:iii, 142, 141-42.

140. MR (11/21/53), 216.

141. PK, p. 126.

142. MR (11/14/53), 212.

143. PK, p. 164: Kate's statement that "my father was passionately fond of colour" supports the possibility that his infrequent references to color are owing neither to indifference nor to ingorance, but to his distate for technical "jargon."

286 THE DICKENS AESTHETIC

144. LD, IV (11/17 & 18/49), 221: the passage is also found in PI, p. 150.
145. PK, p. 164.
146. OR, p. 16. SB, p. 237.
147. "The Ghost of Art," UT, p. 439.
148. See e.g. LD, IV (7/18/46), 586.
149. LD, IV (3/18/45), 281; (3/18/45), 283.
150. Pp. 186-87.
151. P. 703.
152. CP, II:351, 355. *The Complete Letters of Vincent Van Gogh* (Greenwich, Conn.: New York Graphic Society, 1958; repr. 1978), I, #241, 479.
153. LD, III (12/26/42), 401-02.
154. OR, pp. 13-14. F, VII:v, 174: Dickens' praise of Collins here gives weight to the possibility that his professed contempt for his friend's technical discussions of art (see above) was directed at such discussion, not at Collins.
155. BC (1/10/56), 161.
156. F, VII:v, 173-74: Forster agreed with Dickens that "the eyes and the mouth" of the portrait gave "the sense of a general unlikeness."
157. Ibid.
158. LC, II (9/28/61), 174.
159. Ibid., p. 127. "Reminiscences of my Father," *Windsor Magazine*, Christmas Supplement (1934), repr. IR, I:138. IR, I:xvii. IR, I:33. Ir, II:42, 49, 55; 57; see also 58, 81, 83, 85.
160. MR (5/5/56), 247.
161. LD, V (10/22/49), 630.
162. OR, p. 131: the editors of the Pilgrim *Letters* affirm that there is nothing "testy" or "contradictory" in the portrait of Clark; Dickens is trying to find a way of expressing his dissatisfaction with mere surface fidelity, and not succeeding.
163. PK, p. 129.
164. PI, p. 150.

165. PK, p. 129.

166. PK, p. 126.

167. CJ, p. 7.

168. WA, p. 194; LD, IV (3/18/45), 283-84.

169. LE, p. 83.

170. "Old Lamps for New," HW (6/15/50), 265-66.

171. HH, p. 126.

172. OR, p. 20. Letter to the *Times* (May 1851), reprinted in *Realism and Tradition in Art, 1848-1900*, Linda Nochlin, ed.; *Sources and Documents in the History of Art Series*, H. W. Janson, ed. (Englewood Cliffs, N. J.: Prentice-Hall, 1966), p. 119.

173. *Times* editorial (1851), reprinted in book of preceding note.

174. See note 172.

175. Ibid., p. 119.

176. Michael Hollington, "D the Flaneur," D, LXXVII:394 (1981), 79. "Dickens Among the Pre-Raphaelites: Mr. Merdle and Holman Hunt's 'The Light of the World," D, 72 (9/1976), 159. OR, pp. 159-60.

177. JE, II:1131.

178. PK, p. 166.

179. S, pp. 104, 130.

180. F, VII:iii, 172.

181. "Insularities," HW (1/19/56), reprinted in CP, I:626-27.

182. F, VII:v, 172.

Chapter 2

Architecture and Sculpture:
Georgeous Work and Exquisite Shapes

1. LE, p. 58. See e.g. p. 61. LD, IV (3/18/45), 280.
2. LD, IV (7/22/44), 160; (9/1/44), 190. PI, p .83. LD, IV (11/12/44), 217.
3. PI, p. 97. PI, p. 68. LC, II ((10/19/59), 122. PI, p. 68; p. 111; p. 90; p. 123.
4. LD, IV (1/31/45), 258.
5. LD, IV (3/18/45), 282; (3/26/45), 288. PI, pp. 121, 166. LC, I (11/14/53), 386.
6. PI, p. 40. LD, IV (4/2-4?/45), 289.
7. LD, V ((1/12/49), 473. AN, p. 145. DG, p. 119. AN, p. 145; p. 162.
8. AN, p. 164; p. 165; p. 170; p. 249; p. 163.
9. LD, IV (4/12/45), 294. F, VI:iii, 57. HCD (3/16/52), 198. HCD (4/18/52), 198.
10. PI, p. 16.
11. LC, I (9/7/51), 305; (9/21/51), 306; II (7/7/58), 57.
12. CP. I:3. L (11/13/66), 353. LC, II (1/27/69), 477; (4/4/69), 486. DG, pp. 82, 171.
13. F, VI:iv, 146-47. LC, II (1/1/69), 475.
14. For a record of references to architecture in Dickens' novels, see LE, pp. 63-73.
15. S, p. 190.
16. LD, V, 260; III (12/29/46), 686. Article in *Atlantic Monthly*, 26 (1870), 478, quoted in LD II, 18n4.
17. LD, II (4/8/41), 255; II (4/27/41), 271; III (7/31/42), 291.
18. AN, p. 164.
19. PI, p. 37; p. 103.

20. PI, pp. 151-52; p 123; p. 153; p. 166.
21. LD, V (7/8/48), 366 & n.   HCD (11/1/52), 212.
22.   "Threatening Letter to Thomas Hood, from an Ancient
Gentleman," *Hood's Magazine and Comic Miscellany* (5/44), reprinted
in CP, I:27.   HW (8/24/50), 505-507.   "The Good
Hippopotamus," HW (10/12/50), reprinted in CP. I:256-61.
"Proposals for Amusing Posterity," HW (2/12/53), reprinted in CP,
I:422.   "Why?" HW (3/1/56), reprinted in CP, I:641.

Chapter 3

Drama: The Fanciful Reality

1. "Some Literary Reflections" (1884), repr. IR, II:216.
2. "Charles Dickens," *Dial* (11/21/1921), repr. *Essays in Literary Criticism* (New York: 1957), quoted in BT, p. 187. F, I:i, 9. *Memoirs of Joseph Grimaldi* (1838): T. Edgar Pemberton said that Dickens' editing of this book "might alone stand in evidence of Dickens's intense interest in the stage": DS, p. 15. F, I:i, 13.
3. F, I:ii, 28; I:iii, 41.   "A School-fellow and Friend," "Recollections,of Charles Dickens," D, 7 (1911), repr. IR, I:8.
4. PP, repr. IR, I:11-12. F, I:ii, 44.   "Private Theatricals," *Evening Chronicle* (8/11/35), repr. DTR, p. 50.
5. LD, IV (12/30-31?/44), 245: John Hamilton developed a system for teaching languages "by observation, not by rules." F, I:iv, 50.
6. LD, I (12/29/?38), 481. PD, pp. 5-6; p. 9: for a modern assessment of Dickens' plays, see R. C. Churchill, "The Diversity of Dickens," paper read to the Doughty Society (11/1937), and

"Dickens, Drama, and Tradition," *Scrutiny* (10/1942).

7. F, I:v, 62; II:i, 79. LD, V (10/48/47), 200.

8. DS, pp. 2ff.

9. DS, p. 159.

10. F, VI:v, 68: Dickens wrote a letter to Bulwer expressing similar sentiments: NL, II (3/23/51), 286.

11. NL II:619, quoted by PC, p. 213: though Dickens was not good in a little space, he was capable of appreciating its potential: he said that "a short story was the best test for writing fiction," and "in its way it is a higher art than the long story or novel." Constance Cross, "Charles Dickens: A Memory," *New Liberal Review* (10/1901), repr. IR, II:347. Of course we must not forget the *Sketches by Boz*, but in requiring length for his greatest work, Dickens was like other novelists, e.g. Flaubert: ". . . It's impossible for me to produce anything short. I can't express an idea without going the whole way." *Flaubert and Turgenev: A Friendship in Letters* (New York: Norton and Co., 1985), ed. Barbara Beaumont, letter to Turgenev (7/25/74).

12. MR (12/28/54), 233. LD, V (6/10/48), 330; (10/23/48), 429; (12/8/49), 668. WC (1/18/53), 13. LC, II (12/28/60), 156-57, repr. W, p. 75.

13. F, IV:iv, 323; VII:iv, 153; VIII:vi, 245.

14. HCD (1/13/52), 193. L (11/11/62), 324.

15. "Dickens in Relation to Criticism," *Fortnightly Review*, 17 (1872), repr. IR, I:26. LC, I (2/16/55), 451; (11/21/55), 474.

16. LC, II (8/25/58), 73; (11/4/62), 215: *Rothomago* was probably the one-act pantomime by John Laurent, first performed in 1847. Percy Fitzgerald, *Memories of Charles Dickens* (1913), repr. IR, II:230.

17. LC, II (6/11/61), 166; (12/27/62), 217; (6/2/70), 516.

18. SD (2/14/66), 358; (4/6/57), 231. "The Theatrical Young Gentleman," DTR, p. 47. PP, repr. IR, II:352.

19. LD, I (1838-39), 487. LC, II (12/28/60), 156; (7/19/57), 24. LD, V (2/2/49), 486. SD (4/2/55), 184. "Astley's," DTR, p.

44. Dickens loved Astley's Circus; he made it the subject of one of his sketches, and mentioned it in *The Old Curiosity Shop*. Annie Fields, one of his American friends, wrote that she was "astounded at the knowledge Charles Dickens showed of everything before him" when she and her husband took him to a circus. "He knew how the horses were stenciled, how tight the wire bridles were, etc. . . " See diaries drawn from James T. Fields: *Biographical Notes and Personal Sketches*, ed. Annie Fields (1881), repr. IR, II:321. DTR, p. 23. See also L (9/24/58), 246.

20. CP, II:203. AN, p. 76. LC, I (7/2/56), 517. L (11/4/62), 314. LC, I (1/16/54), 403. LC, II (1/4/68), 383.

21. And beyond: Dickens' grave in Westminster Abbey lies directly before the monument to David Garrick.

22. "The Last Cab-Driver, and the First Omnibus Cad," SB, p. 134. WA, p. 21. W, p. 14.

23. See John Payne Collier, *An Old Man's Diary: Forty Years Ago* (1872), repr. IR, I:13. DTR, pp. 3-4. K, p. 13. *Nicholas Nickleby*, Ch. 23.

24. CJ, p. 82: after their conversion to Congregationalism, Dickens' sister Fanny and her husband, Henry Burnett (who had been active in the theater), never went to another play.

25. F, VII:v, 166.

26. JE, I:263. DTR, p. 79. DS, pp. 4, 186. F, VI:v, 81. LC, I (12/9/50), 268. "Fechter as Hamlet," *Atlantic Monthly*, 26 (1870), 558.

27. WA, pp. 3, 11. DTR, p. 20. F, VII:v, 159.

28. WA, p. 185. DS, p. 243: Dickens was not "always" careful: there was at least one exception, at a dramatization of *Nicholas Nickleby*; see below.

29. LD, III (9/27/42), 333: "Young Betty" was Henry Thomas Betty, whom Talfourd, at least, admired; he was called "young" because his father was also an actor.

30. "The Restoration of Shakespeare's Lear to the Stage," *Examiner* (2/4/38), repr. CP, I:141 and in DTR, pp. 151-54.

31.   George Lear, in PP, repr. IR, I:12.   "Scott and his Publishers," (3/31/39), repr. CP, I:141:   Dickens writes of Scott's readers, "in whose mouths the creations of his brain are familiar as household words. . . ."   "Mrs. Joseph Porter," SB, repr. DTR, p. 26.

32.   Robert Langton, *The Childhood and Youth of Charles Dickens*, enlarged edition (1912), repr. IR, I:2-3.

33.   LD, IV (8/7/45), 348; (9/8/45), 372; (9/10/45), 376; (9/18/45), 383.

34.   LD, IV (8/13/45), 353; (9/2/45), 368; (9/18/45), 382. *Diaries*, I:475.   LD, IV (9/11/45), 376; (9/24/45), 385.   F, V:i, 377. LD, IV (9/27/45), 387-89: Forster agreed: the play was performed, he said, "with a success that outran the wildest expectation; and turned our little enterprise into one of the small sensations of the day."   F, V:i, 376.

35.   LD, IV (9/27/45), 390.

36.   LD, IV (12/25/45), 455; (12/25/45), 454.

37.   LD, IV (1/1/46), 463.   *Diaries*, II:318; quoted in LD, IV:463n2.

38.   LD, V (7/9-19?/47), 131-32: the editors guess that B. is Stone, H. is Cruikshank, and Leech and Egg are among the others.

39.   LD, V (8/2/47), 136; (8/6/47), 144; (2/18/48), 249; (2/24/48), 250; (2/28/48), 252; (4/12/48), 277.

40.   LD, V (4/14/48), 277-79; (4/14/48), 281: they played in Liverpool, Birmingham (twice), Edinburgh, and Glasgow (twice). Anne Romer played Laura in *Love, Law, and Physic*, and Mary in *Used Up* in the Glasgow performances.

41.   LD, V (7/12/48), 372.

42.   LD, V (4/30/48), 293; (5/6/48), 299; (5/9/48), 302.

43.   LD, V:701: the rules were written 11/47.

44.   FW, (1/5/51), 175.   WC (3/8/51), 7-8.   HCD (3/23/51), 82-83.

45.   F. VII:ii, 127-28: the second play was *Fortunio and His Seven Gifted Servants*, by James Robinson Planche.   HCD, p.   251n2; p.

281n3. WC (12/17/54), 21.

46. HCD (5/24/55), 302. F, VII:11, 129; VIII:1, 186, repr. IR, I:95. HCD, p. 281n3.

47. NL, II (5/9/56), 772. F, VIII:i, 188; ii, 195.

48. NL, II (1/20/57), 829.

49. F, V:1, 377. DS, p. 121. In *No Name*, Collins describes a manager who sounds much like Dickens: "He was an active little man, of a sweet and cheerful temper; aand he gave the signal to begin, with as patient an interest in the proceedings as if they had caused him no trouble in the past, and promised him no difficulty in the future." (Chapter 6.)

50. WA, p. 94: Alexander Woolcott agrees: "How good an actor he was, it is difficult to tell from the written criticism."--W, p. 22. F, V:1, 374, 376. Quoted by William Howitt (1/15/1857), in Carl Woodring, *Victorian Samplers: William and Mary Howitt* (Lawrence, Kansas: 1952), p. 184, repr. PC, p. xlvi: according to Jane Carlyle, Dickens could also have made a good living as a magician; after a party for Mrs. Macready she wrote, "Only think of the excellent Dickens playing the conjurer for one whole hour--the best conjurer I ever saw--(and I have paid money to see several). . . . [His performance] would enable him to make a handsome subsistence, let the bookseller trade go as it please--!" *Jane Welsh Carlyle: a Selection of her Letters* (1959 ed.), ed. Trudy Bliss, repr. IR, I:61.

51. DS, p. 130. K, p. 13. Charles and Mary Cowden Clark, *Recollections of Writers* (1878), repr. IR, I:92. K, p. 255.

52. LD, V (4/1/48), 270; (9/1/48), 405; for Dickens' opinion of Fanny Kelly's character, see (7/23/48), 375; (12/5/49), 666.

53. LD, V (2/29/48), 255; (10/16?/48), 427; (1/13/49), 476.

54. LD, V (9/20/49), 610. NL, II (2/9/54), 541. F, VI:ii, 124. LC, I (6/29/52), 322. NL, III (2/1/59), 93. LD, V (11/16/49), 649.

55. IR, I:99. NL, III (11/7/64), 404. DS, p. 234.

56. F, VIII:vii, 248.

57.   NL, III (4/30/62), 293: see also 294n.; (9/4/67), 545; (9/13/67), 549.

58.   CJ, p. 186.   SD, p. 3; p. 113; p. 275; PP, 76, 79; p.   333. See e.g. SD, p. 359.   DS, pp. 247, 253, repr.   LD, IV:504n. Gerald Grubb, "Dickens's Influence as an Editor," *Studies in Philology*, 42 (1945), 814.

59.   "Books that Dickens Read," D, 45 (3/1949), 83.   LC, I (7/26/39), 29.   NL, II (12/12/57), 896; III (9/12/67), 547.   LD, IV (2/24/46), 505.

60.   DTR, p. ix.   LD, I (12/23/38), 475.

61.   LC, II (9/4/66), 303.   LD, V (2/14/47), 28-29.

62.   LD, I (12/12/39), 616; (1/16/38), 355; (1/18/38), 356.   NL, III (10/25/67), 562.

63.   LD, I (11/1/39), 596; see 596n.   *Examiner* (7/26/40).   LD, II (7/23/40), 104; 12/20/40), 163.   *Diaries*, II:95.   NL, II (9/3/50), 230; 6/29/52), 399; III (6/6/62), 296.   SD (3/1/51), 116.

64.   LD, II (10/20/40), 138; (9/13/41), 382; IV (7/9/45), 329.   LD, V (12/18/49), 674.   DS, pp. 234.   LC, II (2/3/58), 49, 50: Mme. de Giradin wrote *La Joie fait Peur*.   LC, (2/11/58), 51.

65.   LD, III (11/25/42), 381-82; (11/26/42), 383.

66.   LD, V (11/29/49), 660.

67.   LC, II (2/19/63), 225; I (1/3/55), 444-45.

68.   LD, I (3/5/39), 523; (3/5/39), 520.

69.   LD, IV (9/2/45), 386-69.

70.   Quoted from *Recollections and Experiences* (1884), ii, by Philip Collins, "Some Uncollected Speeches by Dickens," D, 73:382, and part 2 (5/1977), 91.   Harry Furmin, "A Shakespeare Birthday: A Reminiscence of Charles Dickens," *Pall Mall Magazine* (4/1906), 427-28, quoted by Collins in above article, p. 92.   "Forster's Life of Dickens," *Quarterly Review*, 132 (1872), repr. IR, I:115.

71.   Dickens' authorship of this review has been challenged: see William J. Carlton, "Dickens, or Forster?   Some King Lear Criticism Re-Examined," D, 61 (1965), 133-40, and Leslie C. Staples, "Dickens and Macready's Lear," D, 44 (3/1948),

78-80. But I accept Dickens' authorship as, according to Robert F. Fleissner, Graham Storey does; see "Lear's Poor Fool and Dickens, *Essays in Criticism*, 14 (10/1964), 425.

72. "The Restoration of Shakespeare's Lear to the Stage," *Examiner* (2/4/38); DTR, pp. 152-54.

73. "The Poor Fool," *Essays in Criticism*, 14 (4/1964), 209. See Leslie C. Staples, "Dickens and Macready's Lear," D, 44 (3/1948), 78-80.

74. LC, I (1/31/52), 320. NL, II (1854), 560. *Nigger* certainly was used more carelessly in 1854 than it is today, but Dickens did share some of the racism of his age, despite his hatred of American slavery.

75. LD, V (1/27/47), 14: inaccurately dated in DTR as 1/24/47. LD, IV:180n.: the play was *Kean, ou desorde et Genie*, 1836. LD, V (3/24/47), 42: again, it is often difficult to tell whether Dickens refers to the play in such comments, or to its performance only. Since his letters were usually written after seeing a play, they naturally combine the two judgments. Here I think "worked out" refers to the dramatist's effort, but it may be to the production; elsewhere in the letter Dickens definitely concentrates on performance, as he compliments the acting of Rose Cheri. LD, V (8/6/47), 144. CP, I:205.

76. F, VII:v, 163.

77. F, VII:V, 163; 164.

78. F, VII:v, 165-66. LC, I (5/5/56), 521. LD, V (1/28/47), 19-20.

79. LC, I (1/7/56), 488.

80. WC (4/13/56), 46. F, VII:v, 164.

81. F, VII:v, 167. LC, II (2/16/55), 452.

82. "The Unknown Dickens," DSA, 1 (1970), 4. CA, 11; JE, I:127.

83. CA, pp. 12-14; 14.

84. LC, I (10/26/54), 429-30.

85. *Morning Chronicle* (1/21/35), repr. CA, 12; (10/8/35), repr. CA,

p. 14; (11/16/35), reprinted in CA, p. 18.   NL, II (12/25/68), 692.

86.   LD, I (1/14/37), 223; (11/1/39), 596; V (6/10/48), 330; III (8/7/43), 537; V (8/10/48), 391.

87.   SD (3/25/50), 111.   *Morning Chronicle* (10/19/35), repr. CA, p. 16.   L (4/18/54), 125-26.   NL, III (1/3/59), 85.

88.   LC, II (11/16/59), 124; (2/19/63), 225.

89.   *Examiner* (7/26/40), repr. LD, I:103n1.   LD, II (12/29?/41), 454.   "The Restoration of Shakespeare's Lear to the Stage," *Examiner* (2/4/38), repr. CP, III:123, and in DTR, 151.   LD, I (4/39), 539: Macready resigned in July.   LD, I (1839?), 625.

90.   "The Lazy Tour of Two Idle Apprentices," HW (10/31/57), 412.   CP, I:47-48.   "That Other Public," HW 11, 1.

91.   LD, V (9/10/47), 163; see (8/29/47), 153-54.   SD (4/16/57), 230.

92.   "Astley's," SB, repr. DTR, p. 43.   L (4/12/54), 122-23: the table was in the office of *Household Words*.

93.   SD (3/25/50), 110.

94.   L (9/2/58), 145.   LC, II (8/25/58), 73.

95.   F, IV:iv, 324.   PI, pp. 51-52.

96.   F, VII:iii, 139; 141.   PI, pp. 183-84, and see LD, IV (2/23 & 25/45), 273.

97.   LD, V (1/27/47), 14.   F, VII:iv, 149.

98.   LC, I (2/16/55), 451; (11/21/55), 482.   F, VII:v, 162.   DS, p. 232.   "New Year's Day," HW (1/1/59), repr. CP, I:717.

99.   AN, p. 143; p. 76: the two theaters were the Tremont and Warren (later National).   DG, p. 110.

100.   L (3/26/65), 344.   "Astley's," SB, repr. DTR, p. 37.   "The Amusements of the People, I," HW (3/30/50), repr. DTR, p. 239.   HW (2/25/55), repr. DTR, p. 294.

101.   LC, I (5/5/56), 511-12.

102.   *My Lifetime* (1895), repr. IR, II:222.   LD, IV (12/19/46), 680-81.   *Morning Chronicle* (10/26/35), repr. CA, p. 17; (10/14/34), repr. CA, p. 11.   LD, II (12/29?/41), 455.

103. LD, II (12/29?/41), 455. NL, III (3/3/69), 709.

104. *Morning Chronicle* (1/21/35), repr. CA, p. 12; see also (9/7/35), repr. Ca, p. 13, and (11/23/35), repr. CA, p. 21.

105. *Morning Chronicle* (10/26/35), repr. CA, p. 17. LD, V (12/18/49), 674.

106. *Examiner* (7/26/40): see LD, II:103n1. LD, II (7?/23/40), 104; III (11/13/43), 597-98. FW (11/3/51), 191.

107. MR (7/28/50), 140. L (6/24/50), 28. DS, p. 233. "Glimpses of Charles Dickens," *North American Review* (60), repr. IR, I:136. NL, II (3/1/54), 541.

108. LD, IV (1/27/44), 14; V (3/24/47), 42. LC, I (2/19/63), 225; I (12/3/55), 483; (11/21/55), 482; (5/9/53), 353; (11/21/55), 483; II (5/20/70), 510.

109. F, VII:v, 159-60: the French original, by Victor Ducange, was *Trente Ans, ou la vue du'n jouer.*

110. LD, IV (12/31/45), 460; V (4/9/47), 55; (late 1847), 219; (2/10/48), 245. SD (4/2/55), 186-87.

111. SD (4/2/55), 187; (2/14/66), 359. DS, p. 234. LC, II (5/31/70), 512.

112. DS, p. 234. LC, II (7/30/57), 25; (2/3/58), 50. DS, p. 238.

113. LC, II (1/6/66), 286.

114. LC, II (2/19/63), 225-26.

115. LC, I (8/8/56), 530; II (5/15/58), 56. "'Virginie' and 'Black-Eyed Susan,'" *Examiner* (5/12/49), repr. CP, I:206.

116. "'Virginie' and 'Black-Eyed Susan,'" *Examiner* (5/12/49), repr. CP, I:206. NL, II (10/22/57), 893. *Morning Chronicle* (11/23/35), 21.

117. See LD, I (3/5/39), 521; (1/9/38), 352. *Diaries*, II (9/7/40), 78; (9/13/41), 143. LD, I (3/5/39), 520. SD (7/21/58), 275.

118. WC (3/4/55), 22-23. SD (4/4/63), 312. WC (4/4/55), 30. LD, I (11/18/36), 197; II (12?/41), 497; IV (12/13?/44), 239. WC (3/4/55), 23. LD, V (8/12/47), 148.

119. NL, III (5/6/67), 526.

120. LD, II (5/24/40), 73-74; (5/6?/41), 280.

121. "Macready as Benedick," *Examiner* (3/4/43), repr.   CP, I:144-46.

122. LD, III (9/1/43), 548. See e.g. LD, IV (1/2/44), 4; (1/3/44), 11; (9/30?/44), 196; (5/21/46), 551. LD, V (11/23/47), 200. SD (3/29/47), 79.

123. LC, I (2/27/51), 287-88. SD (3/1/51), 115.

124. LC, II (3/16/62), 207-208: in the *Dictionary of National Biography*, which calls Fechter "the best lover on the English stage" (c.f. Dickens' comment, below), G. H. Lewes said that Fechter was the best Hamlet and the worst Othello of his time.

125. LC, II (5/28/63), 234.

126. "On Mr. Fechter's Acting," *Atlantic Monthly* (8/69), repr. CP, I:116-20.

127. NL, III (9/17/67), 551: Claude, the son of a gardener, had deceived a lady into marrying him.

128. NL, III (1/14/70), 759.

129. "Dickens and the Theatre," *Charles Dickens: 1812:1870* (New York: Simon and Schuster, 1969), ed. E. W. F. Tomlin, p.   187. *Examiner* (7/26/40): see LD, II:103n1. HW (4/30/50), repr. DTR, p.   238.   "Macready as Benedick," *Examiner* (3/4/43), repr. CP, I:144.   "Private Theaters," quoted in DS, p. 9. LD, III (8/9/43), 537.

130. LD, IV (12/28/45), 458.

131. LD, V (11/7/48), 437. SD (3/29/47), 79. DS, p. 237.

132. SD (5/21/49), 96; (3/25/50), 110. NL, III (10/27/58), 66; (1/3/59), 85. LD, I:63. LD, III (3/22/42), 149.

133. SD (4/14/51), 124.

Chapter 4

The Dramatic Readings: The Fairy Immortality

1. "A Christmas Tree," opening story of the first Christmas number of *Household Words*, 2 (12/21/50), 292; green was the usual color for theater curtains; does this explain why green was Dickens' favorite color?
2. F, I:ii, 13.
3. K, p. 14. DG, p. 35.
4. F, XI:iii, 399. "In Memoriam," *Macmillan's Magazine*, 22 (1870), repr. IR, II:335.
5. "It Is Not Generally Known," HW (9/2/54), repr. CP, I:502. SH, p. 626. SD (4/6/46), 76; (4/14/51), 122.
6. F, I:ii, 31. SD (4/2/55), 186.
7. HW (1/17/52), repr. SH, p. 384.
8. "Private Theatres," *Evening Chronicle* (8/11/35), repr. DTR, p. 50. LD, IV (2/21/44), 50. Review quoted by CA, pp. 23-24.
9. LD, IV (12/13?/44), 239. F, VII:v, 162. LC, II (5/2/70), 510; Dickens may have been speaking of Plessy's writing, not his acting.
10. LD, IV (2/25/45), 273. Review in the *Examiner* (5/16/49), repr. CP, I:205. DS, p. 238.
11. LD, III (9/1/43), 548. Review in the *Examiner* (10/27/49), quoted by Leslie C. Staples in "Dickens and Macready's Lear," D, 44 (3/1948), 80. "On Mr. Fechter's Acting," *Atlantic Monthly* (8/69), repr. CP, I:116-120.

12. F, VIII:vii, 248. WC (3/4/55), 22-23. "Macready as 'Benedick,'" *Examiner* (3/4/43), repr. CP, I:144-46. DG, p. 442. NL, III (10/14/67), 560. LD, III (12/10/42), 392: date given incorrectly in LC, I, as 11/42.

13. F, VII:v, 159-60: the play, by Victor Ducange, was *Trente Ans, ou la vie d'un jouer.* LC, II (1/1/67), 315.

14. "Why?" HW (3/1/56); repr. CP, I:640. NL, II (3/25/53), 450. *The Almanac of the Month* (1/46); repr. SD, p. 159.

15. LD, I (9/27/39), 587-88. "Astley's," *Evening Chronicle* (5/9/35), repr. DTR, p. 44. DTR, pp. 48-49. DS, p. 232.

16. LC, I (2/27/51), 287-88.

17. Review in the *Examiner* (5/16/49), repr. CP, I:205. "On Mr. Fechter's Acting," *Atlantic Monthly* (8/69), repr. CP, I:116-120. DS, p. 234. NL, II (4/25/52), 390.

18. SD (3/29/47), 79. "On Mr. Fechter's Acting," *Atlantic Monthly* (8/69); repr. CP, I:118. Review in the *Morning Chronicle* (9/7/35), quoted by CA, p. 13. LC, II (2/19/63), 225.

19. "The Theatrical Young Gentleman," DTR, p. 47. SD (1839), p. 3: (4/6/57), 229. LC, II (3/16/62), 207-8.

20. "The Restoration of Shakespeare's Lear to the Stage," *Examiner* (2/4/38); repr. CP, I:123-24, and DTR, pp. 152-54. F, X:i, 324.

21. F, II:i, 70. LD, V (1/18/47), 9; IV (10/29?/44), 207.

22. S, p. 93. LD, V (1/27/47), 13.

23. F, IX:1, 272..

24. Neither, of course, have many of his readers: as Northrop Frye points out, "When . . . we pick up a novel of Dickens, our immediate impulse, a habit fostered in us by all the criticism we know, is to compare it with 'life,' whether as lived by us or by Dickens' contemporaries. Then we meet such characters as Heep or Quilp, and, as neither we nor the Victorians have ever known anything much 'like' these curious monsters, the method promptly breaks down. Some readers will complain that Dickens has relapsed into 'mere caricature' . . . others . . . simply give up the criterion of lifelikeness. . . . *Anatomy of Criticism: Four Essays*

(Princeton: Princeton University Press, 1957.

25. SD (3/29/58), 262. F, V:i, 374; VII, 1, 120.

26. LD, IV (6/24/44), 150. In 1861 Dickens wrote to the *Times*, "I believe it is in the power of any English writer of fiction legally to prevent any work of his from being dramatized or adapted for the stage without his consent," and announced that he and Collins had taken this step, presumably on behalf of *The Frozen Deep*, against "the proprieter of the Britannia Theatre." Letter to the *Times* (1/12/61), repr. CP I:96. LD, I (11/29?/38), 463.

27. LD, I (12/28/38), 479. LC, II (10/19/59), 121.

28. F, IV:iii, 305. LD, IV (12/19/46), 680; (12/21/46), 682; (6/22/44), 150.

29. F, IV:iii, 305; x:1, 324. LD, V (12/18/48), 459; (12/19/48), 460.

30. DS, p. 172. LD, IV (11/27/46), 663. F II:iv, 100. LD, I (1/23?/38), 459: see n.

31. LC, II (1/6/66), 288; (10/19/59), 121.

32. SD (4/29/58), 264. NL, III (4/17/67), 523.

33. LD, III (6/2/43), 500; V (2/49), 494; IV, (9/29/45), 392; V (10/5/48), 419. L (4/18/54), 124; (9/5/55), 172.

34. LD, IV (3/2/46), 510. F VI:vi, 96. HCD (8/17/51), 184.

35. HCD (2/19/56), 316); (8/29/57), 346. NL, II (5/4/55), 658.

36. LD, IV (12/6/46), 622. F, IX:v, 292.

37. HCD (9/22/50), 177. HCD (1/13/52), 193; (6/1/52), 201.

38. LD, V (7/28/49), 583. F, VII:ii, 123. L (4/20/54), 128. LC, I (9/24/50), 263; II (3/15/58), 53.

39. LC, II (3/29/64), 252. DG, p. 435. LC, I (7/22/52), 326: John Romano, in his attempt to show that Dickens was a realist, argues that "the realist signifies . . . with great longing, the world that lies beyond the farthest border of his power to portray." *Dickens and Reality* (New York: Columbia University Press, 1978), p. 7. I suggest, however, that it was not the world of reality which Dickens signified his longing to portray, but the world of his "real" imagination.

40. F, I:iv, 50. LD, IV (12/30-31?/44), 244. "Charles Dickens: Recollections of the Great Writer," New York *Daily Tribune* (7/5/70), repr. IR, II:236. LD, III (5/21/44), 244.

41. LD, V (11/47), 701. NL, II (9/30/50), 224.

42. K, pp. 263-64, quoted by DS, pp. 99-100.

43. EW, p. 59. *The Leader* (1/10/57), quoted by Francesco Berger, *Reminiscences, Impressions and Anecdotes* (1913), repr. IR, II:239-40.

44. *Cheltenham Examiner* (1/8/62), quoted by PC, p. 251. *Scotsman* (12/8/68),quoted by PC, p. xlvii. *Charles Dickens as a Reader* (1872) repr. IR, II:246. PC, p. lv.

45. PK, 125-30; (2/1903), 164-69, p. 129. *Charles Dickens as a Reader* (1872), repr. IR, I:124. PC, p. lviii. K, p. 95.

46. DG, p. 447: Dickens wrote Collins that there was one thing he preferred even to reading: "I would rather, by a great deal, act." WC (8/11/58), 85: this, though, was in 1858, before the triumphs of the later readings. D, 11 (1915), 134, repr. IR, II:205. *Life*, Ley edition, p. 646; PC, p. xx. WC (8/29/57), 81. *Life*, Ley edition, p. 641; PC, p. xxi.

47. Mary Cowden Clarke quotes him as saying, "There's nothing in the world equal to seeing the house rise at you, one sea of delightful faces, one hurrah of applause!" *Recollection of Writers* (1878), p. 324, quoted by PC, p. xxi. But it was not only their approval in which he took pleasure; in his letters he frequently mentioned "their intelligence" as well: e. g. NL, III, 50. New York *Tribune* (12/10 & 11/ 67), quoted by PC, p. liii. IR, II:268.

48. The admiration of Dickens' readings was not unanimous, and there was some qualification among those who praised him, but Philip Collins, who has probably read more contemporary comment on Dickens' readings than anyone else, concludes that Dickens was a great reader; for a summary of his findings, see PC, pp. lviff. DS, p. 135. J. A. Froude, *Thomas Carlyle: A History of his Life in London* (1884), ii, 270. K, p. 97. DTR, p. 357: Dickens was probably helped in his ability to act many different roles by his

early imitation of Charles Mathews, who was known for his ability to "assume a dozen characters": PC, p. xvii.

49. *Scotsman* (11/28/61), quoted by PC, p. xvii. *Charles Dickens* (1882), p. 82, quoted by PC, p. lxi. Portland *Transcript* (2/4/68); Lady Priestly, *The Story of a Lifetime* (1904), p. 174, quoted by PC, p. 4. Clara Burdett Patterson, *Angela Burdett Coutts and the Victorians* (1953), p. 151, repr. IR, I:20.

50. DG, p. 442. PC, p. lvii. NL, III, 276-77. Sir Nevil Macready, *Annals of an Active Life* (1924), I, repr. IR, I:31. NL, III:704.

51. DG, p. 8. F, VIII:vii, 258. L (1/29/63), 324.

52. Lady Pollock, *Macready as I Knew Him* (1884), repr. IR, I:31. Justin MaCarthy, *Reminiscences* (1899), repr. IR, II:295. *The Selected Letters of Charles Dickens*, ed. F. W. Dupee, (New York: Farrar, Straus, and Cudahy, 1960) (11/3/51), 191.

53. PC, p 77. *Charles Dickens as a Reader* (1872), repr. IR, II:245. Kate Field, *Pen Photographs of Charles Dickens's Readings* (1871), repr. IR, I:70; PC, p. 128.

54. *Glasgow Daily Herald* (2/23/69), quoted by PC, p. 469. *Bath Chronicle* (2/4/69),quoted by PC, p. 469. *Chester Chronicle* (1/26/67), quoted by PC, p. 197. PC, p. 197. Kate Field, *Pen Photographs of Charles Dickens's Readings* (1871), p. 92, quoted by PC, p. 365. *Yorkshire Post* (2/1/67), quoted by PC, p. 422.

57. "Dickens in Relation to Criticism," *Fortnightly Review*, 16 (1872), repr. IR, I:26. 97 (1931); repr. IR, II:241. *Scotsman* (11/28/61), quoted by PC, p. lix. *Saturday Review* (6/19/58), quoted by PC, p. 154. *Spectator* (2/7/74), p. 175, repr. *Dickens: The Critical Heritage*, p. 585; PC, p. lxii; p. lxii.

58. PC, p. lxiii; p. lviii.

59. "Macready as Benedick," *Examiner* (3/4/43), repr. CP, I:144.

60. PC, p. 184. DG, p. 176.

61. *Critic* (9/4/58) p. 538, quoted by PC, p. 184. *Manchester Guardian* (2/4/67), quoted by PC, p. 197.

62. Kate Field, *Pen Photographs of Charles Dickens's Readings*

(1871), p. 92, quoted by PC, p. 365; p. 103, quoted by PC, p. 197.

63.   WC (10/31/61), 106. *Recollections* (1908), p. 50, quoted by PC, p. lvi.   HCD (8/23/58), 362-63: the "Boots story" was the second of the stories in "The Holly-Tree Inn," the Christmas number of HW for 1855; in it a Boots at the inn tells of a boy and a girl, ages eight and seven respectively, who elope to Gretna Green.

64.   Quoted in D, 5 (1909), 66; PC, p. lviii.   Quoted by Robert Brannan in "Under the management of Mr. CD: his Production of *The Frozen Deep*" (Ithaca, N. Y.: Cornell University Press, 1966), p. 82; PC, p. lx.

65.   HCD (11/3/61), 372. WC (10/31/61), 106. L (2/4/63), 328.

66.   K, pp. 123-24. *Yesterdays and Authors* (Boston, 1872),repr. IR, II:315. L (9/24/580, 246. NL, II:377.

Chapter 5

Music: Such Sweet Sounds

1.   JE II:1130: in a letter to John Hullah, with whom he collaborated on *The Village Coquettes*, Dickens praised "the beauty of many of the old English operas. . . ." LD, I (12/29?/35), 113.   Thus once more a judgment of the Dickens aesthetic starts with deprecation and ends with some support.

2.   SH, p. 416n: see also Forster: "His eldest sister's musical attainments and connections had introduced him to many cultivators and professors of that art. . . ." F I:v, 62.   LD, I:54n2.   L

(8/31/61), 286. "First Fruits," HW (5/125/52); SH, p. 416. LD, I:97n1. See e.g. CA, 13.

3. PP, repr. IR, I:7. Robert Langton, *The Childhood and Youth of Charles Dickens* (1912), repr. IR, I:2-3; 3. LC, II (11/21/67), 356. JL, p. 19.

4. JL, p. 1. LD, III (3/22/42), 165-66. LD, III (8/7/42), 305. LD, IV (7/22/44), 158.

5. LD, IV (6/16/46), 563; (8/15-17?/46), 605; V (6/20/48), 343: perhaps Dickens would have rejected anything once owned by the wicked Byron. Reverend Dr. G. D. Carrow, reprinted from *University* (Princeton, N. J., winter 1965-66) in D, 63 (1967), repr. IR, II:325.

6. JL, p. vii. *Everyman and His Music* (Freeport, N. Y.: Books for Librarians Press, 1969), 116. JL, p. 19.

7. MR (11/21/53), 217. LD, III (5/3/42), 233.

8. LD, III (8/24/43), 545; IV (8/30/46), 614; V (12/29/49), 684; LC, II (10/25/64), 260. *The Selected Letters of Charles Dickens.* ed. F. W. Dupee (New York: Farrar. Straus, and Cudahy, 1960), ((2/22/55), 214.

9. LD, III (8/7/43), 538.

10. LD, III (8/20/43), 544; (9/5/43), 554: the flageolet was a flute similar to the recorder, though in the nineteenth century it sometimes had keys. LD, V (9/8-9?/47), 162-63.

11. LD, V (11/27/48), 448. NL, II: 575. HW, 10, 269.

12. HCD (11/13/53), 242. LC, I (7/22/52), 325.

13. NL, III (5/64), 389. MR (11/21/53), 217. AN, p. 13; p. 181; p. 262. LC, II (6/11/59), 112.

14. "The Influence of Dickens on the Contemporary Stage," D, 34 (12/1937), 57. LD, V (4/26/49), 528; (5/14/49), 539; (7/3/49), 563. NL, II (5/8/52), 394.

15. LC, I (11/25/53), 396. MR (12/5/53), 226. MR (11/27/53), 221; (12/5/53), 226. F, VII:v, 167. BC (11/13/53), 137.

16. LD, IV (12/13?/44), 239; (1/25/45), 251. LC, II (2/1/63), 222. Mr. George in *Bleak House* and Mrs. Wilfer in *Our Mutual*

Friend.

17. SD (3/17/56), 220. L (1/22/62), 305: Wills wrote on the letter, "I think CD lost, for 'Masaniello' was produced as a ballet." LC, II (7/7/58), 58.

18. JL, p. 83; p. 135; p. 7. LD, I (7/18/38), 417; III (2/10/42), 55; (2/17/42), 69.

19. LD, IV (3/2/46), 510-11; V (5/26/47), 72; (12/22/48), 461.

20. LD, IV (5/13/44), 126: Kathleen Tillotson suggests that Dickens may have thought the Liverpool and Manchester papers "excessive" in their praise of Miss Weller. LD, IV (5/27/44), 132; (6/14/44), 148: notices of the performance were favorable. PA, p. 38.

21. LD, V (4/9/49), 521: Stone took the advice for a painting entitled *Duet Andante con moto* exhibited at the Royal Academy in June, 1849. JL, p. 27; p. 33.

22. JL, p. 36. NL, II (11/3/52), 426. JL, p. 46. NL, II (1/29/50), 201.

23. LD, V (7/7/47), 120: *La Gazza Ladra* is by Rossini. LD, V (5/3/48), 295: for pieces performed, see note. JL, p. 14. Percy A. Scholes, *Everyman and His Music* (Freeport, N.Y.: Books for Libraries Press, 1969), 117.

24. SD (3/8/60), 296. AN, p. 107. "A Sleep to Startle Us," HW (3/13/52), repr. CP, I:395.

25. LC, II (11/4/61), 181. "It Is Not Generally Known," HW (9/2/54), repr. CP, I:502. "The Poor Man and His Beer," HW (4/30/59), repr. CP, II:11.

26. LD, V (11/3/47), 186; (12/12/47), 208; (2/3/48), 244; (2/8/48), 246; (5/10/48), 303.

27. LD, V (9/19/48), 410; (2/5/49), 491; (12/28/49), 563. AN, p. 117; p. 182.

28. LD, V (6/30/48), 353. L (6/3/52), 81. NL, II (4/10/51), 296. LE, p. 39.

29. Herbert Sullivan and Newman Flower, *Sir Arthur Sullivan: His Life, Letters, and Diaries* (New York: Doran, 1927), p. 59; LE, p. 40; JL, p. 13. JL, P. 8. Mary Dickens, *My Father as I recall*

Him [sic] (London: Roxburghe Press, 1896), 114.

30. LD, V (7/48), 382. SD (3/8/60), 294.

Chapter 6

Poetry: Earnest Admiration

1. Arthur Adrian, "Charles Dickens as Verse Editor," *Modern Philology*, 58 (11/1960), 100. LD, V (10/7/49), 621. F, VI:iv, 65. L (8/7/54), 137; (2/12/65), 343.

2. L (9/25/54), 150; (10/14/54), 154; (10/2/58), 248; (11/4/62), 314.

3. L (10/7/52), 85; (6/27/53), 105; (12/29/52), 94.

4. L (2/17/53), 99; (8/12/54), 139; (11/?/52), 92; (11/24/55), 189.

5. L (1/1/56), 198: Howitt is a relative of Mary Howitt, the first translator into English of Andersen.

6. L (8/19/54), 141; (7/17/53), 108; (7/25/53), 110; (12/11/61), 298-99; see e.g. (1/2/62), 303.

7. L (5/30/54), 129; (10/17/62), 311; (1/19/63), 322; (1/4/57), 228.

8. L (11/5/52), 91: Dickens disliked what he considered the excessive fuss over Wellington's funeral; his willingness here to be topical, and to let audience taste dictate his own, is not typical.

9. NL, II (1/12/50), 199-200. NL II (12/28/52), 438. L (9/18/53), 117; (11/24/55), 189; (2/17/56), 213; (11/25/62), 322.

10. L (4/12/54), 121. LC, I (12/17/54), 438-40. F, XI:iii, 385. JL, p. 80.

11. LD, V (3/31/48), 269; (1/1/48), 270.

12. LD, V (5/7/49), 534; 535; (5/11/49), 537; (6/21/49), 557; IV

(7/9/45), 330.

13. F, VIII:vii, 256. NL, II (4/10/52), 386.

14. LD, I (10/8/39), 590; (9/27/39), 587; (12/28/39), 622; II (2/16/40), 30.

15. LD, II (11/26/40), 158; (1/21/41), 189; (10/12/41), 403; III (4/4/44), 96.

16. LD, II (11/25/40), 154-56: the quotation from Shakespeare is from *As You Like It* II:i, 12-13.

17. LD II (1/15/41), 186.

18. LD, II (4/1/41), 247; III (9/14/42), 323: I have not discovered whether the poem was accepted. LD, III (12/2/42), 388.

19. Thus, for example, to Henry Cook, LD II (6/3/41), 296.

20. LD, III (5/16/42), 240. SH, pp. 532-34.

21. LD, III (1-2/43), 449. TN, p. 1577: Stang cites articles in HW (6/55), 414 and (9/54), 68, and in AYR (9/67), 277. Arthur Adrian, "Charles Dickens as Verse Editor," *Modern Philology*, 58 (11/1960), 99. L (10/12/52), 87; (8/19/54), 141.

22. LD, III: 106n6.

23. CP, I:106. 24. JE, I:68-70. CP, I:281. WA, p. 101. LD, I (7/26/37),

287; III (4/29/42), 220; V (12/3/49), 708; (2?/49), 496.

25. LD, III:370n4. PD, p. 126. LD, III:379n2: for a list of Dickens' verse, see PD, p. 3ff.

26. PD, p. 59; pp. 84-5; p. 138; pp. 145f., 175. HH, pp. 131-32. CP, I:283.

27. "Books that Dickens Read," D, 45 (3/49), 88.

28. LD, III (2/14/42), 59.

29. LD, V (2/23/49), 500: *King Arthur* (1849) is an epic poem in two volumes; it was praised by the *Examiner*. NL, III (3/15/64), 382; (1.10.66), 454-55.

30. See JE, II:350-51. WA, p. 292. LD, II (11/25/40), 155. R. Shelton Mackensie, *Life of Charles Dickens* (Philadelphia, 1870), repr, IR, II:342. L (9/18/53), 117.

31. LD, II (7/9/40), 103. LC, II (8/20/66), 303. See LC, II

(1/2/57), 6; (12/8/58), 97; (3/19/59), 106.

32. LD, IV (12/27/46), 685. CP, I:23. James T. Fields, "Some Memories of Charles Dickens," *Atlantic Monthly*, 26 (1870), 240. In *Alderman Cobden of Manchester*. see LD III, 576-77n1.

33. LD, III (3/26/44), 86. Fields, see note 32. BC (3/18/45), 66.

34. LD, III (10/17/42), 355; (5/24/42), 131. SH, p. 534.

35. LD, I (1839), 576. NL, II (5/4/55), 658. "Circular Sent to Friends of Leigh Hunt About Performances for His Benefit," June, 1847, repr. LD, V:692.

36. LD, IV (6/16-21?/45), 322: fireflies are mentioned in PI as "famous" along the coast between Genoa and Spezzia. LD, IV (8/9/44), 171 & n. LC, I (9/8/53), 366. LD, IV (5/9/45), 304. CP, II:449.

37. LD, III (2/28/42), 96; (7/11/42), 266; (7/27/42), 290; (10/13/42), 340; (10/17/42), 349. L, p. 21. SD (4/5/70), 419.

38. NL, III (6/12/62), 296; (8/27/62), 302; (8/23/65), 434; (12/29/65), 449; (2/10/66), 460; (11/23/66), 492.

39. LD, IV (3/25/44), 85. WA, p. 148. "The Late Mr. Justice Talfourd," HW, 9:117-18. DG, p. 454.

40. *The New Spirit of the Age* (1844), repr. IR, I:70. F, III:viii, 259. LD, III (8/7/42), 306; (9/28/42), 335; (3/9/43), 460.

41. LD, IV (3/1/44), 58; (8/12/44), 178, see *Catalog of the Library of Charles Dickens*, ed. J. H. Stonehouse, p. 109. LD, IV (10/6?/44), 199; LC, II (8/25/59), 115. *Mary Boyle: Her Book* (1901), ed. Sir Courtenay Boyle, repr. IR, I:86.

42. SD, p. 56. L (11/24/55), 189. LC, I (2/27/51), 287.

43. F, III:v, 418. HCD (9/18/53), 235. LD, III (57n7. F, V:v, 418.

44. HCD (5/19/53), 226.

INDEX

326

Index

(Simond), 60
Tovey, Samuel, 23
Townshend, Chauncy, 242, 244
Trafalgar Square, 98
Tremont Theater, ccxcvi
Trollope, Anthony, 15
"Trysting Tree, The" (Overs), 248
Turgenev, Ivan, 8, 15, 210, 216
Turner, Joseph Mallord William, 21, 25, 26
Tussaud, Mme., 30

U

Unequal Match, The (Compton), 132
Urania Cottage, 237-38
Used Up (Bulwer), 134

V

Vanbrugh, John, 15
Vandyke, Anthony, 63, 64, cclxxix
Van Gogh, Vincent, 38, 72
Verdi, Guiseppi, 231
Veronese, Paul, 161, 231, 232, 238
Vestris, Lucia, 133
Viardot, Pauline, 161, 231, 232, 238
Victoria, Queen, 99, 123
Victoria Theater, 108, 111
Victory (Stanfield), 54
Villa Bagnerello, 226
Vining, Mr. (actor), 165
Virgil, 259
Virginie (St. Ytres), 143, 152, 164
"Vision of Old Babylon, A" (Ollier), 245
"Voice of the Sluggard, The" (Watts), 118
"Voices of the Night"

(Longfellow), 264
Voltaire, 7

W

Wagner, Richard, 224
Walker, W. C., 34
"Walk, The" (Hunt), 262
Wallach, James, 160, 188
Waller, Edmund, 15
Walpole, Horace, 15
Ward, Adolphus, 213, 220, 258
Ward, Edward, 21
Ward, Frederick, 262
Warner, John R., 5
Warner, Mrs. (actress), 128
Warren, Samuel, 255
Warren Theater, ccxcvi
Warren's Blacking, 256
Washington, George, 95
Watson, Mrs. Richard, 9, 21, 33, 114
Watteau, Jean, 21
Watts, Dr. (composer), 118
Waugh, Col., 126
"We Are Seven" (Wordsworth), 267
Weber, Carl von, 231
Webster, Benjamin, 151, 152, 178, 201, 217
Webster, Daniel, 15
Webster, John, 15, 177
Webster, Thomas, 21
Weller, Anna, 234,
Weller, Christiana, 233-34, 266
Weller, Mary, 118, 225
Wellington, Duke of, 31, 95, 97, 98
Werner (Byron), 167
West, Benjamin, 21
Whewell, William, 9
White, James, 130, 132
Whitehead, Charles, 247
Whitman, Walt, 15
Wilkie, David, 20, 24, 57, 197, 198, 267